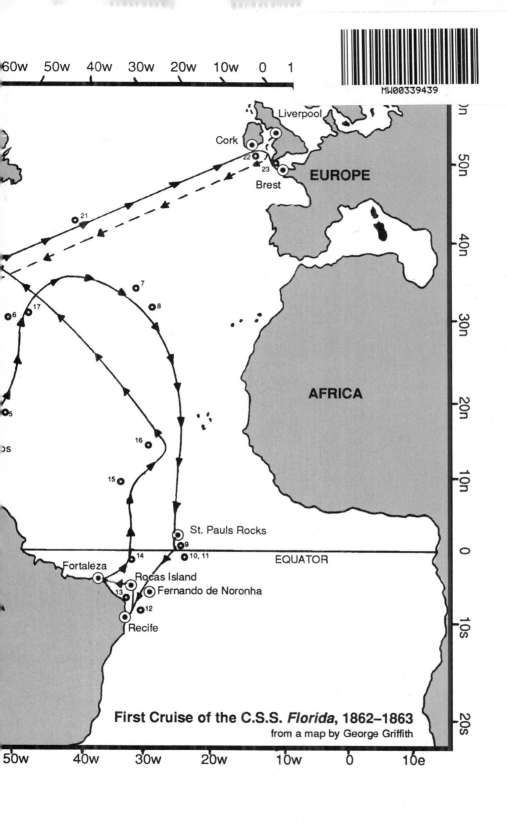

First Cruise of the C.S.S. *Florida*, 1862–1863
from a map by George Griffith

HIGH SEAS CONFEDERATE

Studies in Maritime History
William N. Still, Jr., General Editor

HIGH SEAS CONFEDERATE

The Life and Times of John Newland Maffitt

by Royce Shingleton

UNIVERSITY OF SOUTH CAROLINA PRESS

Copyright © 1994 University of South Carolina

Published in Columbia, South Carolina, by the
University of South Carolina

Second Printing 1995

Manufactured in the United States of America

Library of Congress Cataloging-in-Publication Data

Shingleton, Royce.
   High seas confederate : the life and times of John Newland Maffitt
/ by Royce Shingleton.
      p. cm.—(Studies in maritime history)
   Includes bibliographical references and index.
   ISBN 0–87249–986–3 (acid-free)
   1. Maffitt, John Newland, 1819–1886. 2. United States—History—
Civil War, 1861–1865—Blockades. 3. United States—History—Civil
War, 1861–1865—Naval operations. 4. Ship captains—Confederate
States of America—Biography. 5. Confederate States of America.
Navy—Biography. I. Title. II. Series.
E467.1.M35S55 1994
973.7′57—dc20   93-41981
                                                                 CIP

For
Norman and Hallie
whose own production
Ruth
has enhanced my life

Contents

Preface

The first work on Maffitt was *The Life and Services of John Newland Maffitt* (1906), compiled by Emma Martin Maffitt, his widow. The book, which contains a wealth of information, is basically a collection of original documents, many of which are now housed in the Maffitt Papers in the Southern Historical Collection, University of North Carolina, Chapel Hill. James Sprunt, who was originally associated with Maffitt as a seventeen-year-old blockade runner, also made valuable contributions to this biography. A native of Glasgow, Scotland, Sprunt came to America at the age of six and never foreswore his British citizenship. After the Civil War, he settled in Wilmington and remained a lifelong friend of Maffitt's. Studious and well read, Sprunt recorded the history of the Cape Fear region in his *Chronicles of the Cape Fear River* (1916) and *Derelicts* (1920).

In 1928, Joseph Hergesheimer included a chapter on Maffitt titled "Shadows on the Sea" in his *Swords and Roses*. The Maffitt Papers had not yet been made public, and it is believed that Hergesheimer was unaware of their existence. In 1935, Duncan Rose set forth *The Romantic Career of a Naval Officer, Federal and Confederate: Captain Maffitt, of the U.S.S. "Crusader" and the C.S.S. "Florida."* Rose printed this brief volume (sixty-eight pages) on his own printing press in Spray, North Carolina. The author was familiar with the locale of Maffitt's boyhood home, and that knowledge is probably Rose's most significant contribution to this biography. Edward Boykin's *Sea Devil of the Confederacy: The Story of the "Florida" and Her Captain, John Newland Maffitt* (1959) is a well-written account that includes some material other than the cruise of the *Florida*. Boykin was familiar with the sources and might have seen the Maffitt Papers (available for the first time in 1950), but his work is not documented, and he invented dialogue. The first documented work on Maffitt was *The C.S.S. Florida: Her Building and Operations* (1965), by Frank L. Owsley, Jr. This is an excellent book by a respected historian, but since it is limited to the *Florida*, the work falls short of a biography.

Grateful appreciation is extended to all who helped in the production of the present study. This includes Richard Shrader, research archivist at the Southern Historical Collection, University of North Carolina, Chapel Hill; Sherrill Reid Cook, my cousin, who while living in London aided with the research in the British Public Record Office; DeAnne Blanton and Barry L. Zerby of the Military Reference Branch of the National Archives, Washington, D.C.; Peter Drummey, librarian, Massachusetts Historical Society, Boston; Linda McCurdy, head of Public Services for Special Collections, Duke University, Durham, North Carolina; Michael E. Pollock, of Lineage Search Associates, who conducted research in the Museum of the Confederacy, Richmond, Virginia; Anna D. Sherman, genealogist, Fayetteville, North Carolina; and Renoda Hoffmann, city historian, White Plains, New York.

The Darton College Library professional and support staff have been most helpful, especially Debbie Hardin and Kay Lowry of the Interlibrary Loan Division. Another Darton staff member, Joyce Shalack, typed the manuscript in the most capable fashion. My wife, Ruth, as always has been most helpful, even inspirational.

HIGH SEAS CONFEDERATE

The grand mistake of the South was
neglecting her navy.

John Newland Maffitt

Chapter 1

To the Sea Born

John Newland Maffitt exhilarated in bold action. He demonstrated this in the fall of 1862, when he challenged the Union blockaders in brilliant sunshine off Mobile Bay. These "constables of the sea" dotted the horizon across the shimmering blue waters of the Gulf as Maffitt approached in command of the C.S.S. *Florida*. On board Maffitt's ship, yellow fever ravaged the few crew members, and he was himself barely able to stand from its effects. Moreover, the Confederate raider's guns were useless, for the vessel had been only partially equipped and manned when Maffitt took command at Nassau. Now, he was determined to make a mad dash through the blockade into the friendly port of Mobile to complete the equipment and recruiting. Flying the English colors and under full steam, the *Florida* stood for Mobile Bay. The Federal ships, after two warning shots, hurled a fierce fusillade upon the intruder. Wrote Maffitt: "In truth, so terrible became the bombardment, every hope of escape fled from my mind."[1]

What kind of man was this Confederate naval officer? Maffitt was well-known throughout the Union and Confederate navies for his skill and courage. As ship's captain, he was the perfection of coolness and the consummate navigator. He was one of the best officers, capable of filling any naval position with honor and distinction. Among the many different duties he carried out during his career were the protection of American commerce in distant ports, technical assignments, patrols against the slave trade, commerce destroying, and blockade running. "He is not only a thorough seaman and game to the backbone," wrote a colleague, "but a man of superior intellect, a humorist of rare excellence, and one of the most delightful companions."[2]

Because of his appealing features, bright intelligence, and ready wit, Maffitt's magnetism was irresistible. This was especially true for women, who were charmed by his manner. In pro-Confederate Barbados, a chagrined reporter for a Northern newspaper wrote during the war: "All

1

the ladies are Maffitt mad. It is Maffitt this and Maffitt that. Oh! Does he not talk beautifully! What a voice! What wit and humor!"[3]

Cultivated and gentlemanly, Maffitt had a talent for phrase making and possessed a kind of intellectual chic. He was quite fond of poetry and, throughout the Civil War, carried a tiny volume of *Childe Harold's Pilgrimage,* Byron's narrative poem that describes the impressions of a youth during his wanderings. And at any moment, lines from Homer might issue from Maffitt's lips. His conversation sparkled with a flow of *bons mots,* and his faultless gallantries reflected his usual debonair and friendly personality. Playing the host was one of his strong suits, and when his ship was in port, his cabin often served as a social center.

As a young naval lieutenant, Maffitt was as handsome as they come. His body spare in figure, his head was of fine cast, with a great wave of black hair. By middle age, he wore a strong tuft of whiskers on his chin. Dark, deep-set eyes were his most striking feature. Their twinkling quality lingered in the minds of those who knew him, as did the stern quality of those eyes when he was angered or facing the enemy. His firm mouth seemed to express his determination of character. He had a dignified appearance as he stepped about in his naval uniform. In dress he was attentive if not meticulous—a characteristic, among others, undoubtedly inherited or learned from his father. He always donned his finery when dining with prominent officials in various ports, as well as when ladies came aboard his ship.

Maffitt was born to command a ship. Indeed, he was born at sea in the middle of the Atlantic Ocean, on Washington's birthday, 22 February 1819. Later, with a characteristic flash of wit, this son of Neptune fixed his place of birth as longitude 40° w, latitude 50° n. The exploits of the legendary American captains of the Undeclared Naval War with France and the War of 1812 influenced him during his rise from midshipman to the quarterdeck.[4] Maffitt probably attempted to live up to the family name as well, for his father, also named John Newland, was a nationally renowned figure. According to a Northern newspaper, "Captain Maffitt likes to produce on the ocean the same sensation, in a different form, which his father used to produce in the pulpit" and, unless the Union navy captures him, "will most certainly produce as much discussion and sensation as his father ever did in this country."[5]

Maffitt's father, John Newland Maffitt, Sr., first saw the light of day in Dublin, Ireland, on 28 December 1794. "When a child, the influence of divine things made deep and serious impressions on my mind," wrote Maffitt, Sr. His parents belonged to the "Methodist Society," a religious association within the pale of the Church of England. After a brief stage of repugnance toward religion as a youth, he resolved to become a

Methodist minister. His early passion for reading novels helped shape his oratorical style that brought future eminence in America, but first brought notoriety in Ireland. The senior Maffitt's early experiences as a Methodist preacher included his unsuccessful attempt to break up a gala ball by a loud and stirring exhortation followed by a prayer; on another occasion, when he attempted to hold a service he was stoned by angry Irish Catholics.[6]

Early in life Maffitt, Sr., married Ann Carnic, a beautiful woman with grey eyes set in a proud face. Her other attributes included industry and domesticity, but, in the words of the elder Maffitt's biographer, "she delighted in the practical art of 'turning a penny,' and would not have given a potato for all the poetry in the universe." Ann and John were not suited to be partners; his imagination could not blend with her materialism. The bickering that followed was not diminished by the birth of their children. In 1819, Maffitt, Sr., decided to start a new life in America.[7]

Upon his arrival in the United States, Maffitt found that Methodism was more acceptable here than in Ireland, but at that time, the church did not provide for married preachers, who were expected to "locate" and supplement their income by some other means. This fact must have caused him much anxious deliberation, yet he made his decision to become an itinerant preacher. After 1822, when he began his career in the New England Conference, his family disintegrated. In 1824, Dr. William Maffitt, his brother who had settled in North Carolina, visited the family in Connecticut and adopted five-year-old John. Ann Maffitt, with other children, journeyed to Galveston, Texas, where she opened a small boardinghouse and, through her own exertions, built it into a fashionable hotel.[8]

In the early nineteenth century, a tidal wave of reaction known as the Second Great Awakening roiled against Catholicism, Deism, and Unitarianism. The Second Great Awakening was one of the most momentous episodes in American religion. Methodists and Baptists converted the most souls; personal conversion and democratic control of church affairs appealed to the masses, as did rousing emotionalism. The Reverend John Newland Maffitt, "the Methodist meteor," burst upon the country and coursed alongside the likes of Henry B. Bascom, Peter Cartwright, and Charles G. Finney. The personal experience of religion of these men probably gave form to their style of preaching; filled to overflowing with inspiration, their words, modulation, and action were highly spontaneous.[9]

The most dramatic development of the Second Great Awakening, and one that blended quite well with the elder Maffitt's plans, was the rise of the professional itinerant evangelist in the urban churches. The practice had precedents in frontier itineracy, wherein a scattered population coped with a shortage of ministers, and where, unlike the urban evangelist, the circuit rider was both pastor and evangelist. Maffitt was one of the few Methodists to achieve success as both frontier and urban evangelist. As a full-time professional itinerant, he was unconcerned with the long-term spiritual life of his audiences, but simply became the major attraction in one church after another. He was the novelty that would draw the crowds from secular attractions. Show bills would popularize the revivals, and Maffitt's sermons would be characterized by striking illustrations rather than depth of thought. There was some danger of a post-revival reaction, but for the moment, the mystique of Maffitt's appearance could be electrifying.[10]

The "exile from Erin" had a love of personal finery (although he disdained his father's trade of fashionable tailoring). As a devotee of fashion, the Reverend Maffitt usually dressed in the latest style which was cut to show off his figure.[11] In physical appearance he was striking. He was of medium to slightly undersized stature, with a high forehead and an expressive face that offset a harelip. Coal-black hair and eyes gave a radiance to his features that glowed brightly when, in the words of one newspaper report, he "vaulted away in what were really extraordinary flights of oratorical display."[12]

Crowds of women followed him from church to church. As Grover C. Loud described it in his *Evangelized America* (1928), "One New York sermon ended with an impassioned appeal for a charity fund. Women threw rings, bracelets, brooches, and necklaces into the collection plates." Maffitt's pulpit specialty, at which he was perhaps unrivaled by any minister of his day, was word painting—dramatically presenting a common thought. For example, in describing "eternity," he said if a bird came from another planet and took in its bill a grain of sand from the huge mass of the earth, flew away with it, and did not return for a thousand years to take another, ages would be required to carry away the entire planet, with its thousands of miles of diameter; yet this fact would but dimly shadow the meaning of eternity. In another sermon, according to Loud, "he dwelt upon the beauties of paradise till his hearers spontaneously burst into a united shout of 'Glory!' "[13]

As the star attraction, Maffitt constantly worked to develop his delivery, which together with his physique, made him a magnetic personality. His figures of speech, which drew upon a wealth of Shakespeare, were fashioned with skill and delivered with beauty, so that he captivated the most sluggish mind and became for the moment the master of human impulse. One newspaperman wrote that Maffitt was "finished, flowery, and dazzling, a scintillating genius, a perfect master of rhetoric."[14]

Following his sermon, Maffitt would come down from the pulpit and invite penitents to come forward to join the church, but he asked the congregation not to join in the hymn. He was fond of singing by himself. From his true Irish heart came songs remarkable for clearness, force, and variety. He could be soft as a lute, then loud as a trumpet. Indeed, he rather acted than sang: "It was", according to a writer for the *Raleigh Christian Advocate,* "a sort of operatic, scenic recitation."[15]

America contained no assembly hall large enough for the revivalist. Once in Boston, the Reverend Benjamin F. Tefft announced at morning service that the Reverend Maffitt would appear in the largest hall in the city that afternoon. Soon, a storm blew in from the ocean, bringing heavy wind and rain. The clouds were so dark that gaslights were lit inside the building. No other man in Massachusetts except Daniel Webster could have attracted a hundred people under the circumstances.

> The place was the old Federal street theatre; it was packed from pit to dome with the *elite* of Boston; not only were all the seats, but the aisles and corners were densely crowded, hundreds of ladies being obliged to stand, below and in all the four galleries, because the whole living mass was so wedged in that no gentleman could move out of his place to make a vacancy; the more venturesome, crowded more and more by those pushing forward from the doors, clung to the front railings of the galleries, where they seemed to hang like bees when swarming; and when the preacher arose to lead the first hymn, and the full head of gas was poured on the scene, it was both curious and exhilarating to behold what multitudes of human beings, gathered by so brief a notice, could be so crammed together.[16]

From the 1820s through the 1840s, Reverend Maffitt preached in the major cities from Boston to New Orleans as well as frontier camp meetings. In the winter of 1831–1832, Ormsby M. Mitchell, traveling by stage from Canterbury, New York, to New York City, learned from the driver that the gentleman in the back seat was the great Methodist preacher. Maffitt had just concluded a fortnight in Newburgh, preaching nightly to crowded houses and converting large numbers. During the day's journey, while Maffitt talked freely of politics (he was a friend and admirer of President Andrew Jackson), he carefully avoided disclosing to Mitchell who he was, which caused Mitchell to think he was eccentric. Mitchell later met him several times in Cincinnati and other western cities, both in church and in private homes. According to Mitchell, the revivalist was an agreeable companion, but very exacting in his demands in the house. Also, "it was his custom to break into a wine glass a raw egg, fill it with brandy, and swallow it, just before going to preach."[17]

Maffitt sometimes remained for months at one church, preaching in the morning, discussing religious questions in the afternoon with penitents, preaching again in the evening, and spending the late evening thinking of ways to improve. In the early 1830s he left the New England Conference and, in 1833, helped establish in Nashville, Tennessee, what became the *Christian Advocate,* the major newspaper of Southern Methodists. In the mid-1830s he served a nominal stint in the chair of elocution at La Grange College, Georgia. For the next several years he appeared in Tennessee, Kentucky, and Ohio. In the winter of 1840–1841 he brought President-elect William Henry Harrison to conversion, which assured Maffitt even wider fame and perhaps explains his election in 1841 as chaplain of the United States House of Representatives. In 1845–1846, Maffitt founded and edited the *Calvary Token* at Auburn, New York.[18]

In 1847 the "Prince of the Pulpit" remarried, this time to a well-to-do young girl, Fanny Smith Pierce of New York, one of the thousands of his feminine admirers who, apparently because of his extroverted nature and good looks, had succumbed to man worship. She proved to be another marital thorn. In his biographer's words: "After a few short months he separated from his second and beautiful bride; and ere the next new moon, the fact was known to the herdsmen of Iowa, and the hunters of Texas."[19] The press began to challenge Maffitt's moral credibility, and Methodists developed a "diversity of views" concerning his religious experience. The controversy weakened his drawing power, and he left New York to join the Methodist Episcopal Church, South, which had been formed in 1845 after a split from the General Conference over the slavery issue. Fanny Maffitt died shortly afterward, and two years later, the Reverend John Newland Maffitt suffered a cardiac rupture while conducting a mission near Mobile, Alabama. He died 28 May 1850 and was buried in Magnolia Cemetery, Mobile.[20] By that time, his son was making his mark in the United States Navy.

Chapter 2

Midshipman Maffitt

Ellerslie, near Fayetteville, North Carolina, was the residence of Dr. William Maffitt. It was said that the frame house took its name from the Maffitt ancestral home in Dublin. Ellerslie stood on an elevation near the head of Blount's Creek about half way between Fayetteville and present-day Fort Bragg.[1] The locale was at the head of navigation of the Cape Fear River and had been settled by the Highland Scots, who in 1762 incorporated the town as Campbellton (or Campbelltown). Cross Creek, a nearby settlement where two creeks seemed to cross without their currents mixing, later merged with Campbellton. In 1783 the town took the name Fayetteville after the Marquis de Lafayette and, because of a good road network, prospered as an exporting center for the wagon trade over a vast region. From 1789 to 1795, Fayetteville served as the seat of state government. By 1820 the town had a population of 3,532 and was second in size only to New Bern in North Carolina.[2]

In 1824, when he was five years old, John Maffitt, Jr., arrived at Ellerslie. Here he would live with his uncle, Dr. Maffitt, and his first cousin Eliza Maffitt.[3] It was a home of refinement. Dr. Maffitt had a small family, no son of his own, and enjoyed a rewarding practice as a physician. He could easily rear and educate young Maffitt. For school, young Maffitt was sent to Fayetteville. He became devoted to his adopted family, and although he would live only a few years at Ellerslie, he was henceforth to consider himself a North Carolinian.

Young Maffitt grew into a bright and friendly boy. He easily gave and attracted affection as a result of his generous and unselfish nature. Full of restless energy, he enjoyed his river-port surroundings that included two creeks and numerous artificial lakes, or mill ponds, within five miles of Ellerslie.[4] From this environment he would rise to join James W. Cooke of the C.S.S. *Albermarle* and James I. Waddell of the C.S.S. *Shenandoah* as the most notable officers from North Carolina to serve in the Confederate Navy.[5]

A boyhood friend and playmate of Maffitt was Duncan K. McRae. The

McRae family came to the town from Scotland just prior to the Revolutionary War and became leaders in local public affairs. Like Maffitt, young McRae (born in Fayetteville in 1820) would serve the Confederacy with distinction. The latter would lead a desperate charge at Williamsburg that an English war correspondent ranked "with that of the Old Guard at Waterloo and the Light Brigade at Balaklava."[6] In later years, McRae recalled that Maffitt as a boy "was a leader in all our sports. He was a born leader."[7]

The most dramatic event to occur in Fayetteville during Maffitt's years at Ellerslie was the visit of Lafayette. His triumphal tour of the United States marked the fiftieth anniversary of the beginning of the Revolutionary War. The anniversary was a period of great national pride. In each town and city, large crowds greeted Lafayette with wild enthusiasm. He and his entourage arrived in Fayetteville from Raleigh amid pouring rain on 4 March 1825. Outside the town, men and boys on horseback and militia on foot greeted the living symbol of a heroic era. In town, elegantly dressed women cheerfully ignored the deluge to approach the general's carriage.[8] After welcoming ceremonies in front of city hall, Lafayette was conducted to his lodgings at the home of young McRae's grandfather, Duncan McRae, a prominent banker.[9] The next day, Lafayette wrote that "we are given honors, tenderness, fetes and escorts."[10]

The visit of the great hero reflected the environment from which Maffitt developed his sense of responsibility. One of his duties during the happy boyhood years at Ellerslie was to guard a neighbor's orchard against predators. Later as a midshipman aboard the U.S.S. *St. Louis,* he wrote that he "used to run among the woods like a Mohawk Indian." He described himself as "that wild little fellow who used to protect . . . cherry trees from the red head wood birds," and added with teen-aged pride that he was "now protecting our country's commerce on the great ocean."[11]

In 1828, Dr. Maffitt sent nine-year-old Maffitt to school in White Plains, New York. With his ticket pinned to his jacket, the stripling boarded a stagecoach for the long journey northward.[12] Maffitt had developed strong ties to his adopted family, being obviously fond of his uncle William, his cousin Eliza, and Fayetteville.[13] As for Ellerslie, he said late in life: "I love every blade of grass that grows on the old place."[14] Judging from Maffitt's leadership in sports and "Mohawk Indian" style as a boy, and his journey from Fayetteville to White Plains alone at age nine, two of his primary characteristics were love of adventure and absence of fear.

Maffitt rolled into White Plains amid the usual flurry of horns, the jingle of harness, and the shouted commands that added to the excitement of stagecoach arrivals. White Plains, founded by Connecticut Puritans in

1683, is situated midway between Long Island Sound and the Hudson River, twenty-three miles north of New York City. Early traders gave the site its name from the local groves of white balsam, and it is best known for the Battle of White Plains (1776) during the Revolutionary War. When Maffitt arrived, the village consisted of twenty-five houses, three churches, and several stores situated along Village Street (now Broadway). There were few shade trees, and cattle and poultry still used the town common. It was something of a "Sleepy Hollow." Since life in the farming community moved at a leisurely pace most of the time, Maffitt's arrival created something of a sensation as townspeople came to see the little boy who had made the trek alone from the South.

The White Plains Academy, which Maffitt attended, was a new school founded by the Methodists. Located in a building constructed for that purpose on the east side of North Broadway at Hamilton Avenue, it was managed by a board of trustees and a principal, and operated on the semester system. It was a classical private boarding school of the English model. Maffitt applied himself to his studies, and his later intellectual make-up reflected strongly not only courses such as literature, grammar, composition, and elocution, but also math and science. Athletics were also part of the daily routine, and the common in front of the academy served as a ball field. Maffitt remained at White Plains Academy for four years; then his education continued at sea.[15]

On 25 February 1832, President Andrew Jackson appointed the precocious thirteen-year-old as acting midshipman in the navy.[16] He was actually a cadet on officer track, but prior to the establishment of the Naval Academy in 1845, cadet training consisted of years of apprenticeship at sea followed by a comprehensive examination. Many failed the examination; the successful ones were passed midshipmen and presumably had careers as naval officers. The U.S. Army had established West Point in 1802, but for American midshipmen, it was mostly "learn by doing." Chaplains or underpaid schoolmasters and professors, depending on the size of the ship, conducted classes at sea in makeshift rooms created by partitioning off a part of the deck. Classes were not taken very seriously, and were often interrupted for midshipmen to attend to "more important duties."[17]

On 8 August 1832, Maffitt was ordered to report to the U.S.S. *St. Louis*,[18] a 700-ton sloop of war.[19] Sloops, or corvettes, along with frigates, made up the bulk of the old navy. All usually carried square sails on three masts. The distinguishing nomenclature, although not entirely reliable, was based on the number of decks having complete batteries. A sloop mounted from eighteen to thirty guns on the spar (upper) deck, sometimes including the quarterdeck and forecastle. A brig or schooner carrying guns on one deck might belong to the sloop or corvette class—roughly equivalent to destroyers of the present.[20]

The *St. Louis* at the time cruised on the waters of the West Indies. In the Caribbean, Maffitt began to learn the duties of a seaman by firsthand experience: sails and ropes, knotting and splicing, charting a course, the lore of the sun and stars, the winds and currents, steering, and gunnery. He went aloft with the crew, but he also learned the duties of command in anticipation of advancing someday to the quarterdeck.[21]

The *St. Louis* anchored at the Pensacola Navy Yard on 8 December 1832 to be overhauled and to take on supplies. Maffitt visited the city and unexpectedly ran into a friend of the family. He was delighted to hear about his friends in Fayetteville. "It afforded me the greatest pleasure I have experienced in some time," Maffitt wrote his adopted father, "but how much greater and unbounded would be my pleasure to see you and Eliza."[22] Then it was back to sea for another cruise to show the flag, the highlight of which was a stopover in Havana. Back in Pensacola, Maffitt was able to obtain an extended leave of absence beginning 30 January 1834.[23] His correspondence reveals a very literate, and somewhat nostalgic, midshipman who longed for "the extreme felicity" of visiting Ellerslie.[24]

The Boston Navy Yard was Maffitt's next duty station. Under orders dated 18 September 1834, he reported for duty at the time of the restoration of the historic U.S.S. *Constitution*.[25] The vessel is undoubtedly the most famous ship in American history. No ship trained more men; none has so glorious a history. It was one of four fighting ships built in the 1790s that gave birth to an adequate navy to protect the nation's commerce. First assigned to rid American waters of French privateers in 1798, the vessel in 1803–1804 served as Commodore Edward Preble's flagship in the brilliant campaign against the Barbary Pirates, and under the command of Captain Isaac Hull, it won its most famous victory in 1812 against the English *Guerriere*. Though the *Constitution* was condemned as unseaworthy in 1830 and ordered to be dismantled, Oliver Wendell Holmes's poem "Old Ironsides" forced reconsideration. Work began in 1833, and the *Constitution* became the first vessel to enter the new dry dock at the Boston Navy Yard. The keel, which was found to be out of line, was straightened, and the ship was otherwise extensively rebuilt.[26]

The *Constitution*'s lines and history particularly impressed naval men like Maffitt. Its hull curved inward at the top, which narrowed the upper deck. The vessel was a frigate originally designed to carry forty-four guns, but it had sometimes carried over fifty. Frigates carried guns on two decks, with the more complete battery carried on the main or gun deck, rather than on the upper or spar deck, to reduce top heaviness and the danger of capsizing. Ship-rigged (three masts with square sails), the *Constitution* was heavily sparred. Its original tonnage was 1,576; it showed a speed of 12½ knots. The ship's tanks held 48,600 gallons of water, and its hold stowed six months' provisions for 475 officers and men.[27] The vessel was comparable to a modern heavy cruiser.[28]

In Boston, Maffitt found the period of the restoration of the *Constitution* enlivened by a running controversy over the choice of a likeness of Andrew Jackson for the ship's figurehead. The central character in this unseemly episode was the commandant of the Navy Yard, Captain Jesse D. Elliott. One of the most inflexible of officers, and a hero of the War of 1812,[29] Elliott ordered the full-length figure carved after witnessing Boston's enthusiastic reception of President Jackson during his 1833 visit. Local citizens, especially Whigs, differed with Elliott on the propriety of Jackson as a figurehead for their favorite ship: he was a living president, he represented Democratic views, and he had a military, not a naval, background. In spite of numerous threats, Elliott had the figurehead mounted, whereupon merchant skipper Samuel Dewey (a cousin of George Dewey, later the hero of Manila Bay), under cover of darkness and a storm, rowed out to the ship and sawed off the head of the figure through the chin and carried it away in a coffee sack.[30]

Following the "heinous crime" by Dewey, the Navy Department, which had approved the figurehead but now wanted conciliation, ordered the decapitated figure of Jackson covered with canvas. During the next eight months, the *Constitution* was fitted for sea, and on 17 February 1835, Maffitt was ordered to the vessel. The next month, with Elliott as commander, the great frigate stood out of Boston Harbor amid threats of artillery fire at the Narrows because the remains of the figurehead were still on the ship's bow. However, instead of guns booming, observers saw simply an American flag painted on the canvas with the stripes of New England missing as a sign of disloyalty. Repaired in New York, the figurehead (or one like it) remained on the *Constitution* for forty years before being sent to the Naval Academy.[31]

Where Maffitt stood in the figurehead controversy is unclear, but his zest for life doubtless caused him to enjoy the episode immensely. His private feelings were probably on the side of Elliott because both had been appointed midshipmen by Democratic presidents (Jefferson had appointed Elliott) and both had Southern ties (Elliott was from Maryland and had married a Virginia woman). Maffitt's outward attitude toward the controversy certainly did not offend Elliott, who appointed Maffitt his aide. The appointment reflects well on Maffitt's ability and personality because Elliott was difficult to please. Robust in figure, Elliott was rough in manner, was a severe disciplinarian, and had a facility for making enemies. However, he had warm friends, for whom he would make sacrifices. Elliott also had ability, and he was unquestionably brave.[32]

In New York, the *Constitution*, with final adjustments made and stores loaded, was ready for active service for the first time in seven years.[33] The vessel was ordered to France to bring home American minister Edward Livingston and his family. The United States and France had severed diplomatic relations, and war seemed likely because France refused to pay the "spoilation claims." These were claims of American citizens against France based on that nation's Napoleonic-era destruction of American property. In 1831 the French, who had paid similar European claims, had agreed to pay Americans, but by 1835 no payment had been made. Jackson ordered the navy on alert status and threatened possible reprisals against French property. The angered French then recalled their minister to Washington and suggested that Livingston leave Paris.[34]

Maffitt considered himself fortunate to have succeeded in gaining assignment to the *Constitution*, for he enjoyed the company of other midshipmen in the "reefer's den" aboard ship. On 16 March 1835, the vessel stood out to sea, bound for Havre. Soon, Elliott noticed the warning of the barometer and the signs of nature. The mercury continued to fall, the winds increased, and the waves rolled in a cross pattern. Dark clouds hid the horizon. Lights were shut in, guns housed, topsails and foresail reefed. Life lines were fitted; barrels and casks not under hatches were lashed to stanchions. The crew secured everything liable to displacement by the plunging ship or rushing waters. However, one gun, left by a sick gunner to the charge of a raw yeoman, was not secured to the carriage.

The ship, with spray round its bows, ploughed into fearful surges of the sea as a full gale lashed the ocean. Cold rain accompanied thunder and lightning. The crew received a double ration of grog. Maffitt was the midshipman of the watch. The officer of the deck had doubts about carrying so much canvas during such a storm, and sang out from the ward-room hatch ordering Maffitt to have axes placed by the main mast.

The force of the gale increased with every hour. The frigate creaked and groaned. Seasickness—the great equalizer aboard ship—swept through the crew from the highest to the lowest rank. Then came the relatively calm eye of the storm, followed by a heavy roar of wind and sea that jolted the ship, knocking some of the men ten feet or more. Tattered sail whipped in the wind, and spars snapped like pipe stems. A tremendous wave broke over the stern and curled around the guns; it stove in the captain's gig, sending the thin planks upon the water, one of which contained the word "Constitution" in white letters. A cry of distress came from forward, where a heavy thump could be heard above the storm. The forecastle gun had sprung from its carriage, fallen overboard, and was hanging from its port by its breeching rope. As the ship rolled through the water, the gun thumped against the starboard bow, forming a dangerous iron plumb of four thousand pounds.

Elliott now appeared, a long red cap on his head, the tail of which streamed out to leeward. Booming through a trumpet, he ordered the starboard bow gun cut away. The gleam of an axe could be seen forward, followed by a grating noise, and the gun went down to the silence of the mysterious deep. The major danger had passed. The ship hove to and put its bows to the wind. The laboring of the masts and timbers eased as the vessel sprang to meet the crest of the waves.[35]

The frigate arrived at Havre on 10 April 1835 and took Livingston aboard.[36] It then crossed over to Plymouth, England, and on May 16, sailed for New York. On the evening of the fifth day, beating down the English Channel and making its last tack from the French coast, the *Constitution* ran into another gale. The great danger this time was the ship's being smashed against the granite rocks to leeward—the location of the Scilly Islands off Cornwall, England, which had been the scene of many shipwrecks. It was a very close call as the *Constitution* passed between a rock and island breakers at night in high wind at a crucial nine knots. And all the while, the bolts holding the masts were about to give way. Elliott's seamanship saved the vessel. When the danger had passed, he gave the order to "splice the main brace"—lay aft for a tot. Accordingly, the crew "gathered about the grog tub and luxuriated in a full allowance of old rye."[37] The frigate arrived in New York on 22 June 1835, fulfilling its mission of transporting Livingston from France.[38]

Chapter 3

Acting Lieutenant Maffitt

Upon returning from France, Maffitt remained on the *Constitution* and continued as aide to Elliott. The frigate's new assignment was an extended cruise of three years (1835–1838) as the flagship of the Mediterranean Squadron, with Elliott in command as commodore of the fleet. For two months, the crew busily engaged in the nautical preparation incidental to refitting for the cruise. Weighing anchor 19 August 1835, the vessel sailed to Gibraltar, then on to Port Mahon, the latter a Minorca-Balearic Islands port that continued its traditional status as the base of operations for the Mediterranean Squadron. From Port Mahon, America had fought its naval wars against the Barbary pirates. Numerous future naval commanders of the Civil War served at the base, and like Maffitt, they socialized at their favorite restaurant on shore—Cachio's.

Maffitt seemed to enjoy the cruise, which extended throughout the Mediterranean area. The *Constitution* sometimes remained in exotic ports for weeks and visited some of them several times. Maffitt inspected relics of ancient civilizations and attended balls and parties given by local aristocrats. The excitement and the bustle appealed to him. Many distinguished and high-ranking officials visited the *Constitution,* since the ship was partly on a good-will tour and because such a visit was customary. These occasions often found Maffitt, as aide to Elliott, in the mainstream of events—a situation that complemented his fondness for society.

The cruise also displayed the young republic's naval power. Under the critical eye of British and other European naval officers, the frigate was a model of spit and polish. Ancient forts welcomed the Stars and Stripes with salvos, and the frigate's broadsides returned the salutes.[1] The itinerary included many ports of call: from Athens to Smyrna; then, westward to Malta; to Lisbon, where a royal wedding took place; back to Port Mahon; to Palermo and Messina; to Milo and to Athens again; to Sidon and then to Beirut. At Tripoli, Ibrahim Pasha, Turkish-Egyptian naval commander and governor of the coast of Syria, came on board with his captains and inspected the crew at quarters. A light repast followed at which Ibrahim

14

Pasha toasted President Jackson, whose likeness adorned the frigate's bow and whose portrait hung in the captain's cabin. (The French surgeon acting as interpreter appeared uncomfortable with the sentiment.) After one of the visiting captains spoke of the sailing qualities of his ship, a ninety-mile race ensued, during which the frigate "under a stiff breeze, sailed around the Turk twice."[2]

The months fell away as the *Constitution* continued its circuit. At Alexandria, the viceroy of Egypt, Mehemet Ali, and his entourage went on board. Then, the ship sailed on to Tripoli (scene of former hostilities for the ship), to Tunis, and back to Port Mahon. Cruising from there, the frigate fell in with the *Perseverance,* a dismasted English schooner, and towed the vessel in to Cadiz. At Lisbon a large party of ambassadors, consuls, and admirals from England, France, Denmark, and Belgium visited the ship.[3]

On 28 April 1837, the *Constitution* dropped anchor at Marseilles. When the flagship departed three days later, Lewis Cass, with his family and entourage, was on board. A veteran of the War of 1812, a former governor of the Michigan Territory (1813–1831), and the Secretary of War (1831–1836) under Jackson, Cass was now the new American minister to France. He advocated a strong navy and worked against British efforts to maintain the right of search on the high seas. Cass boarded the frigate on a diplomatic fact-finding mission. He hoped to establish commercial ties with Egypt, a country that had been usurped from the Turkish Empire by Mehemet Ali. Nothing came of the talks because Washington had second thoughts concerning Egypt's sovereignty. However, as a result of his long tour on the frigate, Cass, the future presidential candidate, wrote articles on various locations in the eastern Mediterranean, replete with history and philosophy that enhanced his reputation for scholarship.[4]

One of the most memorable visits paid to the frigate took place on the third stopover at Athens. Shortly after the ship arrived from Malta on 15 June 1837, the king and queen of Greece and their retinue went aboard. As aide to the commodore, Maffitt drew the assignment of escorting the royal party from shore. A dozen hardy, tanned seamen manned the oars of the commodore's barge as the detail headed for the seaport of Piraeus. Maffitt sat in the stern in full dress uniform—his handsome features accented by gold lace, high collar, and cocked hat. On shore, King Otho and Queen Amalie arrived at Piraeus with attendants in a cortege escorted by cavalry. With modest assurance, Maffitt handed the queen to her seat in the barge. She was only fifteen, but full-blown and gaily dressed. When a breeze sprinkled the party with spray from the oars, Maffitt gallantly draped his blue cloak around the queen. The party went aboard and, together with the ship's officers, gathered on the quarterdeck. The marine guard presented arms, and the band played the Greek anthem.[5]

The queen was particularly fond of dancing, and the irascible Elliott—during a speech in his hometown six years later—recalled the occasion with some degree of amiability:

> Having a fine band on board, I ordered a portion of them to the quarter-deck, and to play one of their most animated waltzes. The music electrified the Queen. She looked at me wistfully, and I imagined I could read in her eyes, "Do let's waltz. . . ." I beckoned for one of my aids, Midshipman Maffitt, son of Rev. John N. Maffitt, who was quite adept at the business, presented him to the Queen, stepped aside, and motioned to him to be off. He did so, and in less than thirty minutes at least twenty couples, including the King, were whirling upon the deck to their hearts' content. The evening closing in upon us, the awnings were spread, and the muskets of the marines placed around the capstan with sperm candles in the muzzles instead of cartridges, forming a splendid chandelier, and thus converting the quarter-deck into a beautiful ball-room. The dance continued until two o'clock in the morning, when the King proposed being taken on shore. The boats were accordingly manned, the yards and masts of the ship splendidly illuminated, and a salute of twenty-one guns fired when they had left. Before leaving the ship, the Queen remarked to Mr. Maffitt that she would give a return ball on shore, at the same time extending an invitation to him.
>
> She did so, and sent invitations on board for General Cass, his family, my captain and myself. From the English frigate the captain alone was invited. Mr. Maffitt came to me, informed me of his invitation to the Queen's ball, and asked permission to attend. I promptly answered him, "No! what will be the feelings of the other young men if you should go, and they excluded. And, further, no one has been invited from the British frigate but the captain, and your attendance may cause complaint by the British Ambassador."[6]

One day later, the frigate sailed away through the calm and picturesque Aegean Sea, but Maffitt always remembered dancing with the queen on the deck, which the sight-seeing and the masque balls of Port Mahon could not obliterate. His naval cloak that had briefly wrapped the queen remained a treasured memento.

The frigate was now making its final eastern Mediterranean tour, the crew visiting historic sites that included the Temple of Minerva, Corinth, the Plains of Marathon, the plains of Troy, Gallipoli, and Constantinople. Back the *Constitution* glided through the Dardanelles and Grecian Archipelago to the Holy Land, with numerous stops, then on to Alexandria, Malta, and back to Port Mahon. The ship arrived at the friendly port 24 October 1837 for three months of overhauling and provisioning.[7] During that time, his probationary period as midshipman having ended, Maffitt was ordered back to the United States.

Maffitt sailed home in March 1838 aboard the U.S.S. *Shark*.[8] En route, trouble developed when the crew of the schooner gained access to the storeroom that held the provisions of spirits. Maffitt, although not an officer of the deck with a regular watch, was entrusted with the deck on several occasions. The incident proved him efficient in his duties, and foreshadowed his promptness in emergencies. Years later, an officer aboard the *Shark* at the time testified: "Maffitt displayed great activity and energy on that occasion in quelling the difficulty, by going among them, and assisting to secure the ring-leaders. . . . I don't mean to convey the idea that there was a mutiny, but that the men were ungovernably drunk, and had possession of the vessel for a moment, and Mr. Maffitt was mainly instrumental in quelling it. He was a midshipman."[9]

On 27 March 1838, with the *Shark* tied up at Norfolk, Maffitt obtained three months leave to study for his examination. Unlike many of the midshipmen, Maffitt did not have a college education. He journeyed to Baltimore, where the examination was to take place, to prepare. It had been five years since his appointment, and he was now nineteen years old. The board of senior officers questioning the candidates included the stern Commodore Isaac Hull, hero of the War of 1812. Maffitt's appearance before the tribunal was a day of triumph, including a most satisfactory response to Hull's favorite question (because Hull had executed it during the war) of how to recover tow boats while underway with the enemy in pursuit. Therefore, as of 23 June 1838, Maffitt was a passed midshipman.[10]

Three more months of leave followed for Maffitt, and this time he visited relatives. He saw Eliza Maffitt, his cousin, in Portsmouth. She was on her way to school in Bordentown, New Jersey. Maffitt also made a rare visit to his biological family (probably in Galveston, Texas). He expressed delight in seeing his three sisters —Eliza, Matilda Caroline, and Henreitta —terming them "three of the prettiest and most charming girls Heaven ever created." He added that they "desired me to send oceans of love and many hopes of yet meeting with their North Carolina cousin, Eliza."[11]

Following duty aboard the government packet U.S.S. *Woodbury,* a schooner running in the Gulf of Mexico,[12] Maffitt on 20 November 1838 was ordered to the U.S.S. *Vandalia,* a sloop of war at Pensacola. In order to be on hand for any violations of the Monroe Doctrine, the vessel sailed to police a French naval expedition on a punitive mission against Vera Cruz. Maffitt observed the French bombard and capture the castle fortification San Juan de Uloa. He then went ashore. "I wandered about like a second Don Quixote, in search of adventures," he wrote. But his major objective was to observe the effects of naval gunfire. He found the city completely deserted, and heavily damaged by the guns of the French.

The *Vandalia* had a rough cruise because of tropical storms in the Gulf of Mexico. A lieutenant on the vessel was blown overboard and drowned, and Maffitt took his position with the rank of acting lieutenant as of 11 March 1839. He was ordered to perform the duty of sailing master, which gave him experience with navigation. Maffitt himself was nearly killed while attempting to cross a dangerous bar in a storm off Matamoras. He was engaged in rescuing vessels that had been blown upon the beach by the storms. Details are sketchy, but Maffitt was stranded on an island for two days, where he and some of his companions found shelter in a few fishermen's hovels. He wrote: "they had the impudence to call the place Baghdad, from one of the most luxurious . . . cities of the past." He had no food, only water—in great abundance: "It appeared as if the very heavens were laboring with all the pent-up hurricanes that ever existed."[13]

Maffitt wrote that he "had the good fortune to save several ships from the beach . . . after old Lieuts. had made failures." On one occasion at St. Rosa's beach twenty miles east of Pensacola, Maffitt went ashore in a launch full of men at the oars to investigate a beached schooner. He sprang ashore, approached a "bean pole" of a man, and inquired if he was the owner. The captain and owner of the schooner was desperate; he had been en route from St. Mark's to Mobile with a cargo of corn when the storm drove him ashore. He was now on the brink of total financial ruin. Maffitt boarded the vessel, named the *Mary Ann,* which was rocking from the heavy seas, and determined its starboard side must be caulked. To steady the vessel, Maffitt went offshore in a boat to position an anchor attached to a hawser from the schooner. He almost lost his life when the boat went down in a roller, but was hauled out by a lifeline he had extended from the beach. At one point, word came from the *Vandalia* for Maffitt to abandon the project as hopeless. He bluntly refused, to the chorus of "bully" from his men. After several days' hard work, Maffitt rendered the *Mary Ann* to some extent seaworthy. He sent his men back to the ship—except for four, whom he kept as a crew—then set sail in the schooner for Pensacola, where he relinquished it to the delighted owner for more complete repairs.[14]

In Pensacola, Maffitt received orders, dated 20 October 1839, for transfer to the U.S.S. *Macedonian*. The frigate had been captured from the British during the War of 1812, repaired, and placed into service. It saw duty against the Barbary pirates in 1815, and was rebuilt as a sloop of war in 1835–1836 at Norfolk. Maffitt went aboard the frigate, now assigned to the West India Squadron, as acting master. Its cruising grounds off Mexico were familiar to Maffitt. Writing from Vera Cruz in the summer of 1840, he noted that the fortifications had been rebuilt a year after the French bombardment. Stormy times continued, and yellow fever at the ports prohibited visitations. Mexico, he wrote, was "in a wretched state, nothing but anarchy and confusion." After a visit to Tampico, the *Macedonian* returned to Pensacola for the hurricane months.[15]

For some time, Maffitt had been thinking of marriage. "I will not be over-particular," he wrote in describing his ideal for a wife, "should like an amiable disposition and fine mind. Riches would be *no objection*." [16] When he was detached from the *Macedonian* on 22 October 1840 and granted three months leave, his main interest was Miss Mary Florence Murrell. She was from Mobile, and Maffitt had met her while she was visiting in Pensacola. They were married in Mobile on 17 November 1840. Now more interested in shore duty, Maffitt obtained an assignment to the Pensacola Navy Yard for most of the following year.

When the Navy Department posted Maffitt to sea duty 26 October 1841, it was again as acting master on the *Macedonian*. The vessel was now the flagship of the Home Squadron under the command of Commodore Jesse Wilkinson. Maffitt performed his duties as deck officer and navigator so efficiently that Wilkinson spoke of him as a first-rate officer. Fellow officers allowed that no officer on board the vessel was more esteemed than Maffitt. In February 1841, while he was at sea, his first child, Mary Florence "Florie" was born in Mobile. Maffitt learned the good news by letter shortly after in Pensacola. He immediately sent for his family and had Florie baptized by the chaplain aboard the *Macedonian*.[17]

Chapter 4

With the U.S. Coast Survey

Maffitt's next assignment, as of 20 April 1842, was the U.S. Coast Survey.[1] The Coast Survey at the time was a bureau attached to the Treasury Department.[2] Although the ships on this duty carried naval personnel, they were not fighting ships. The Coast Survey was considered a normal tour of duty, and most officers did not remain with it over a few years. Maffitt, however, because of his mathematical bent, was ultimately to find that he performed this duty too well. Equally ironic, the work he did in hydrography provided helpful guides to U.S. naval squadrons along the southern coast during the Civil War. Yet he was to know the southern coastline like the back of his hand—useful information indeed for a blockade runner.

When Maffitt found that his work with the Coast Survey would be on the east coast, he rented a house in Baltimore and moved his family there. At first, Maffitt's assignment was at Baltimore, where he served as acting master on the receiving vessel. On 9 May 1843, he was assigned to actual survey duty. To look after his family while he was away, Maffitt hired an Irishman whom he had long known. In November 1844, his second child, Eugene Anderson, was born in Baltimore. Maffitt's happiness seemed complete, but then, for some reason that remains unexplained, his marriage ended unhappily. Decades later, Maffitt's third wife and widow commented only that Maffitt went on with his life, but that the "scars remained."[3]

Maffitt's major work with the Coast Survey was in hydrography. Charting waters followed naturally from his experience as navigator on various ships. It was exacting work, and dangerous, especially in bad weather because of the treacherous rocks and bottoms along inlets and channels. During this time, on 3 February 1844, he was commissioned a lieutenant (effective 25 June 1843).[4]

The year 1846 was a critical one for Maffitt. He was extremely skilled at soundings and triangulations, but at the beginning of the War with Mexico, he applied for an assignment at the seat of war. Writing from the surveying schooner U.S.S. *Gallatin* at Newport, Rhode Island, he applied directly to Secretary of the Navy George Bancroft: "Sir, I have the honor to request orders to the squadron employed off the coast of Mexico."[5]

Bancroft denied Maffitt's request because of the intervention of the superintendent of the Coast Survey in Washington, Alexander D. Bache. It was a major decision in Maffitt's career. Bache, a physicist, was one of the most distinguished scientists of the nineteenth century. He was the great-grandson of Benjamin Franklin, grandson of "Sally" Bache (Franklin's only daughter, who administered to soldiers during the Revolutionary War) and, on his mother's side, grandson of Alexander J. Dallas, secretary of the treasury in President James Madison's cabinet. Bache had inherited not only Franklin's taste for science, but also his skill as a diplomat—both of which contributed to the success of the Coast Survey.[6]

In countermanding Maffitt's request to participate in the War with Mexico, Bache explained: "I have upon my own responsibility, and from grounds of public duty, interfered to prevent his detachment from the Coast Survey. . . . His qualifications for this work are so peculiar, that I should not have felt justified in doing otherwise."[7] Bache was correct in that Maffitt was best serving his country as a member of the Coast Survey because the information he gathered was invaluable to commercial maritime interests as well as the navy. However, the accumulated years with the Coast Survey on his naval record would later cause difficulty for Maffitt.

Appointed chief of a hydrographic party on 8 February 1848, Maffitt for the first time commanded a ship, the Coast Survey schooner U.S.S. *Gallatin*.[8] No one excelled Maffitt as a surveying officer. He mapped the Atlantic coast, accumulating astounding totals: 100,006 soundings taken; 2,746 miles of soundings run: 7,347 angles observed.[9] "His vessel was always a model of efficiency and neatness—his surveying expenditures always amongst the smallest—his work has been upon the most dangerous parts of the coast, and he has encountered the dangers without shrinking, and has always drawn his command out of them with great success," commented Bache.[10]

Coast Survey reports reveal Maffitt's movements: Nantucket shoals, Boston harbor, Hyannis harbor, New Bedford, Cape Hatteras, Cape Fear, Beaufort harbor, St. Mary's River, Charleston harbor, Georgetown, Edisto harbor, the James River, and the Gulf Stream. In addition to soundings, topography, reductions and plotting, and sailing directions, Maffitt took specimens from bottoms, installed tide gauges, and recommended locations for lighthouses and buoys. By 1850 he had become an assistant in the Coast Survey, which had a system of multiple assistants.

He often compiled his reports ashore, and while afloat sometimes used several vessels in a surveying squadron.[11]

It was becoming clear by 1850 that Maffitt had discovered a new channel at Charleston harbor, located east of Fort Sumter near Sullivan's Island. Bache wrote in his annual report: "There seems to be no doubt that Lieutenant Commanding Maffitt has discovered a new channel across the bar, through which the same depth of water can be carried as through the main ship channel, more direct for vessels coming from the eastward and northward, but narrow, interrupted by lumps, and not straight. When proper sea marks are placed for this channel it may be used."[12]

About June 1851, Maffitt and his hydrographic party aboard the *Gallatin* established headquarters at Fort Johnson (Fort Pender), North Carolina, on the lower Cape Fear River.[13] Here his off-duty hours were quite pleasant. Up the river near Fayetteville was Ellerslie. Near the mouth of the river was Southport (Smithville), which served as a summer resort for Wilmington society, and where cotillions, picnics, and strolls through exquisite gardens were available to Maffitt. Finding local gossip distasteful, he diverted attention by organizing a theater company and produced at least a dozen plays.[14] Local homes were opened to Maffitt. The grandest setting for entertainment was Orton Plantation, in full flower during the antebellum years. Maffitt was a guest at Orton in August 1851 and was moved to write (under the name "Crowquill") an account of the elaborate series of tableaux and dancing for a newspaper in Wilmington.[15]

During 1852, Maffitt carried out some supplemental survey work at Charleston and surveyed the bars of the Cape Fear River and New River. In June, Maffitt, having completed a survey of the Savannah River, sailed for New York, where he was ordered to exchange ships, departing the next month as commander of the schooner U.S.S. *Crawford* for Charleston. Arriving on July 9 he immediately began a resurvey of the channels. Then he was on to Georgetown to oversee a recommendation for beacon and range lights in the South Carolina harbor. Superintendent Bache wrote of Maffitt's efforts that "the labors of this party have, in amount, as compared with means, in constancy, and in success, exceeded any which have yet come under my observation in the progress of the survey."[16]

Maffitt was usually popular wherever he went, and Charleston was no exception. Here he found a new wife. She was lovely Caroline Laurens Read, a widow of fellow officer James W. Read, and a member of a prominent South Carolina family. The wedding took place 3 August 1852 in St. Paul's Church, Charleston. They began life together in a house at Fort Johnson near Southport,[17] as Maffitt made surveys at Charleston, Cape Fear, and Cape Hatteras. He also made soundings across the Gulf

Stream off Charleston and discovered a ridge on the bottom. His work in the area made him a favorite of local commercial interests in Charleston.

On 16 December 1853, Maffitt was detached from the *Crawford* and, for the first time, assumed command of a steamer, the U.S.S. *Legare*.[18] Since he was beginning a survey near the entrance of the James River, Maffitt moved his family from Southport to a house he purchased on the James. They called the place "Carrieville," in honor of his wife Caroline. Maffitt believed he could enjoy family life while he surveyed the James, but fevers stalked the family in that location. Indeed, his wife's health began to fail during their residence of some four years.[19]

At times during 1854, Maffitt was away on the *Legare,* surveying Beaufort harbor in North Carolina and resurveying Sullivan's Island Channel at Charleston. After giving the composition of the bar at Beaufort as "coarse and fine marine sand, mixed with dead shells," he noted a universal for mariners: "like all southern sand-bars, it is subject to the extraneous influences of sea and current."[20] This made resurveys necessary. At Charleston, the resurvey of Sullivan's Island Channel (from two years earlier) showed it had "moved northward while retaining its general direction, to have diminished in width and slightly increased in depth."[21]

The president of the Charleston Chamber of Commerce, George A. Trenholm (future Confederate secretary of the treasury), tendered a public appreciation dinner in June 1854 to honor Maffitt and other members of a special board that had been created to examine and report on Maffitt's suggestion for deepening the waters over a bar in the harbor. Bache attended and presented to the Chamber "a very large map of the Harbor and vicinity, executed in a most masterly style" that the Chamber had requested. Maffitt and others were toasted at the dinner, and he was undoubtedly one of those who "responded in a pithy and spirited style."[22] The citizens of Charleston were so pleased with Maffitt's work in the harbor that they renamed Sullivan's Island Channel, which he had discovered, Maffitt's Channel.[23] The discovery, wrote a Charleston reporter, "linked his name inseparably with the commerce of our city."[24]

On 18 October 1854, Maffitt returned to command of the familiar *Crawford*[25] and, during the next several months, continued his examination of Charleston harbor. Amid apprehensions that a recent hurricane had deteriorated Maffitt's Channel, he resurveyed it to find the fears groundless; the waterway had actually improved. The Coast Survey numbered among its maps and charts several comparative sketches of Maffitt's Channel. Maffitt also examined other east-coast harbors, including the channels of the Cape Fear. Next, nearer home, he surveyed the James River as far upstream as Jamestown Island, personally executing the necessary preliminary triangulation. He then drew and sent a two-part chart of the river to the Coast Survey office in Washington.[26]

One of Maffitt's acting masters in 1855 later wrote of him: "I was very fond of him, as no doubt every one was who sailed with him. My recollection of that period is that we had lots of hard work and no end of fun; for Maffitt had the rare art of getting all the work possible out of one with the least amount of friction. He was always in a good humor, nor do I remember ever having seen him lose his temper even under the most trying circumstances."[27] Maffitt's temperament must have been sorely tried when he learned through public print that on 14 September 1855, a Naval Efficiency Board had arbitrarily placed him on the indefinite furlough list. If upheld, the directive meant his forced retirement from the navy.[28]

Maffitt obtained a special dispensation from the secretary of the navy to continue on active duty, and for almost two years his career hung in the balance.[29] During this time he received very strong backing from the Charleston Chamber of Commerce, which passed a resolution of protest, published it in the city press, and sent copies to President Franklin Pierce, Secretary of the Navy James C. Dobbin (a native of Maffitt's hometown, Fayetteville, North Carolina), and other government officials.[30] Secretary Dobbin sent to Maffitt a personal message "of such a complimentary character as to make it a sufficient satisfaction for the endurance of almost any humiliation or injustice."[31]

Naval officers had no experience with the concept of retirement and felt disgraced if placed on the list. Maffitt—only thirty-six and, in his words, unwilling to become "an idle and degraded pensioner of the government"—decided to fight. The idea of the fifteen-member Naval Efficiency Board was to purge the officer corps by sending a list of the "unfit" to Secretary Dobbin, who had favored the purge to make way for junior officers. Dobbin presented the list to President Pierce for the final decision. After conferring with Dobbin, Pierce called in the fifteen officers and questioned them carefully. He and Dobbin did not agree with the decision reached in every case, but believed they had to accept or reject the list as a unit.

When the Court of Inquiry convened in Washington on 6 July 1857, Maffitt conducted his own defense. It quickly became apparent that the court would base its case on "professional fitness," a notion that reflected prejudice by some officers against scientific duty rather than man-of-war duty in the navy. In short, the case against Maffitt was that he had been too long (fifteen years) with the Coast Survey and therefore could not function aboard a man-of-war. One further suspects, as did Maffitt, that he was also considered too literary. When Maffitt requested the government to open its case, the Court of Inquiry presented an abstract of his record from the Navy's Official Register. Maffitt then presented a long succession of testimony from fellow officers; some from the witness stand, and others by deposition. Together they represented his naval service, including ship after ship on which he had served, and fully and impressively declared him professionally, physically, morally, and mentally fit for any naval service.[32] In a masterful defense statement, Maffitt pointed out that the survey of America's coast was *by law* one of the duties of naval officers: "And I might here pause to inquire, whether the Naval Efficiency Board made it a *part of their proceedings to investigate fully into the competency of the officers retained on the 'Active List' to perform the important duties of this branch of the service, to which I have been so long attached,* and often against my wishes."[33] Maffitt fought hard and won. His name should not have been on the list, and the wrong was rectified.

On 18 January 1858, the Navy Department detached Maffitt from command of a hydrographic party and ordered him to the Coast Survey office. A few days later, on January 29, he was officially restored to full rank and grade on the active list. Learning that he would soon be leaving the Coast Survey, Maffitt and his survey party "vigorously prosecuted," in Bache's words, the office work in Washington in order to complete it before his separation. According to Bache, Maffitt directed the plotting of the latest soundings made in the James River and left them at the office in April, "together with twenty-seven volumes containing the original notes of soundings, angles, and tidal observations."[34] Maffitt's long years with the Coast Survey, which almost ended his naval career, nonetheless contributed to the establishment of the bureau as a permanent agency.

Chapter 5

Suppression of the Slave Trade

Maffitt's next command was the U.S.S. *Dolphin*—a 224-ton, 88-foot brig carrying 4 guns. The vessel had been on an extensive oceanographic research voyage in the Atlantic during 1855. But when Maffitt took command of the ship on 1 June 1858, he had a different assignment: protection of American commerce and suppression of the slave trade on the Cuban Station.[1]

Piracy had abated, but the slave trade flourished, reaching a peak between 1840 and 1860. In spite of congressional legislation dating from the early 1800s and obligations under the Webster-Ashburton Treaty of 1842 with England to prevent the trade, American refusal to allow search and seizures by the British navy allowed slavers to fly the American flag as protection from capture. American ships and capital participated in the fitting out of slavers, and the flourishing business centered in New York City. The trade continued mostly to Spanish colonies such as Cuba, but there was strong suspicion that slaves also landed in the southern United States. Profits were enormous as humans were bartered for items such as New England rum, Virginia tobacco, and European gunpowder.[2]

Maffitt set forth on his new venture in the *Dolphin* by cruising off the north coast of Cuba.[3] On 21 August 1858, he observed the suspicious movements of a vessel running westward along the shore between Sagua la Grande and Cardenas. This particular craft seemed to be searching for a place to land its cargo. Maffitt ordered the *Dolphin* in pursuit. Closing in, he hoisted the Union Jack and fired two blank cannon shots. He wanted to see the colors of the other craft and, when that was not forthcoming, fired a shot across its bow, then another. The vessel hoisted the American flag, but continued under sail. Maffitt quickly exchanged American for English colors on the *Dolphin* and sent a shot through the main topsail of the fleeing vessel, which then luffed to.

Maffitt had captured a beautiful clipper named *Echo,* originally from Baltimore. It had a crew of eighteen, several of whom were Americans. Maffitt sent his first lieutenant, Joseph M. Bradford, on board with an armed boat's crew to investigate. The *Echo* claimed no papers or nation. It carried—stowed in a false lower deck only forty-four inches high—some three hundred African slaves. They were separated by sex and almost entirely naked. Maffitt ordered Bradford and Lieutenant Charles C. Carpenter with a prize crew to sail the *Echo* to Charleston to be turned over to the U.S. marshal for disposition in court.[4]

The capture of the *Echo* was the beginning of national prominence for Maffitt. The arrival of the ship and the blacks in Charleston created a sensation in the press, partly because Northerners believed Southerners would attempt to use the incident to reopen the international slave trade. It was often front page news. (For days, details of the case appeared alongside news of the laying of the Atlantic cable and the burning of the Crystal Palace in London.)[5]

Soon Maffitt was back in Washington, posted to the Coast Survey office as of 29 October 1858.[6] He sold his place on the James River and purchased a home at 1214 K Street in Washington. It was furnished with heirlooms such as family portraits, beds, and a piano.[7] Maffitt enjoyed the social life in the capital and had a circle of distinguished friends. There was some time left before distant rumblings of sectional strife led to tension between friends, but there was more immediate sadness for Maffitt. His duties at the Coast Survey office allowed him to be near his ill wife, Caroline, whose years of suffering from disease ended in her death that winter. Wrote Maffitt's daughter Florie: "Our beloved, our noble, beautiful, Mama—died in Papa's arms, surrounded by fond friends and loving children."[8]

That summer Maffitt again went to sea. From orders dated 11 June 1859, he learned his new command was to be the U.S.S. *Crusader*.[9] Much larger than his last ship, the *Crusader* (formerly the *Southern Star*) was a screw steamer of 545 tons, 169 feet in length, and carried 8 guns under 3 masts.[10] Maffitt's assignment, somewhat delayed as it turned out, was again cruising for slavers. (His earlier capture of the *Echo* had touched off great interest in the enterprise and led to a series of captures by other U.S. naval vessels.)[11]

Upon arrival at his duty station in Key West, Maffitt found himself dispatched to the Mississippi River on a special mission. The purpose of the mission was to intercept a suspected filibusterer from New Orleans. Maffitt then, under orders, anchored off New Orleans for months. He wrote that the adventurers were "in large numbers, but afraid to move because of the naval show of force." Indeed, the obsessed American filibusterer William Walker organized a company of followers in New Orleans in 1859, but the group never left the harbor. (Walker did slip out of Mobile the next year, only to face a firing squad in Honduras.) While keeping watch off New Orleans, Maffitt was overwhelmed with visitors. He commented: "Have been so much *oppressed* with company and ceremony, that not one day have I had to myself—or even an opportunity to use my own cabin."[12]

During the winter of 1859–1860, Maffitt visited Warrington Navy Yard near Pensacola. The junior lieutenant of the Yard was a friend, John McIntosh Kell. Kell's wife, Blanche, and their children, had recently moved into the Yard. One afternoon, Maffitt approached two children on the street accompanied by their nurses, and asked who the parents of the older boy were:

> "The Devil!" [Maffitt exclaimed] on learning that he was Kell's. He asked the same question of the nurse holding the baby, after which he exploded with, "The devil! Hell! Kell is raising a navy for himself; here's the Commodore, and here's the first lieutenant!" When Blanche later heard of her nurses' encounter, she told her husband and asked what ship had arrived. Laughing heartily, he replied, "That's John Maffitt and the *Crusader*. Tomorrow dress yourself in your prettiest morning dress for he will call on you about 11 o'clock. Maffitt loves ladies and the children, and I know he will want to see my wife." The next morning, while hurrying to answer the door, Blanche tore her dress but, nevertheless, greeted Maffitt, telling him of her distress over the accident. He replied, "Oh, Madam, you're lovelier in a torn dress than most people are in a whole one." When Blanche commented that he must have kissed the blarney stone, Maffitt admitted that his parents were Irish, but that he was a "son of the ocean—born at sea."[13]

In April 1860, Maffitt was back in Cuban waters, but the *Crusader* developed engine trouble. A resounding crash in the engine room made the hull tremble. Maffitt found a bolt had broken in the port cylinder (he referred to cylinders as the lungs of the engine) that caused the cylinder to burst.[14] The ship having made its way into Key West, a board of engineers recommended that Maffitt return to the North for a new cylinder. Instead, Maffitt ordered temporary repairs by his own first assistant engineer, Jonathan A. Grier. Although Maffitt was in "constant dread of an accident," he returned to station under flowing sails. He believed the trip into Key West had cost him a slaver but, on 22 May 1860, predicted he would catch the next.[15]

The following day, while cruising in the mouth of the Old Bahama Channel off the northern coast of Cuba, one of the few ship channels through the Bahama chain, Maffitt decided to determine the character of a bark in the distance. He bore down—without "letting out," because of the patched cylinder—under English colors. When the *Crusader* fired a warning shot, the square-rigger hoisted a French flag. Maffitt then switched to the Stars and Stripes. The captain of the other vessel lowered his flag, tied it, along with his papers, to a forty-pound weight, and tossed the bundle overboard.

Maffitt, seeing that the ship's hatches were closed and being close enough to detect the strong odor characteristic of slavers, sent over Lieutenant James M. Duncan. When Duncan asked for identification of the vessel, its captain replied: "I have no papers, no flag, no name." Said Duncan: "Then, sir, I am ordered to capture you." At this moment, hundreds of blacks broke open the hatches and, with a great shout, swarmed on board. When they saw the American flag over the *Crusader,* they became frantic with joy. The men danced, shouted, and climbed into the rigging. The women's behavior was quite different. Totally nude, and some with babies in their arms, they withdrew to sit upon the deck, silent tears of appreciation in their eyes.

A cheer went up from the decks of the *Crusader;* then Maffitt's discipline became conspicuous. He sent over a detachment of Marines that promptly restored order on the slaver and clothed the blacks in pieces of canvas. Maffitt ordered the officers and crew of the captured vessel to the *Crusader* and sent over a prize crew under the command of Duncan and Lieutenant Andrew K. Benham. The crew of the slaver surrendered without resistance, such a fate regarded by them as part of the risk. They stated that their ship had no name, but it subsequently was found to be the bark *Bogata,* out of New York. The officials and crew of the bark were rather heterogeneous in their appearance. A few could have been English or American, but they revealed little about themselves. The cargo master spoke English and "might be taken for a Yankee galvanized into a Frenchman or Spaniard, as circumstances might dictate." The captain of the bark was apparently a Frenchman (who spoke English), and a man of pleasant and gentlemanly deportment. When he came on board, Captain Maffitt addressed him: "You declined to manifest your nationality, sir?" The response: "I have no flag, no name, no papers; I am a slaver, sir, and now your prisoner."[16]

Maffitt escorted the *Bogata* to Key West. The blacks, between four and five hundred of them, had been on passage in the *Bogata* for forty-five days from Ouidah, a slave trading base in the People's Republic of Benin (Kingdom of Dahomey). They, like many others, had been prisoners of war sold by the king. Seven had died en route to Cuba. At Key West, the blacks joined others who had been recaptured by the navy. Buildings had been erected to house them at Whitehead Point. At the time, there were some fourteen hundred Africans in the complex awaiting government disposition. Maffitt turned the crew members of the *Bogata* over to the U.S. marshal's office at Key West.[17] After dispensing with his prize, Maffitt immediately stood to his cruising grounds off Cuba.

Official commendation came Maffitt's way, as well as plaudits from the pulpit. Vivid newspaper accounts of the chase and capture were widely read. The famous Maffitt name made him easily stand out as a vigilant naval officer who rescued unfortunates from bondage. Indeed, as the *Wilmington Daily Journal* later declared, "it is a curious fact, for those who maintain that the civil war in America is founded upon the slave question, that [Maffitt] should be the very man who has distinguished himself actively against the slave trade."[18]

The damaged machinery in the *Crusader* still had not forced Maffitt to go north, and he continued to stalk slave ships. His next capture was the *William R. Kirby*. Boarded 23 July 1860, in Cuban waters, the ship was found deserted except for three African boys left aboard. Maffitt's last capture occurred 14 August 1860 off Cuba: the *Young Antonio*, a ship of somewhat doubtful character but with no slaves aboard.[19] (Maffitt believed it was a pirate vessel.) By Maffitt's own account, in the first three of his four captures he rescued a total of 789 slaves.[20]

The faulty boiler in the *Crusader* finally forced Maffitt off the Cuban station for repairs, which could only be performed at a U.S. Navy Yard, and he chose the nearest, Pensacola. On the first leg of the voyage, he transported some mutineers from the ship *Champion* from Havana to Key West, where they would be tried, along with the crews of several slavers, in the district court of southern Florida. Maffitt arrived at Key West to deposit the mutineers 7 November 1860,[21] the day following Abraham Lincoln's election to the presidency, and the day the South Carolina legislature began proceedings that led to secession. By the time Maffitt arrived in Pensacola for repairs in mid-November, other Southern states were following the example of South Carolina.[22]

Southerners were capturing Federal property when Maffitt, after a visit to his family, was again ready for sea.[23] On the evening of 2 January 1861, he sailed from Pensacola in the *Crusader*.[24] He proceeded to Mobile, where as acting purser he presented a check on the collector of the port for the prize money due the officers and crew of the ship for capturing slavers. There was some delay concerning the cashing of a government check because Alabama was seceding. At the same time, the presence of the *Crusader* aroused strong local feeling, and Maffitt learned of a plot to board and capture his ship: "I immediately placed the steamer in a defensive position, got up steam and prepared for action." In an interview with influential citizens, including the editor of the *Mobile Register,* John Forsyth, Maffitt vowed that if boats approached with hostile intent, he would open his broadsides "and sink them in fifteen minutes with every desperado on board of them." The check was paid, and Maffitt departed Mobile.[25] His defiant stand proved his loyalty to the government that had entrusted the ship to him, which was not unusual for Southern naval officers at the time, but Maffitt's action was highly visible.

During the next few days, amid resignations by Southern naval officers, Secretary of the Navy Isaac Toucey—not one of the better navy secretaries—desperately attempted to ascertain Maffitt's whereabouts. It was rumored that the *Crusader* would steam up the Mississippi River to prevent the takeover of strategic forts and arsenals; but on January 9, Maffitt routinely reported his return to the Cuban Station, giving his position as off Havana. The next day, Toucey, not yet in receipt of this information, asked pointedly, "Where has Lieutenant Maffitt gone?"[26]

When new orders finally reached him, Maffitt reported to Key West, arriving by 11 January 1861. The island population was pro-Southern. Florida's secession the previous day created a threat to Federal outposts in the area—Fort Taylor at Key West and Fort Jefferson at Dry Tortugas. Both forts were under-manned, and Fort Jefferson was without guns. Captain Montgomery C. Meigs, the engineer in charge of Fort Jefferson, loaded guns and ammunition aboard the *Horace Beale* at Key West and—towed by the *Joseph Whitney* and convoyed by Maffitt in the *Crusader* "to guard against every possible contingency"—arrived January 23 at Dry Tortugas to arm Fort Jefferson. Maffitt also, along with Lieutenant T. Augustus Craven of the U.S.S. *Mohawk,* sent bluejackets ashore at Forts Taylor and Jefferson, to provide proper garrisons. They received official recognition for their "prompt and efficient assistance in aiding and protecting the two works."[27]

Maffitt's role in protecting the strategic outposts was a material factor for the Union. The forts, which remained in Federal hands throughout the war, controlled the entrance to the Gulf of Mexico. Without them, the Federals would have had a much more difficult task in blockading Florida and the Gulf Coast.[28]

Chapter 6

From Navy Blue to Navy Gray

In spite of Maffitt's contributions to the Federal cause, naval officials in Washington came to view him with increasing suspicion. While he was defending the Federal forts, Secretary Toucey ordered him to proceed immediately with the *Crusader* to New York. In need of funds for the voyage, Maffitt first sailed to Havana, where he attempted to arrange an advance from the Bank of Havana through the U.S. consulate. The times were too uncertain (and Cuba too pro-Southern), however, and Maffitt had to use his own funds in order to finance the voyage. It was his final cruise as a Federal officer.

In New York, Maffitt on 1 March 1861 relinquished command of the *Crusader*. Returning home to Washington, he attempted to settle the ship's accounts. The food and clothing items received prompt attention, but Federal auditors refused to reimburse the advance from Maffitt. For months he constantly applied for settlement, but Federal auditors withheld reimbursement because of his presumed pro-Southern orientation.[1] This rebuff, in contrast to Maffitt's delivery of the *Crusader* to Federal authority, reflects a greater nobility of character on his part than on the U.S. Navy's.

The news of the fall of Fort Sumter reached Washington in the early evening of April 13, causing intense excitement within the city. Maffitt now faced his terrible decision of allegiance. He could hear the tramp of soldiers and the roll of artillery wagons day and night outside his house. Southern families departed daily; resignations were announced "in language of gall and bitterness."[2] Maffitt's relatives were in the South. His property was partly in the North—his Washington home with its valuable furnishings and fine library; and partly in the South—interest in land in South Carolina he inherited from the Laurens family through his second wife, Caroline. Maffitt described himself as a slave owner, a notion that was probably related in some way to the Laurens estate, although his interest was apparently modest. He recoiled against a people who sold slaves to Southerners and then became puritanical in their attitudes:

I fancied that New England, with her well-developed seces-sion proclivities, would offer no material objection to the course of the South. In truth it was natural to presume that her fanatical abolitionism would hail with joy the departure of the un-Godly, slaveholding section of the country from her unwelcome participation in the Union. But material interest gave zest to patriotism, and her war course would lead the world to suppose that she had never contemplated a severance from the Union and forming a Northern Confederation.[3]

Maffitt, acting on the conviction that free government is founded on the consent of the governed, overcame his love of the U.S. Navy and prepared to go South. On April 18 he sent his children out of Washington to his brother-in-law, John Laurens, in Charleston. From there, they would eventually move to the family of Eliza (Maffitt) Hybart at Ellerslie. However, Maffitt was unable to collect funds due him from the navy, nor could he transfer his furniture, or sell his house or bonds. Maffitt sent in his resignation from the navy on 28 April 1861,[4] but again, there was no action until he appeared in the office of recently installed Secretary of the Navy Gideon Welles, who accepted his resignation as of 2 May 1861.[5]

When Maffitt learned that his name was on a list of those subject to arrest, he slipped out of Washington. Approaching the carefully guarded Long Bridge over the Potomac River, Maffitt in some way convinced a Federal officer to allow him to pass over to Alexandria, Virginia. "How 'twas done becomes me not to state even in a private journal," wrote Maffitt. In defense of the officer who soon lost command of his battery of artillery, Maffitt pointed out that not everyone had envisioned the Civil War. Maffitt spent the night in Alexandria and, on the morning of May 3, started for Richmond. Four days later, he arrived in Montgomery, Ala-bama, to offer his services to the Confederacy.[6]

Disappointment awaited Maffitt in the "Cradle of the Confederacy." While Montgomery resounded with the bustle of military preparation, including martial music in the air and volunteer companies in the streets, there was scant attention paid to forming a navy. Wrote Maffitt: "The government instantly seemed to be at sea, without rudder, compass, or charts by which to steer upon the bewildering ocean of absolute neces-sity."[7] Many of the Confederate states had established provisional state navies, consisting of tug boats and small river steamers, that were turned over to the Confederate government. The South had little in the way of seamen, machine shops, and ship yards. In officer personnel, the South was more fortunate; the Confederate navy's chief assets were about a quarter of the officers from the list of the old navy. A total of 322 officers had left the U.S. Navy, 243 of whom were line officers, and they were to engage in some of the war's most heroic episodes.[8]

The Confederacy had called for these "naval sons of the South," and they had left the Federal service at great personal and professional sacrifice. Yet at the time, President Jefferson Davis seemed convinced, based on correspondence he received from the North, that Southern independence would come without war. In an interview with the president, a stunned Maffitt listened to Davis say it was unnecessary for the South to expend funds to form a navy. The president was unmoved when Maffitt described war preparations in the North. Davis believed that Southern officers should have brought their ships with them and undoubtedly knew of Maffitt's defiant refusal to relinquish the *Crusader* at Mobile.[9]

In spite of the nature of their interview, the president would prove a stronger supporter of Maffitt than did Secretary of the Navy Stephen R. Mallory. "I was pained to find that the Cabinet was injudiciously selected," wrote Maffitt. He pointed out that Mallory did not enjoy popular support with Southerners and that the Confederate Senate had repeatedly rejected his nomination. But Mallory finally did gain confirmation after he was endorsed by Southern naval officers such as Captain Josiah Tattnall.[10] Davis had appointed Mallory because the latter was from Florida, a fact which satisfied geographical considerations; because he had been chairman of the U.S. Senate Committee on Naval Affairs; and because he was acquainted with naval officers.[11] Mallory brought to the monumental problems facing him the ability of a clever amateur in the field, but he had a passion for learning about naval affairs and began to enjoy the challenges. He also belatedly developed "a kind of impulsive progressivism."[12]

An interview with Mallory caused even greater consternation for Maffitt. During the mid-1850s, Mallory had been the chief Senate sponsor and defender of the Naval Efficiency Board that had attempted to force Maffitt into retirement. Now, at the meeting in Montgomery, Mallory was so uncomfortable and defensive that, as Maffitt later told a friend, "he had been received by the Secretary of the Navy as if [Maffitt] had designs upon him."[13] Maffitt left the meeting without an offer to serve in the Confederate navy. Disgusted, he went to his hotel room and started packing his trunk for Europe. Suddenly, in rushed a delegation of notables including Robert Toombs and Benjamin Hill. They had just come from President Davis and brought with them an offer for Maffitt to reconsider his departure because the Confederacy needed his services.[14] Maffitt agreed to stay, and Davis approved his appointment as a lieutenant in the Confederate navy effective 8 May 1861.[15]

Maffitt received orders to report to Savannah, where Tattnall was assembling a fleet of small craft to defend the waters off South Carolina and Georgia. The command was further evidence to Maffitt that "the puerile attempt to improvise a navy is a part of the melancholy history of our mistakes." He arrived in Savannah on May 9 to assume command of the C.S.S. *Savannah,* flagship of the mosquito fleet. The 406-ton paddle-wheel steamer was formerly a passenger boat (called the *Everglade*) that had plied the inland route between Savannah, Georgia, and Jacksonville, Florida. Accustomed to the big ships of the U.S. Navy, Maffitt termed the Savannah an "absurd abortion of a man-of-war."[16]

Maffitt journeyed to Norfolk on June 6 to obtain cannon and powder. He arrived to find the Navy Yard in ruins following the Federal evacuation, though the raised U.S.S. *Merrimac* was there, being converted into the C.S.S. *Virginia.* Maffitt obtained three dozen guns. Some of the guns were mounted on the mosquito fleet's vessels, and some went to Beauregard for the defense of Charleston.[17] This was part of the large cache of guns (conservatively estimated at 1,400) that had fallen into Confederate hands at Norfolk. The weapons were shipped south, by way of the Dismal Swamp Canal and the inland waterway, as far as Florida. Without them, the ports of the South would have easily fallen to the Federals, who would have consequently ended blockade running, and probably the war, at a much earlier date.[18]

Back in Savannah, Maffitt's apprehension grew. The frequent inland cruises of the small vessels "gave evidence of their total inability to meet the Federal gunboats with prospect of success." Maffitt made various proposals. One was to destroy the New York Navy Yard, a bold plan that he termed "not difficult at the period." He also advocated running into the South large quantities of arms, clothing, and provisions, as well as powerful engines for large warships before the blockade became effective. None of his suggestions received favorable action by government authorities during the summer, and the months of opportunity were wasted. Maffitt also suggested that a captured prize ship of 1,200 tons be converted into a floating ironclad battery to support the earthen Forts Walker and Beauregard guarding the entrance to Port Royal Sound, and the guns of the two forts be spread along the beaches to deny the enemy a small focus on which to concentrate their fire. The latter suggestion, wrote Maffitt, was "agreed to when too late!"[19]

The Federals were quite interested in Port Royal, located midway between Charleston and Savannah. It was a fine harbor with sufficient water for the largest vessels. If captured, the harbor could serve as a base of operations—providing safe anchorage, coal, provisions, a storage depot, and machine shops and docks for refitting ships—for the Union fleet against the Southern states. Accordingly, on 19 October 1861, a naval task force departed New York with Captain Samuel Francis Du Pont as flag officer aboard the steam frigate U.S.S. *Wabash*. The men-of-war sailed to Hampton Roads, where large troop transports carrying an army corps under General Thomas W. Sherman joined in, making a combined force of fifty vessels, excluding twenty-five coal ships. Never before had there been so large an American fleet. Moving slowly southward against a head wind in the formation of an inverted V, the ships encountered a fierce gale off Cape Hatteras. One transport loaded with stores went down, and a few other store ships were disabled, sunk, or separated from the fleet as phosphorescent ocean waves broke over the decks "in superlative grandeur." November 3 dawned bright as the fleet straggled southward on a smooth sea.[20]

The Federals went to great lengths to keep the fleet's destination a secret, but President Davis in Richmond learned through informants in Hampton Roads that the objective was Port Royal. Davis conveyed the information to Tattnall, who ordered the mosquito fleet from Savannah via Skull Creek to Port Royal Sound. The little navy arrived to find some of the enemy ships already at the entrance to the harbor. For several days during the first week of November, the Federals buoyed the channel in preparation for their attack. Fort Walker on Hilton Head Island, stronger than Fort Beauregard on Bay Point across the harbor, was Du Pont's primary target. Both forts had a combined total of forty-three guns that were manned by inexperienced troops. The *Savannah* mounted one thirty-two-pounder forward and one eighteen-pounder aft; the other Confederate vessels one or two guns each. Du Pont's heavy batteries amounted to 215 guns.[21]

An eyewitness on board the *Savannah* on November 5 counted forty-four enemy ships off the bar. The mosquito fleet approached to within a mile and a half of several Federal vessels taking soundings near the bar, and engaged them for forty minutes before being driven back to Bay Point. The following day, November 6, Tattnall went ashore to confer with Colonel R. G. M. Dunovant, the commander of Fort Beauregard. While Tattnall was ashore, Maffitt steamed out and again engaged the enemy at long range. The *Savannah* received minor damage to its upper works and more serious damage six inches above the waterline. An eleven-inch shell from the U.S.S. *Seneca*, fired at ricochet from 2,500 yards across a glossy sea, entered near the wheelhouse of the "miserable little cockle-shell" of a flagship and carried away bulkheads and stanchions, but failed to explode and caused no casualties. Maffitt returned to Bay Point, where he was forced to run the stricken vessel ashore until a plank could be fitted over the hole. Tattnall disapproved of the action and suspended Maffitt from command of the *Savannah*.[22]

The Federal fleet came into the harbor next morning, November 7, and attached Fort Walker with serial broadsides in line action from an oval sailing pattern in front of the works. The mosquito fleet moved up to a mile from the ships and opened fire, which was ignored at first by the Federals. In due course, two of the enemy ships chased the pesky mosquito boats into Skull Creek.[23] The exchange of fire between the forts and the Federal ships lasted four hours, and ended when the Confederates evacuated their works. Tattnall, not realizing the end was near, ordered his flagship to Savannah for repairs and disembarked men at Seabrook's Landing in Skull Creek in an effort to reinforce Fort Walker across Saint Simons Island. But the fort had already fallen, and Tattnall left the island in the middle of the night, taking many of the men from Fort Walker with him to Savannah on board the *Resolute* and the *Sampson*.[24]

Back in Savannah, the disagreement between Tattnall and Maffitt reached a conclusion. Tattnall maintained the order he gave when he left the *Savannah* at Bay Point was to remain at anchor, but Maffitt wrote: "I did not so understand him, but on the contrary, understood him to direct that no soundings by the enemy should be permitted." When Maffitt saw the Federals sounding he "went at them," causing Tattnall to suspend him for disobedience of orders, after which Tattnall received credit for the bold attack. Maffitt had sent the commander "a very insulting letter," and Tattnall sent friends to ask Maffitt to withdraw it, expressing his regards. Maffitt did so, adding: "We met—he obliterated all that was unkind and harsh." Then at Maffitt's request, and on application of General Robert E. Lee, Tattnall approved the transfer of Maffitt to Lee's staff as naval aide.[25]

Lee had recently assumed command of the department of South Carolina, Georgia, and Florida. Shortly afterward, the Federal navy occupied Tybee Island in preparation for a successful attack on Fort Pulaski at the entrance of the Savannah River. Lee realized the coastal islands were vulnerable, and quickly withdrew troops and supplies to an interior line away from the Federal navy. He chose for his base camp Coosawhatchie, South Carolina, a small village up the Coosawhatchie River four miles beyond the reach of enemy boats. The situation appeared desperate; Lee expected an attack on both Savannah and Charleston.[26]

Maffitt, under orders of 11 November 1861, reported for duty at Lee's headquarters.[27] He was one of three volunteer aides on a headquarters staff that also consisted of two assistant adjutants general and three officers of the general staff. Because of the smallness of the command, all the headquarters officers were in close touch with Lee,[28] and Maffitt's association with his new commander was most agreeable. "I am now well pleased," wrote Maffitt.[29]

As naval aide to Lee, Maffitt was on temporary assignment helping with defense preparations. Maffitt's duties included mapping roads, building forts,[30] and obstructing the Coosaw River (northeast of Beaufort). At first, he had serious misgivings concerning the local soldiers' ability to hold the Charleston and Savannah Railroad. "The troops were raw, badly clad, and almost without organization," Maffitt wrote. But General John C. Pemberton soon arrived, and his energetic efforts brought improvements, so that, according to Maffitt, "hope dawned."[31]

By mid-December, the military situation around Charleston, the most exposed of the two major ports, appeared to be stabilizing.[32] Lee believed that the land defenses around the city "will now give steadiness and security to our troops in any advance of the enemy."[33] The Federal navy, for its part, sank a stone fleet (small sailing vessels loaded with stone) in the Main Ship Channel, and another in Maffitt's Channel, the only two channels that allowed ships of any size to enter the harbor.[34] The enemy's effort to obstruct the harbor failed—and blockade runners continued to be partial to Maffitt's Channel.[35] But the attempt at obstruction suggested that the Federals had no immediate plans to attack Charleston.

Chapter 7

Running the Blockade

Maffitt's duty as naval aide to Lee was nearly complete. Because of his extensive knowledge of the southeastern coastline as a result of his Coast Survey experience, Maffitt occasionally advised Fraser, Trenholm and Company on blockade running. The firm was Charleston's largest shipping enterprise and, with an office in Liverpool, was well-known overseas. George A. Trenholm, one of the most influential men in the South and president of the company, enjoyed unlimited credit abroad. Trenholm regarded Maffitt's advice so highly that he suggested to Secretary of War Judah P. Benjamin that Maffitt be placed in charge of blockade running activities in Nassau.[1] Small wonder that Maffitt wrote: "my efforts are *highly appreciated*."[2]

By 1862, the ever-more effective Union blockade was causing changes. Privateering ended because prizes could not be brought into port. Slow sailing vessels and large, slow steamers could no longer serve as blockade runners, but small steamers could speed into Southern ports at night after goods were transshipped at ports such as Halifax, Bermuda, Havana, and Nassau. An early example of transshipment occurred when a large steamer, the *Gladiator,* heavily laden with 20,240 Enfield rifles and other munitions and stores, arrived in Nassau from England, but became stranded when Union blockaders took up position about the Bahamas. Trenholm, motivated by commercial purposes and patriotic zeal, offered to transship the cargo in two of his small steamers, the *Cecile* and the *Kate.*[3] Maffitt considered the situation critical because the expansion of the war had proved the inadequacy of the South's domestic industry to meet the increased military demand. He later commented: "The pressure on the government at Richmond became alarming and created an uneasiness that could not be concealed. At this tenacious crisis, the mercantile firm of Fraser, Trenholm and Company . . . generously came to the rescue."[4]

On 2 January 1862, Trenholm notified Benjamin that Mosquito Inlet at New Smyrna, Florida, had been chosen as the point of importation. Maffitt probably recommended New Smyrna. From there, the Confederate supplies could be shipped northward via the St. John's River to railroad connections in Jacksonville. New Smyrna was only two days' run from Nassau, and the steamers could follow the Gulf Stream northward, which would reduce the risk of encountering blockaders steaming southward because the blockaders would avoid the Gulf Stream. Most importantly, however, the port was entirely free from blockaders. But Maffitt also advised that two guns be placed at the inlet to drive away any blockaders that might be sent in after the *Cecile* and the *Kate*. Lee accordingly had two guns mounted in a fieldwork at the little harbor. Trenholm, with an air of urgency, wired Benjamin again on January 2: "We took the liberty of telegraphing you this morning in relation to Captain Maffitt. It is important that we should command his services without delay."[5]

While waiting for orders as proposed agent in Nassau, Maffitt now entered a kind of intermediary status, and one for which he was well-suited—blockade running. On January 7, he was ordered to the blockade runner *Cecile*. Built in Wilmington, Delaware, in 1857, the *Cecile* was a 360-ton side-wheeler, 156 feet in length and 29 feet across the beam. The small steamer had been a prewar passenger ship plying the waters between Charleston and Fernandina. The vessel could carry over 300 bales of cotton on its iron hull.[6]

Maffitt now became a direct participant in the New Smyrna project. The *Cecile,* loaded with cotton, departed Charleston 20 February 1862 for Nassau. Upon arrival at Nassau, Maffitt supervised the transshipment of Enfield rifles to New Smyrna via the *Cecile* and the *Kate*. The two vessels operated two to three days apart. The *Cecile* arrived at Mosquito Inlet 2 March 1862, and the ship's six-to-eight-feet draft allowed it to cross the shallow bar into the harbor. In addition to munitions, the *Cecile* also brought in dispatches bound for Richmond. Five days later, it departed for Nassau. The mission of the small steamers had been successful, prompting the Confederate government to rely on private companies for importations by the transshipment method.[7]

Within two weeks of the departure of the *Cecile,* Union troops captured Jacksonville, and the Confederates evacuated New Smyrna. The Federals not only extended their blockade to include New Smyrna, but captured Fernandina, Brunswick, and Fort Pulaski. This accomplishment, together with Union successes in the sounds of North Carolina, basically confined east coast blockade running to Charleston and Wilmington by the spring of 1862. Maffitt made several runs between Wilmington and Nassau as commander of the *Cecile,* importing arms and stores for the Confederacy.

Early in April, Maffitt journeyed to Richmond and personally sought an answer concerning his duties from the new secretary of war, George W. Randolph. Results came quickly. On 11 April 1862, Randolph appointed Maffitt agent in Nassau, and his duties were sweeping: "You are authorized to take entire control of all vessels loaded with arms and munitions for the Confederate States." Maffitt could select ports of entry, and even discharge officers and crews of vessels and replace them. The only limitation to the orders was that he was to confer with Louis Heyliger, Confederate agent in Nassau. Maffitt was to report to his duty station in command of the blockade runner *Nassau*.[8] The wooden side-wheeler, built in New York in 1851, had a powerful engine and was a 518-ton ship, 177 feet long and 27 feet wide. A much-named vessel with a varied career, the craft had been purchased by the Confederate government from Fraser, Trenholm and Company.[9]

Soon an interesting group of passengers boarded the *Nassau* in Wilmington, bound for Nassau. One of them was Maffitt's daughter, Florie.[10] Also on board was recently appointed Confederate agent to Europe, Edwin DeLeon.[11] On the moonlit night of 2 May 1862, Maffitt ran down the Cape Fear River and through the gauntlet of blockaders. Some of them gave chase for a few hours, but Maffitt eluded them. For two days and a night, there was beautiful weather, but on the second night, the little ship encountered an angry sea and sky. Soon a major storm hit with full force. The roar of waves and wind, and the groaning of timbers, made for an anxious night. Above it all, Florie could hear "the calm, steady voice of her father encouraging, and directing his men."[12]

The next day the craft steamed into the harbor at Nassau. The emerald water of the harbor was so clear that the seaweed and shells could be seen on the bottom as "the usual swarm of newsmongers" came on board the blockade runner. Shipping was the lifeblood of Nassau—the only town on the island of New Providence. Before the war, Nassau had attracted only a few wreckers and fisherman, but now throngs of newcomers on an international scale brought prosperity based on blockade running. Overlooking the town was the fashionable Royal Victoria Hotel. Built by the British colonial government, the hotel could accommodate two hundred guests, and commanded a fine view of the harbor.[13]

After the passengers of the *Nassau* had settled into the Royal Victoria, Maffitt received a visitor who brought important news. Master John Low of the Confederate navy, who had arrived earlier in the *Oreto* (*Manassas*) from Liverpool, handed Maffitt a letter from Commander James D. Bulloch, Confederate naval agent in England. The letter offered Maffitt both a great opportunity and an extreme difficulty and, in the end, would secure his place in history. He was offered command of the *Oreto*, anchored nine miles east of Nassau.[14]

Destined to become the raider C.S.S. *Florida*, the *Oreto* could do little to turn the tide of war. It could, however, "repay upon the enemy some of the injuries his vastly superior force alone has enabled him to inflict upon the states of the Confederacy."[15] But obstacles prevented Maffitt from immediately taking the ship to sea. First, a series of protests by U.S. officials, both in England and in Nassau, challenged the vessels' status. Construction of the ship had begun in June 1861, after Bulloch, with Fraser, Trenholm and Company assuming financial responsibility for the Confederacy, secured a contract with shipbuilders William C. Miller and Sons of Liverpool. As building progressed over the next few months, Union diplomats found through their network of spies and dockyard informants that the ship took on menacing characteristics.

The South's first English-built commerce destroyer was modeled after a dispatch gunboat of the Royal Navy. However, Bulloch made some modifications. Increased length allowed the ship to carry more coal and supplies, and would possibly add to its speed. Bulloch also specified more rigging for sail capacity to increase the range. (Because of the Union blockade, Confederate cruisers could not depend on Southern ports for supplies, and foreign neutrality laws limited the use of other ports to once in ninety days. Further, longer periods at sea resulted in more enemy commerce destroyed.) An unusual feature of the ship was a retractable screw. A perpendicular shaft through the stern deck allowed the propeller assembly, attached to a hawser, to be raised by a wench located on deck directly over the shaft. Lifting out of the water the screw of a steamer under sail improved handling and increased speed.[16]

The $225,000 raider-in-the-making was schooner rigged with 3 masts and 2 funnels. The ship was 191 feet long, with a beam of 28 feet and a depth of 14 feet. Constructed of wood (which carried heavy guns better than metal ships of that day), the ship's registry shows an original weight of 410 tons—over 700 tons when fully operational. Its engines consisted of 2 horizontal cylinders, 42 inches in diameter, fired by 2 horizontal boilers—each with 3 furnaces. This power plant, built by Fawcett, Preston and Company of Liverpool, produced 200 horsepower and drove the vessel at an average of 9½ knots, boosted by a favorable wind under canvas to 12 knots.[17]

To keep the ship's purpose secret, officials gave it the dockyard name *Oreto*. The name sounded Italian, and dockyard workers were told the vessel was destined for a firm in Palermo, Sicily. By February 1862, the vessel was afloat and in full view in the Mersey River. Thomas H. Dudley, U.S. consul in Liverpool, became convinced it was destined for use as a Confederate raider. He hired private detectives and bribed seamen to obtain information concerning the vessel's warlike character. It was not fitted out with arms and munitions, but its general appearance, along with portholes for guns, indicated a prospective raider.[18]

The *Oreto* was the first test of British neutral obligations, which prohibited arming, manning, or equipping a warship in British waters. However, British law at the time was silent on structure or intent and was, overall, rather weak.[19] The greatest danger was the effect of determined American protests to the British.[20] The *Oreto* passed the test of British law because the ship had no arms and munitions on board, but because of the intense U.S. diplomatic pressure for its detention, Bulloch devised a daring plan to remove the vessel from Liverpool.

The plan for the departure of the *Oreto* included selection of a commander. Acting from a sense of obligation, Bulloch first approached Lieutenant James North, a fellow Confederate naval agent in England and a procrastinator. North declined as expected, leaving Bulloch free to approach Maffitt, a man he knew from the old navy as having "great natural resources—self-reliant, and fearless." Since Maffitt was running the blockade, the *Oreto* would be sent to him. Bulloch hired an English merchant captain, James A. Duguid, and an English crew of fifty-two men. When it cleared the Mersey River on 22 March 1862, the *Oreto* had on board no arms or munitions. The crew believed the vessel was bound for Palermo, and observers on shore believed it was on a trial run, especially since there were several women and other visitors on board—but, except for John Low, they were all sent ashore in small boats outside the harbor. Ostensibly a passenger, Low was actually in charge of the *Oreto*, with secret orders to deliver the ship to Maffitt in Nassau.[21]

On 28 April 1862, the *Oreto*, under the guise of an English merchant vessel, arrived in Nassau and put into Cochrane's Anchorage, nine miles east of the main harbor, but within the limits of the port of Nassau. By the time Maffitt arrived on May 4, the vessel was already attracting attention and comment. Maffitt promptly relinquished command of the blockade runner *Nassau* and assumed control of the *Oreto*. For a time, he would command incognito and issue orders through Low. Maffitt wrote that his position "was delicate, and required great caution on my part." Since Adams had sent information from London that armaments for the *Oreto* would arrive from Britain on the steamer *Bahama*, Maffitt concluded "it was natural to presume that the American consul would not neglect the interests he represented."[22] Indeed, the U.S. consul in Nassau, Samuel Whiting, now brought diplomatic pressure in Nassau for the British to confiscate the *Oreto*.[23]

Maffitt's next step was to confirm his new command with the Navy Department, and request funds and experienced officers. He reported to Mallory via three blockade runners, including the *Nassau*.[24] Although the latter was captured, a report reached Mallory, who responded with approval of Maffitt's conduct, but still hoped the indecisive James North would arrive in the *Bahama* to assume command of the *Oreto*.[25] When the *Bahama* arrived on 7 June 1862, North was not aboard, and Maffitt, as instructed by Mallory, considered himself officially detailed. No money came, and only two inexperienced officers—Master Otey Bradford, whom Maffitt described as having "little ability of any kind," and Midshipman George T. Sinclair, Jr., who on the passage to Nassau saw the ocean for the first time.[26] Further, the English crew left the *Oreto* because they had never been told, and could not ascertain, the vessel's destination.[27] Wrote Maffitt: "The Secretary complacently ordered me to fit out and cruise, as though I controlled a navy yard, and had engineers, men . . . at my command."[28]

British warships kept careful watch over the *Oreto* at Cochrane's Anchorage. Seeking to avoid seizure of the vessel, Maffitt did not go near it as he attempted to find officers and a crew. The *Oreto* had already been seized by the H.M.S. *Bulldog*, but was released in view of British legal opinion. However, continuing pressure from Consul Whiting and British naval officers forced pro-Confederate Governor Charles J. Bayley to report that the *Oreto* would be prosecuted in the Vice Admiralty Court of the Bahamas for violation of the Foreign Enlistment Act. A prize crew from the H.M.S. *Greyhound* took possession of the vessel.[29]

A decision by the court did not come for six weeks. Maffitt passed the time pleasantly at the spacious Royal Victoria Hotel. The fare was excellent, and the sea breeze made the summer heat more tolerable. With Maffitt were Commander Raphael Semmes (soon to take command of the C.S.S. *Alabama*) and other Confederate officers, and some pretty and musical women—wives and sisters of men engaged in running the blockade. Semmes, commenting on life at the hotel that summer, gives a vivid description of Maffitt's persona:

> Maffitt in particular, was the life of our household. He knew everybody, and everybody knew him, and he passed in and out of all the rooms, *sans ceremonie,* at all hours. Being a jaunty, handsome fellow, young enough, in appearance, to pass for the elder brother of his son, a midshipman who was to go with me to the *Alabama,* he was a great favorite with the ladies. He was equally at home, with men or women, it being all the same to him, whether he was wanted to play a game of billiards, take a hand at whist, or join in a duet with a young lady—except that he had the good taste always to prefer the lady. Social, gay, and convivial, he was much courted and flattered, and there was scarcely ever a dining or an evening party, at which he was not present. But this was the mere outside glitter of the metal.[30]

Maffitt delighted in practical jokes, especially when the focus of the humor was the enemy. While waiting to get the *Oreto* out of irons, he took a brief excursion as a passenger on board the *Kate*. The blockade runner ran to the west end of New Providence Island to meet a British mail steamer. Several prominent inhabitants of Nassau were on board the *Kate* with refreshments in the form of cases of champagne and brandy. After a pleasant hour during which the officers of the two vessels exchanged visits, the *Kate* started back to Nassau. Among the guests on board was Consul Whiting, who had gone along to get his dispatches. He was greatly disliked by the Confederate sympathizers in Nassau. On the return run, the consul, overcome by his numerous potations, lay down with his dispatches and was soon asleep. Back at Nassau, Whiting discovered that his dispatches were missing, "whereupon he accused Maffitt of stealing them, resulting in a grand row all round."[31]

The case of the *Oreto* was coming to a conclusion. Maffitt attended the lengthy and tedious trial, and heard testimony from many principles, including the ship's officers and crew members. Captain Duguid testified he believed the *Oreto* to be an ordinary merchant ship, but members of the crew claimed that it had magazines instead of cargo space and was a warship lacking only guns. The trial resulted in proof that the vessel had left England unarmed and without a battle crew. This convinced the judge, John C. Lees, that regardless of the ship's configuration, it had not violated the Foreign Enlistment Act, and he ordered the release of the *Oreto*.[32] A ship did not violate the law unless it was armed, and the result presumably would have been the same if the case had been tried in Britain. Maffitt had anticipated the outcome of the trial and welcomed the opportunity for action, but he could not have foreseen the new troubles that were nearly to take his life.

Chapter 8

Audacity at Mobile Bay

Surveillance of the *Oreto* had allowed Maffitt no opportunity to arm, equip, or recruit a crew in Nassau. He wrote: "The difficulties are very great; some twelve men-of-war are on the lookout. Seamen, firemen, and engineers are hard to obtain. I have no invoice of what has come for her, and we dare not open the boxes in the bonded warehouse."[1] Maffitt would have to fit out at sea with a scant crew and inexact knowledge of his arms inventory.

As part of Maffitt's deception, clearance papers for the *Oreto* listed his stepson, Laurens Read, as captain. The vessel then steamed to a point outside the harbor at Nassau where Maffitt went aboard and took command.[2] With him was only one officer who had nautical experience, Lieutenant John M. Stribling; there were a handful of junior officers, and just five firemen and fourteen deck hands.[3] The deficit in officers was thirteen, and in crew members, over one hundred. Maffitt sent Stribling back to Nassau to take charge of the schooner *Prince Albert*, load the arms and stores, and rendezvous at sea with the *Oreto*. Once armed and cruising, Maffitt hoped to recruit his crew from among neutral sailors usually found on Northern merchant vessels.[4]

On August 8, Maffitt tested his engines in the outer roads and mapped his strategy for eluding the Federal blockaders off Nassau. Commander Francis Winslow of the U.S.S. *R. R. Cuyler*, alerted by Consul Whiting that the *Oreto* might proceed to sea at any moment, came out of the inner harbor and began to circle the vessel as a shark does its prey. But the British were having none of this in their waters. The H.M.S. *Petrel* came out and ordered the Federal gunboat to move either into the harbor or outside British territorial waters. The *R. R. Cuyler* put to sea and began cruising in the vicinity of Abaco Island, a key lighthouse station for Bahama shipping, with the hope of intercepting the *Oreto*.[5]

For the moment, Maffitt was safe from capture. Under the cover of night, he quietly moved within the shadow of the land to avoid detection by the Federal ships. Threading his way through innumerable rocks and shoals, Maffitt reached the west end of the island. He then set a course southward and, before daylight, met and took in tow the *Prince Albert*. During the afternoon of August 9, the *Oreto* anchored off Green Key, a small uninhabited island some ninety miles south of New Providence. Maffitt had evaded pursuit by stealth and his superior knowledge of the Bahama channels.

In this desolate spot, Maffitt transferred the arms and stores from the tender to the *Oreto*. With so few men, the officers joined in the painful labor in the hot August sun. "All hands undressed to the buff" during "one of the most physically exhausting jobs ever undertaken by naval officers," wrote Maffitt. The hard labor lasted a week. Hoisted on board by the blistered men were two seven-inch pivots and six six-inch side guns, with carriages, powder, shot, shell, and stores. One of the men died and was buried on shore. Maffitt had some misgivings about the yellow appearance of the seaman who had suddenly come to the end of his earthly career, especially since there had been a recent outbreak of yellow fever in Nassau.[6] Finally, Maffitt completed the transfer, but only "after efforts that for heroism rival any saga of the sea."[7]

On August 16, Maffitt steamed down to Blossom Channel. At sunrise the next morning, he ran clear of the Bahamas and called the crew on deck. It was a beautiful day—and nearly five months after the *Oreto* had sailed down the Mersey River. In a short ceremony, Maffitt cast off the tender and put his ship in commission. To the cheers of the men, he ordered the British flag hauled down, had it replaced with the Stars and Bars, and re-christened the vessel—after Secretary Mallory's home state— the C.S.S. *Florida*.[8] During the ceremony, Maffitt read his orders as commander of the *Florida*: "You will cruise at discretion," Mallory had written, "the department being unwilling to circumscribe your movements in this regard by specific instructions. . . . you are to do the enemy's commerce the greatest injury in the shortest time." Maffitt was to observe the rights of neutrals and cultivate friendly relations with their naval and merchant services.[9]

Maffitt set about establishing naval efficiency aboard the new cruiser. But when the guns were run in for loading, an outcry came from Stribling. Investigating, Maffitt found no artillery sights, rammers, sponges, or quoins aboard; these accouterments had been overlooked in the haste and secrecy of loading the *Prince Albert* in Nassau. Without them, it was impossible to fire the guns. Maffitt wrote of that first day aboard the *Florida*: "Beautiful in model, warlike in guns, the absence of important essentials despoiled the reality, and left her afloat the mere typical representation of what a gallant cruiser should be." Further, several more cases of yellow fever ("King Death in His Yellow Robe") appeared among the crew. Maffitt set a course southwestward toward Cuba, hoping the pure ocean air of the trade winds would disinfect the *Florida*.[10]

The *Florida* had barely enough men to handle the ship—and no firepower; Federal warships were about, and there was disease on board. The only help at hand was the indomitable energy of the ship's captain, who, since there was no surgeon on board, personally attended the sick. "You remember my fondness for doctoring the crew," Maffitt wrote to a friend.[11] The increasing numbers of the stricken were separated from those who were still healthy, and the quarterdeck became a hospital. Maffitt attended the crew day and night without intermission as the fever reduced his working force to one fireman and four deck hands.

Reluctantly, Maffitt abandoned the idea of cruising and, before daylight on August 19, slipped into a harbor of refuge at Cardenas, Cuba. He sent Bradford ashore in the cutter to inform local Cuban authorities of the vessel's helpless condition, and received permission (by telegram from Governor Francisco Serrano) to remain in port. The next day Maffitt dispatched Stribling to Havana to obtain through Confederate agent Charles J. Helm more men and a physician.[12]

The acute possibility of the mission's failure weighed heavily on Maffitt. He fought despondency: "The fact of being afloat I knew would excite extraordinary expectations, and to fail, under any circumstances, involved professional extinction."[13] His ship was in a helpless condition, but matters were not yet at their worst. Maffitt's duties as acting physician had weakened him, and in the afternoon of August 22, he felt a slight chill, which he believed originated from his having gotten wet in a thunder squall. Two hours later, however, while attending the sick, he "was seized with a heavy chill, pain in the back and loins, dimness of vision, and disposition to vomit."[14]

Maffitt realized he was stricken with the tropical disease. He took a mustard bath in a tub, followed by several injections, and changed underclothes and sheets. Aware that yellow fever always affects the brain, he gave instructions to a clerk:

> "I've written directions in regard to the sick, and certain orders in relation to the vessel; also some private letters, which you will please take charge of." Upon the clerk's asking him why this was done, he informed him that "he had all the symptoms of yellow fever, and as he was already much broken down, he might not survive the attack." He had made all the necessary preparations for his own treatment, giving minute written directions to those around him how to proceed, and immediately betook himself to his bed—the fever already flushing his

cheeks, and parching his veins. There was now, indeed, nothing but wailing and woe on board the little *Florida*.[15]

At first Maffitt's delirium ebbed and flowed. A throbbing pulsation in his head produced dizzy blindness. Shooting pains in his body gave him excruciating agony. It seemed, her wrote, as if his "bones had been converted into red-hot tubes of iron and the marrow in them boiling with the fervent heat." His mouth and throat felt as if he had consumed molten lead, resulting in a blistered thirst that nothing could alleviate. He retched violently. His eyes held no moisture: "the fountains seemed seared and parched, as if red-hot irons had branded the well-spring of tears." Then came the icy chills. Finally, life itself flickered, and Maffitt lapsed into unconsciousness.

Remembering nothing for a week, Maffitt seemed to be passing into eternity. He regained consciousness during the morning of August 29, just in time to hear a medical consultation in progress. A physician from Cardenas noted the time was 9:20 a.m., and that Maffitt would not survive beyond noon. Maffitt opened his eyes and informed the speaker that he was mistaken: "I have got too much to do, and cannot afford to die." He began to convalesce from that moment.[16]

The next day, Stribling returned from Havana with a dozen men only, in consequence of neutrality laws. Maffitt also received a telegram from Governor Serrano to steam to Havana because Serrano believed Federal gunboats off Cardenas intended to cut out the *Florida*, a violation of Spanish neutrality. Although Serrano had sent two Spanish gunboats to protect Maffitt (one of which anchored alongside the *Florida* to aid the sick), the governor thought the guns of Morro Castle at Havana could better protect the stricken cruiser. At this point Maffitt, now able to sit up, decided to sail immediately for Havana. Yet he was required to give twenty-four hours notice before sailing to allow Northern merchantmen the opportunity to avoid his cruiser. Maffitt promised, however, that he would not interfere with any vessel until after he sailed from Havana. This prompted Cuban officials in Cardenas to wire Havana for instructions. The reply: "Let her sail, the word of a southern gentleman must be taken."[17]

On the evening of August 31, a Spanish mailboat left Cardenas for Havana. When the mailboat was just outside the Cardenas harbor, Federal gunboats chased and fired upon the craft, having mistaken it for the *Florida*. This activity allowed Maffitt to steam unmolested out of the harbor and along the coast. He arrived in Havana late the next morning, where he was welcomed by a large crowd. Since seamen avoided the city at that time of year because of yellow fever, Maffitt could not recruit a crew. Spanish authorities also kept the vessel under strict observation, so that all Maffitt's ingenuity could not procure the equipment needed to work his guns. He decided he must sail for a Confederate port, and the sooner the better, because Federal gunboats had begun to assemble off Morro Castle.[18]

Because he heard it was less well-blockaded at the moment, Maffitt decided to steam for Mobile.[19] That Confederate port had been the most important on the Gulf since the fall of New Orleans. On the evening of September 1, the same day he entered Havana harbor, Maffitt sailed. He ran close to shore for some distance to avoid pursuit by Federal gunboats outside Havana, then headed for open sea. The passage was pleasant, except for some new cases of yellow fever on board. Maffitt himself was still weak, in bed, his health so "wretched" that he could barely attend to his duties.

During the afternoon of 4 September 1862, the *Florida* steamed under a clear sky and over a smooth sea toward Mobile Bay. Stribling went to the captain's cabin for a conference, where he advised Maffitt to wait for the cover of darkness. But because the Confederates had dismantled the lighthouse, Maffitt decided it would be too difficult to find the channel. Then too, the draft of the *Florida* would not allow dalliance with the shoals. Instead, Maffitt would power through the blockade during daylight.[20]

And now Maffitt finally had a bit of good fortune. His information that the blockade off Mobile was under-strength proved correct. Several of the ships of Rear Admiral David G. Farragut's Western Gulf Blockading Squadron were at Pensacola for repairs or coal, and another was west of Mobile on a mission and out of signal distance. Only the screw steamer U.S.S. *Oneida,* carrying ten guns; the screw steamer U.S.S. *Winona,* with four guns; and the mortar schooner U.S.S. *Rachael Seaman,* with only two guns, were on hand to contest Maffitt's entrance into Mobile. Union Commander George H. Preble of the *Oneida,* the senior naval officer off Mobile, ran his flagship out to meet the stranger, and signaled the *Winona* to join the interception. Maffitt ordered his ship charged with explosives; he intended to blow up the *Florida* if necessary to deny it to the enemy.[21]

Maffitt ordered full speed ahead and black smoke poured from the funnels of the *Florida.* Good blockade runner that he was, he added a variable to the mix by flying the ensign of Britain. This was an excellent ruse on Maffitt's part, because his ship very much resembled a British gunboat, and it was quite usual for that government's warships to approach and observe the blockade. Maffitt realized Union naval officers would not quickly open fire on a British vessel because the 1861 "*Trent* Affair" had caused talk of war in Britain against the United States. Maffitt hoped that by capitalizing on the situation, he could gain some precious time. In this he was correct. From three to four critical minutes, Preble hesitated "between the risk of insulting a British vessel of war and running the risk of allowing an enemy to escape."[22] It was the most serious misfortune of Preble's career.

Maffitt set a course directly for the *Oneida*. Preble called his men to quarters and, at some one hundred yards, hailed the intruder. Receiving no answer, he fired a shot across the bow of the *Florida*. Maffitt, too weak to walk, had himself carried on deck. His ship maintained speed, and Preble, still thinking that the *Florida* was a British gunboat, sent two more shots across its bow.[23] He then attempted to cut off the stranger, but the onrushing *Florida* caused him to reverse engines for fear of being run down. This gave Maffitt a momentary advantage. As the Confederate craft raced by with the *Oneida* on the port side, Preble poured out a broadside from his starboard battery and both pivot guns. Most of the shots, however, passed over the *Florida*. The *Winona* and *Rachael Seaman* opened fire as well, and the cannonading from the blockaders became rapid, which artillery "bid fair to send the little *Florida* to the bottom."[24]

Once passed the *Oneida*, Maffitt ordered a starboard helm. Commander James S. Thornton, in command of the *Winona*, noticed the maneuver: "She altered her course, about 4 points, I should judge, as though she intended to heave to."[25] Maffitt sent men aloft to set sail in an effort to catch a sudden breeze and gain speed. But only the top sails could be loosed before the gunboats began firing shrapnel, forcing the men to climb down. "Several were wounded, and the boats, masts, spars, and hulls were cut with thousands of the shrapnel."[26] Maffitt then ordered the crew below; he remained on deck with other officers and two men at the helm. Resuming course, Maffitt pushed rapidly for the entrance to the harbor as shots peppered the *Florida*.

"The loud explosions, roar of shot, crashing spars and rigging, mingling with the moans of our sick and wounded, instead of intimidating, only increased our determination to enter the destined harbor," wrote Maffitt. The Confederates could make no effort at resistance. "Properly manned and equipped, the excitement of battle would have relieved the terrible strain upon our fortitude," Maffitt later commented. A shell exploded near the port gangway and caused serious damage to the *Florida*. Then, a heavy shell entered the hull, causing vibrations from stem to stern. Fired from the *Winona*, it entered the cabin and passed through the pantry, but failed to explode.

A shot from the *Oneida* was the worst of all. The eleven-inch shell went in just above the waterline, passed through the port coal bunkers, bounced off the port forward boiler, decapitated one of the best seamen on board,

James Duncan, and wounded several others as it passed along the berth deck. However, it too failed to explode. If it had, the entire crew would have been lost, except for the two at the helm. The men were able to work the bilge pumps, which, along with a smooth sea, kept the ship from sinking as a result of the hole near the waterline. Faster than its pursuers, the *Florida* gained as the Federals fed their fires with rosin to increase their steam. Enemy artillery roared fiercely until Maffitt came under the protection of the guns of Fort Morgan.[27]

The press excoriated Gideon Welles as a result of Maffitt's bold entry into Mobile Bay. Even a London magazine poetically chimed in:

> There was an old fogy named Welles,
> Quite worthy of cap and of bells,
> For he tho't that a pirate,
> Who steamed at a great rate,
> Would wait to be riddled with shells.[28]

Welles in turn was incensed with Preble. The latter, in his first brief report to Farragut, had noted the "unparalleled audacity" (an unfortunate choice of words for Preble) of the intruder's commander, and had signed off "with great mortification."[29] Farragut forwarded Preble's report to Welles, with the comment that the success of the *Florida* "was owing to two things— first, not firing at her in time when she was so close that they could not miss her; second, bad firing."[30] Welles believed Preble was guilty of neglect. An example must be made of him to encourage a more aggressive style of fighting by naval officers. When Welles presented the case to Abraham Lincoln, the President precipitously ordered Preble dismissed from the naval service.[31]

Preble made his excuses in subsequent reports of the action. At first encounter, the men of the *Florida* had trained its guns on the *Oneida*, so Preble's masthead lookout had reported. This apparently rattled the *Oneida*'s crew, and its critical first broadside was too high. Another problem for Preble was that he "had full steam only on one boiler, and we were raising it on the other, and could not immediately get up full speed. A mile or so of distance, and a few minutes more of daylight, and she must have been ours." Finally, Preble complained that he had not been informed that a Confederate cruiser "was expected or on the ocean"; otherwise, he maintained, he would have known the true character of the *Florida* and could have run the vessel down.[32] This affirms Maffitt's strategy of boldness and English disguise in entering Mobile Bay.

Maffitt wrote of Preble's dismissal: "Never was an officer more unjustly dealt with, for I can vouch for his promptness of destructive energy, on the occasion of my entering Mobile Bay." Indeed, according to Maffitt, the *Florida* had "limped like a wounded stag into the friendly port." Its fore-topmast and fore-gaff were swept away and the main rigging set adrift. Its hammock nettings on one side were gone, and its boats had been virtually destroyed. The hull was perforated. In looking over the damage, Maffitt noted "1400 shrapnell shot in our hull, and our masts were pitted like a case of smallpox." Maffitt's conclusion: "We were torn to pieces."[33]

Chapter 9

Escape of the *Florida*

Maffitt's courage and determination during his entry into Mobile Bay was one of the most dashing scenes of the war. Danger for the moment had passed, and Maffitt found "the reaction from overstrained anxiety to quiescent repose pleasurable beyond expression."[1] He did not forget his emaciated little crew, writing that despite all their trials, "everyone acted well his part."[2]

Professional congratulations were extensive. Admiral Franklin Buchanan, the Confederacy's ranking naval officer and commander of the Mobile station, visited the *Florida* the next day and was moved to find many of the officers and crew prostrated by yellow fever and few capable of resisting the enemy. He wrote Maffitt: "The gallantry and energy displayed by *yourself,* officers and crew of the *Florida* in forcing an entrance into this port on the 4th instance through the enemy's blockading squadron, reflect great credit upon you all." The admiral promised to inform the secretary of the navy, who "I feel convinced will bring such commendable conduct to the notice of the president."[3] Buchanan clearly believed Maffitt had earned a promotion.

Secretary Mallory offered official thanks to Maffitt: "The escape of your defenseless vessel from an overwhelming force . . . was alone due to the handsome manner in which she was handled, and I do not remember that the union of thorough professional skill, coolness, and daring have ever been better exhibited in a naval dash of a single ship." But Mallory did not hint of a promotion for Maffitt. Mallory instead inquired of the "future movements of your vessel."[4] Maffitt's friend Raphael Semmes termed the Mobile affair "the most daring and gallant running of a blockade that occurred during a war so fruitful of daring and gallant exploits."[5] Even the enemy appeared somewhat awed. Robert W. Shufeldt, U.S. consul in Havana, wrote that Maffitt "escaped Preble in a cool and dashing manner."[6]

Fellow officers from Fort Morgan and commands afloat visited Maffitt, their boat crews cheering as they approached the *Florida*. Other visitors crowded toward the vessel, some of whom had to be interdicted because Maffitt was too debilitated to entertain much company. He said in a letter to his daughter Florie at Ellerslie:

> Thank God I did my duty so well as to call forth *extreme adulation*. The papers are full of it—the crowd who visit me annoy with compliments.
>
> I am still very weak and look like a poor ghost. To write this requires pillows and mental determination absolutely at war with my physical ability, but, my darling, I am determined to write *home*.
>
> All the officers say I must be promptly promoted—well, the Richmond people flatter but do not always act with justice.
>
> When stronger and able will write fully. My cabin is like a flower garden—and as for jellies, cakes and delicacies, the young ladies seem to exert great industry and gentle courtesy.[7]

Because of yellow fever on board, the *Florida* was placed in quarantine. After the gallant Lieutenant Stribling came down with a fatal case and was buried on shore, and because Maffitt remained weak from the disease, visitations were often restricted to boats beside the ship.

For three weeks, little could be done but try to clear the wreckage made by the Federal guns and keep the ship clean. On September 30, the quarantine ended, but repairs were slow and tedious. There was a shortage of skilled workers, and they were reluctant to board the ship until after the first fever-killing frost. Repairs had to be made nearly thirty miles below Mobile in open water because of the draft of the ship. The standing rigging, the worst damage of all, had to be spliced or replaced, a task which bad winter weather often hampered or stopped completely. The scarcity of ordnance supplies in the Confederacy caused delays in securing the equipment for the guns.[8] Buchanan eased frustrations by aiding materially in providing medical care, fumigating the ship, and repairing damages.[9]

During the months the *Florida* was undergoing repairs, Maffitt assembled a crew. So daring a commander attracted some of the best young officers, and Maffitt made several changes. Probably the most noteworthy officer to serve under Maffitt was Lieutenant Charles W. Read. Maffitt had personally applied for Read, who had acquired a reputation for coolness and determination in the battle of New Orleans, where he fought the C.S.S. *McRae* until the Federals riddled the ship beyond further service. He had also served on the ram C.S.S. *Arkansas* that fought Federal gunboats on the Mississippi River. Maffitt applauded Read's courage and was glad to have him on board where Read would find work to his liking. But Read seemed impatient with naval routine. Wrote Maffitt: "As a military officer of the deck he is not equal to many—time will remedy this." Lieutenant Samuel W. Averett reported for duty as executive officer. Averett had served on the Mississippi River and on the ironclad C.S.S. *Atlanta*. "His frank, manly manner pleases me much," Maffitt declared.[10]

Collecting able rank-and-file seamen in the South was a problem for Maffitt. There was a dearth of them. They came on board "in driblets—many rated as seamen who in the old service would merely pass as very ordinary, ordinary seamen." Finally, Maffitt got together some one hundred men, many of them from among the soldiers at Fort Morgan and from the merchant service, men who would have to be taught duties aboard a warship. Some were Southerners; most were foreign born; but they were openly recruited in a Confederate port for the Confederate navy.[11] Maffitt, in a telling statement that goes far to explain life aboard his ship, as well as his motivation, instructed his executive officer Averett: "Perfect the crew of this vessel. Go to night quarters frequently, and think only of the great and grand object in view: southern success, southern independence, southern chivalry. So far as God gives us the opportunity, let us to the full extent of our ability, illustrate the Confederate States Navy."[12]

On 25 October 1862, new cruising orders arrived from Richmond that, much like the earlier orders Maffitt received at Nassau, were vintage Mallory: "The Department does not deem it necessary to give detailed instructions for your guidance, relying as it does upon your judgement and discretion in the conduct of your cruise, and believing that your success will depend entirely upon your freedom of action." Mallory pointed out that since any attempt to run prizes through the blockade into Confederate ports was impractical, Maffitt would have to make some other disposition of prizes. To finance the cruise, the department sent $35,000 in coin and a $30,000 letter of credit (Maffitt had on hand $15,000), all of which was to be accounted for by Paymaster Junius Lynch.[13]

For Maffitt, part of the preparation for the cruise was to put his personal affairs in order. He set up a trust fund for his daughter Florie, and wrote instructions to his young son John. Maffitt advised John that it would be well for him to start attending school in Fayetteville and to be serious in his studies. John was also advised to maintain an honorable and manly demeanor: "You must prove yourself worthy of the commander of the *Florida*—that I may be proud of my son if I live, and if I am killed, you will then have to take care of your sisters—and to do that you must be well educated and be a gentleman."[14]

As refitting of the *Florida* neared completion, Maffitt celebr
mas Eve of 1862 by providing a lively artillery show for the (
at Fort Morgan and the Federals on the blockaders. Steaming
western side of Sand Island near the entrance of the bay, Maffitt positioned
the *Florida* inside the bar and opened on a blockader across the bar in the
Gulf. The vessel was the U.S.S. *New London*, a screw steamer carrying five
guns. During the afternoon spectacle the *Florida* reportedly was not
struck, but three of its shots were believed to have hit the enemy ship since
all the other shots were seen to strike the water. After the *New London*
backed out of the long-range duel, it signaled the fleet, and a ship ran
down and lay alongside for several hours, apparently rendering assistance.
Maffitt had actually engaged in a training maneuver, exercising his guns
with the enemy serving as a target.[15]

Maffitt's stay in port, which exceeded his expectations, at first was due
to slowness in refitting; then it was lack of a sustained storm front to give
cover to the exit of the *Florida*. "All hands are very restive," wrote Maffitt.
Lieutenant Read, especially, considered every passing squall as making it
a good night for running out, although the storms lasted less than an
hour. Maffitt knew that winter gales lasting several days were prevalent;
they were accompanied by a misty sky and a heavy sea upon the bar—
both favorable to a safe exit. It was vital that he slip out intact; his orders
were to attack Northern commerce vessels, not warships. The *Alabama*
and *Florida* were the only two cruisers the Confederacy had at the time,
and Maffitt believed it would be "perfect absurdity" to tilt against Union
warships. Everyone but Admiral Buchanan was impatient. He seemed to
think the *Florida* served a useful purpose in keeping a large a fleet offshore
to watch it. To be sure, the number of Federal warships off Mobile had
been steadily increasing in order to block the exit of the *Florida*.

Because of the delay in port, Secretary Mallory summarily detached
Maffitt on 30 December 1862. Maffitt's consternation could hardly be
contained: "Tis easy for Mr. Mallory to say, do this and do that—seated
in his easy chair in Richmond."[16] And further, "Mr. Mallory, with
characteristic littleness of mind, has permitted surreptitious naval gossip
to operate, with the least magnanimity of soul or manliness of purpose."[17]
Many references in Maffitt's writings are critical of Mallory's conduct in
office. They suggest Maffitt considered Mallory a poor secretary of the
navy because Mallory failed to understand the Confederacy's needs, and
because he favored a small coterie of officers, including Lieutenant Joseph
N. Barney, Maffitt's designated relief as the *Florida*'s commander.[18]

Maffitt believed his services on the *Florida* thus far entitled him "to a
slight consideration and call for information." He also suspected that
Buchanan "was indirectly hit over my shoulder."[19] Fortunately, President

Davis happened to be in Mobile, and Buchanan saw him in person to declare Mallory's order unjustified. Davis telegraphed Mallory on December 31 to suspend the order in relation to Maffitt, and added that Buchanan would send a full report.[20] In a letter to his daughter, Maffitt quoted Davis as saying that "Maffitt brought her in gallantly and *he* will take her out."[21]

Restored to command, Maffitt was impatient for a sustained gale. He realized he could make more captures the sooner he could sail. Meanwhile, at Buchanan's suggestion, he painted the *Florida* a dull lead color. Maffitt did not particularly like the color because he thought it detracted from the beauty of the ship, but blockade runners had learned that the color blended well with the horizon at night. "When you sail," Buchanan told him, "have the *Florida* prepared in all respects for a fight, hammock nettings taken down, men at quarters, . . . escape the blockaders if possible, without using your guns, as they would give the alarm to the whole squadron at anchor and to those cruising off the coast."[22] This advice was hardly needed by a commander of Maffitt's experience and ability.[23]

On the night of 10 January 1863, Maffitt ran down to the bar, but the overcast sky suddenly cleared, leaving enemy ships plainly in sight. Wrote Maffitt: "I knew I could not pass without having sixty guns fired at me— and we would no doubt be lost. So I must abide a better time, though exceedingly disappointed."[24] He made another reconnaissance on January 13, and the pilot grounded the vessel off City Point. The crew had to unload the guns and coal, a two-day task, before two steamers towed the vessel free. On January 15, with his ship again afloat, Maffitt made still another effort to get out of port. Because the inexperienced crew of the *Florida* previously had reported phantom ships when approaching the bar in the darkness off Mobile, officers took positions some twenty feet apart along the deck, forming a continuous line aft to the wheel, where stood Maffitt. That night, conditions were again unfavorable, however, and a blockader appeared in the raider's path.[25]

Reports from deserters out of Mobile had kept the blockading fleet on alert. Commanding officers and gun crews spent sleepless nights. Picket boats reconnoitered the entrances of the bay. The fleet adopted special signals to speed information concerning Maffitt's movements. The Federals had even prepared a written program for attacking, boarding, and chasing the *Florida* whenever it appeared, day or night. In short, the capture of the raider was the absorbing topic aboard the ships stationed off Mobile Bay.[26]

Cold winds swept Mobile Bay on 16 January 1863. The frigid blasts heralded the coming of the tardy northeaster. Waves swelled and broke in the surf, roaring with wrath—music much desired by Maffitt. By evening, pouring rain reduced visibility to twenty yards. The ship was kept at ready, with steam up, the crew resting in their clothes, and the sails specially rigged to deploy without sending the top-crew aloft. At 2:00 a.m., Maffitt came on deck. The rain had ceased, and the stars were visible. Mist hung on the water's surface. The wind was still puffing, coming north by northwest. Maffitt called all hands. Within twenty minutes, the *Florida* was bearing over the bar of the main channel, burning coke.

Maffitt passed undetected hard by one blockader, then another. The *Florida*'s firemen, running low on coke, changed to soft coal. When Maffitt's vessel came abreast of a third blockader, orange-red flame from the soft coal shot from the stacks of the *Florida*. Drums on the blockaders beat the Federals to quarters, feet tramped on deck, lights flashed, and cables were slipped amid great excitement. The Federals who had sighted the *Florida* near Fort Morgan the previous day had expected Maffitt to run out during the storm, but their vigilance had begun to decline after midnight. Maffitt believed that the bitter cold had caused Federal lookouts to seek partial shelter from the stinging blasts.[27] Federal Commander George F. Emmons of the U.S.S. *Cuyler*, thinking Maffitt would have attempted to run out during the peak of the storm, had gone to bed. The *Cuyler*, rated faster than the *Florida*, had been ordered to Mobile especially to catch the cruiser. When summoned from his quarters, Emmons appeared on deck partly dressed; he ordered the signal to the other blockaders, delayed somewhat because the crewman had trouble lighting the lamp in the damp, windy weather.[28]

At this critical moment, the *Florida* had zigzagged to a point about three hundred yards beyond the inner semicircular cordon of the enemy.[29] "Let fall and sheet home your topsails," ordered Maffitt.[30] The heavy pressure of the gale on the canvas shot the vessel forward like a deer. Commodore Robert B. Hitchcock, on his flagship, the U.S.S. *Susquehanna*, had directed the *Oneida* and *Cuyler* as the principal chase vessels. But Captain Samuel F. Hazard of the *Oneida*, unable to sight the *Florida*, failed to chase and still rolled at anchor the next morning.[31] Emmons turned his ship, the *Cuyler*, about and began the chase, running south-southeast. Lieutenant Commander William G. Temple in the U.S.S. *Pembina* also chased during the night, following the light at the peak of the *Cuyler*, which had cut across his bow. After daylight, Temple, who caught a glimpse of the *Florida*'s upper spars twelve miles ahead through his glass, found he was rapidly dropping astern and returned to the blockade.[32]

It was Emmons against Maffitt. Emmons was an energetic officer, and confident that during the day, he could overhaul the *Florida*. The *Cuyler*, which (under another commander) had earlier threatened the *Florida* at

Nassau, was a 1,200-ton screw steamer with a crew of 134 and 10 guns.[33] Both vessels crowded on sail. The heavy sea kept the *Cuyler's* deck covered with water and constantly threw the propeller entirely out of the water, where it raced wildly and endangered the ship's machinery. In an effort to trim his ship by pushing the propeller deeper into the water, Emmons ordered 10 tons of coal and all hands aft. The *Cuyler* had formerly made 14 knots on steam alone, but on this day under steam and sail, its utmost was 12½ knots. The *Florida,* its speed logged for the first time under steam and sail, made 14½ knots, the best of the vessel's career. Maffitt noted that the *Florida* was very wet but that it rode the sea like a pilot boat in spite of seas rolling on board from stem to stern. In the heavy pitching, the *Cuyler* lost its topsail yard and had no replacement. The *Florida* sprung its fore-topsail yard, and Maffitt ordered the spar lowered to the deck and repaired. The temporary reduction of canvass allowed the *Cuyler* to gain to within three miles of the *Florida.*

Maffitt realized his sails made a white and fleecy guidon for his pursuer. Toward evening, he decided on a blockade running ruse to end the chase. The crew was sent aloft to shorten sail. Shorn of its plumage, and with the engines at rest, the vessel's silhouette was lost betweeen the high waves. Maffitt knew that clear daylight was necessary to enable the enemy to distinguish the low hull of the raider. The *Cuyler* swiftly passed by, and the *Florida* plunged through the high waves to the south. Emmons, with unusual frankness, wrote: "From fancying myself near promotion in the morning, I gradually dwindled down to a court of enquiry at dark, when I lost sight of the enemy."[34]

Maffitt's escape was another great embarrassment to the Union navy. But it did not prevent some of the enemy from expressing their admiration. Wrote one: "There were seven of us off the port, we had fifteen hours' warning, and her only way out was through the main ship-channel, which at the bar is less than a mile wide. They ran a big risk and won."[35] On the Confederate side, Raphael Semmes penned in his journal: "Gratified to learn of the escape of the *Florida.* We have thus doubled our means of destroying the enemy's commerce."[36] A *Charleston Mercury* correspondent in Mobile filed this report that included a prediction: "Maffitt is as brave as Nelson, as shrewd as a fox, and as thorough a seaman as ever trod a deck. . . . Yankee journals will soon teem with the details of his operations."[37] It was a true prophecy. The ill luck that had dogged Maffitt's ship for months was finally over, and at last, the actual cruise of the *Florida* began.

Chapter 10

First Cruise of the *Florida,*
Tortugas to Barbados

Maffitt took his first prize 19 January 1863. It was the *Estelle,* a brig on its maiden voyage, running in heavy seas off Tortugas. Out of Santa Cruz, Cuba, the handsome Yankee craft was cutting through the waters of Florida Strait, bound for Boston. Stored in its hold was a large cargo of honey for Federal troops, and molasses for the rum factories of New England. The *Florida,* flying American colors, bore in under a full press of canvas and steam. Maffitt fired a shot across the bow of the *Estelle,* and the master of the brig, John Brown, saw that the raider had hoisted the Confederate flag. Maffitt approached the vessel's stern, lowered his boats, and sent a party on board to order Brown and his crew to the *Florida.* The Confederates also sent the brig's chronometer, charts, instruments, and topsail (Maffitt's had been carried away) on board the steamer, then fired the brig fore and aft. In a few minutes, the *Estelle* was a mass of flames.[1]

Prisoners aboard the *Florida* were treated well, much better than Master Brown and his crew had expected—a fact that set the pattern for the cruise of the raider, and reflected, in spite of the war, the unyielding personal style of Maffitt. According to Brown: "Captain Maffitt received me with great courtesy, invited me into his cabin, and said that it was necessary for him to burn my vessel, that the consequences of this unnatural war often fell most heavily upon those who disapproved of it—he trusted the vessel was owned by abolitionists." Maffitt allowed the *Estelle*'s crew to keep their personal effects. He regarded the men as prisoners of war but gave them the run of the ship, provided they obeyed ship's rules. They were integrated among Maffitt's men as messmates and consumed the same fare. Brown, who was given a stateroom on board, did justice to his captors. He thought the nature of his treatment should not pass unheeded, regardless of his enemy status; the rigors of war, he later affirmed, "may be somewhat mitigated by politeness and manly forbearance."[2] Indeed, Brown seemed to understand that burning ships and cargoes at sea was equivalent to destroying buildings and corncribs on land.

Maffitt waited to ensure that the flames would burn the *Estelle* to the waterline; then, against the faint glow of the burning ship as a backdrop, he set a course for Havana. The sustained run across the Gulf had depleted the *Florida*'s coal bunkers. The following evening, January 20, the vessel steamed through rainy and disagreeable weather past Morro Castle and into the harbor at Havana. Spanish neutrality law allowed Maffitt twenty-four hours to refuel, but in entering after sundown and without clearance from the health officer, he had unknowingly violated port rules. To make amends to Spanish officials, including Governor Serrano, Maffitt donned his dress uniform, had his gig lowered, and was rowed ashore by eight men in whites. He was able to gain a few extra hours from the Spanish and to arrange parole for his prisoners. He also obtained coal and provisions through the Confederate agent Charles J. Helm.[3]

The *Florida* created a sensation in Havana, where Confederates were much more popular than Federals.[4] The ship was far from being the disease-ridden and helpless craft it had been the past August. Gifts of fine liquors and cigars, as well as flowers and fruits, were brought out to the gangway by cheering local inhabitants. A Northerner wrote from Havana: "Captain Maffitt is no ordinary character. He is vigorous, energetic, bold, quick, and dashing, and the sooner he is caught and hung, the better will it be for the interests of our commercial community. He is decidedly popular here, and you can scarcely imagine the anxiety evinced to get a glance at him."[5] Another Northern account, in a sketch of Maffitt, compared him with his father. Reverend Maffitt was "a well-known sensation preacher," and "Captain Maffitt likes to produce on the ocean the same sensation, in a different form, which his father used to produce in the pulpit, and if Mr. Secretary Welles does not look sharply after him he will most certainly produce as much discussion and sensation as his father ever did in this country."[6]

The officer whom Welles chose to lead the search for Maffitt was Acting Rear Admiral Charles Wilkes, commander of the West Indian Squadron. Like Maffitt, Wilkes was noteworthy for his ability as a naval scientist, but he was also insubordinate and impulsive. Wilkes had seven relatively fast ships. According to his orders from Secretary Welles, "the first great imperative duty" of his command was the capture and destruction of the *Florida* and "similar cruisers of a semi-piratical character."[7] Maffitt knew that Robert W. Shufeldt, U.S. consul in Havana, had sent word—by express steamer, to the gathering place of the squadron at Key West—that the *Florida* was in Havana.[8] It was imperative for Maffitt to coal and leave at once. At dawn on January 22, the *Florida* steamed out of Havana. Later that day, Wilkes arrived in his flagship, the new screw sloop U.S.S.

Wachusett. He soon departed and searched for Maffitt on the south side of the island—the wrong location.[9]

Maffitt set a course along the northern coast of Cuba, where numerous inlets could provide a haven if the Federal warships appeared in strength. Four miles off Matanzas he spotted a brig. Sailing under a British flag, Maffitt switched to Confederate colors and brought the unfortunate *Windward* to by a shot across its bow. The brig had just cleared Matanzas, bound for New York with a cargo of sugar and molasses. Since they were near land, Maffitt allowed the captain of the *Windward,* Richard Roberts, and his crew to pull for land in their boats. Maffitt then had the prize stripped of valuables and set afire.

Cruising in mid-afternoon, Maffitt detected a brig bearing toward the channel leading into Cardenas. The *Corris Ann* was easy prey. Brought to and boarded with the usual alternating flags and bow shot, the vessel was found to be carrying timber and barrel staves from Philadelphia to Cardenas. Its unsuspecting captain, Fredrick H. Small, protested in vain the use of the British flag and the fact that he was inside Spanish waters. He had fifteen minutes to gather his personal effects and take to his boats; his ship's instruments went to the *Florida*. At sunset, the inhabitants of Cardenas could see the blazing *Corris Ann* drifting into their harbor.[10]

That evening Maffitt anchored for a few hours near Cardenas to adjust his engine valves, then stood out to sea. On the morning of January 23, he discovered the coal obtained at Havana was faulty. It failed to burn properly and drove the ship at a paltry three knots. Federal warships were nearby, and the *Florida* would be extremely vulnerable in a fight without proper steam power. Maffitt ordered much of the inferior coal overboard in order to reach the good coal from Mobile; the resulting shortage forced him toward Nassau. Moving slowly along the coast, and passing Green Key of recent lamentable memory, the *Florida* on the morning of January 26 steamed into Nassau.[11]

The previous day, Maffitt had anchored and squared away the ship,[12] so that upon entering the harbor, "the *Florida* presented a man-of-war-like appearance, her masts being well set, yards neatly squared, and the brass work well polished."[13] U.S. Consul Whiting quickly sent off a schooner to alert Federal cruisers off Abaco Light, and initiated vigorous objections concerning the treatment of the *Florida* by local colonial officials: "This pirate ship entered this port without any restrictions, with the secession flag *at her peak* and the secession war pennant *at the main*." He noted with disapproval that Maffitt and his officers were escorted to land in the garrison boat of Her Majesty's Second West Indian Regiment. British authorities had also established a rule against entering port without the governor's permission, and Maffitt's trip to shore in the garrison boat was not so much an escort of honor, but an effort to make amends to Governor Bayley. When the governor allowed Maffitt to coal without restrictions, but allegedly limited a Union gunboat to 20 tons, Whiting was even more outraged, writing sarcastically that the coal allowed Maffitt was "evidence of the perfect neutrality which exists here."[14] Bayley denied the allegations and regretted that Washington "should have given credence to the mis-representations of a person of such inferior judgment and excitable temperament as Mr. Whiting has proven himself to be."[15] Whiting's days as consul at Nassau were numbered.

Nassau gave Maffitt a most joyful welcome. At the Royal Victoria Hotel, he was greeted, as Whiting described it, with "a display of secession bunting."[16] Maffitt wrote that "all my friends were astounded to see me— reception cordial in the extreme." He received visitors on the *Florida,* including British naval and army officers.[17] In the harbor were several blockade runners, the commanders of which greeted him, including Lieutenant John Wilkinson.

The *Florida*'s brief stay in Nassau was marred by a not-uncommon incident for a ship in port. On the morning of January 27, when the vessel had finished coaling, a muster of all hands on board revealed that twenty-six men were missing. "Our hard cases," Maffitt termed the deserters. He quickly gained permission from Bayley to remain three hours longer to arrange for a few replacements.[18] Maffitt got underway about noon, stood out of the harbor, and came to anchor. This movement allowed the *Florida* to exit on time and to take on several new crewmen outside the three mile limit in order to avoid violating the Foreign Enlistment Act.[19] Maffitt also waited until after dark to up anchor, thus foiling any attempt by Whiting to discern his course. He set a course for Green Key, where he spent three days servicing the ship. Provisions had been hurriedly loaded in Nassau and were in disarray. The crew washed the interior of the vessel, restored the hold, scraped the whitewash off the exterior, and painted the ship black.[20]

On the morning of February 1, while cruising away from Green Key across the Bahama Banks toward Queen's Channel, Maffitt sighted one of Wilkes's "flying squadron"—a side-wheel steamer of four guns, the U.S.S. *Sonoma.* From his distance, Maffitt overestimated its firepower at ten guns. "As our cruise had just begun and its object was the destruction of commerce," he wrote; "I did not think it my duty to seek an engagement and run the risk of injury to our engine—so kept away." Maffitt turned and made full sail, whereupon the *Sonoma* gave chase. Its skipper, Com-mander Thomas H. Stevens, correctly identified the now-famous cruiser despite its Union Jack. Under full sail and steam, he began to gain in this unequal hare-and-hound episode. Both commanders beat to quarters.

Maffitt quickly shifted two of his broadside guns to aft-quarter ports and (together with his aft pivot) fired three guns astern. Stevens dropped back some but continued the chase for thirty-four hours over a distance of three hundred miles. On three occasions when Stevens approached to within gun range, his engine's blower belt split, and his vessel fell back. The sea began to run rough on the second day, giving some advantage to the excellent hull design of the *Florida*. Still, Maffitt believed his pursuer could have closed and fought. Probably Stevens hoped to keep the raider in sight until other Federal gunboats could join him before engaging what he knew to be superior firepower. When last seen at dark on February 2, the *Florida* was bearing eastward. During the night, Maffitt altered course northward to elude his pursuer and deliver to the North "a small appreciation of war troubles."[21]

Maffitt's destination was the coast of New England.[22] The weather became increasingly squally as the *Florida* cruised up the Southern coast. Maffitt's quick thinking and ability to deceive the enemy at sea was soon needed to save the ship from destruction. On the misty night of February 5, a large steamer was sighted off the starboard beam. As the stranger changed course and sped toward him, Maffitt quickly cut his speed, ordered the hinged twin funnels lowered to the deck, and extinguished all lights except for a small lantern hung over the side. The Confederate *Florida* could now be taken for a sailing vessel of the West Indian trade. What Maffitt believed to be the U.S.S. *Vanderbilt*—a 3,360-ton steamer with 15 guns—approached and circled, and then, with a great roar of its massive paddlewheels, steamed away in the mist. Ironically, the *Vanderbilt*, one of the largest U.S. warships, was searching for the *Florida* but had failed to recognize it. The Federals lost an easy opportunity to destroy the raider.[23]

Cruising on through drizzle and heavy wind and sea, the *Florida* encountered a powerful gale off Cape Hatteras, North Carolina. Maffitt was forced to cross the Gulf Stream, steaming to the southeast to escape the fury of the storm. He again noted that although the vessel "behaved well," it ran low in the water and was wet below decks fore and aft. The storm damaged the *Florida*'s bow pivot ports, topsail yard, and hammock rail, stove in the boats, and carried away the captain's launch. A few ships were sighted, but the seas were too heavy for boarding them. Even worse, the *Florida*'s heavy use of coal during five days of bad weather seriously depleted the bunkers, which had a maximum capacity for nine days' steaming. Reluctantly, for lack of fuel, Maffitt changed his plans to cruise off New England. He wrote: "Deeply did I regret my inability to make the anticipated visit."[24]

The bad weather began to moderate by February 7, and the *Florida*'s prow pointed toward the southeast and a West Indian port, where Maffitt hoped to obtain coal. He took advantage of the good weather to make repairs and cruise under canvas—saving for emergency use his remaining fuel. In order to avoid Federal ships in his recent cruising grounds in the West Indies, Maffitt kept far out in the Atlantic around the Bahamas. Steering east of Cuba and Haiti, he continued southward and reached the Leeward Islands, in the upper part of the Lesser Antilles, then sailed along the Leeward Islands toward the Windward Islands, in the lower part of the Lesser Antilles.[25]

On 12 February 1863, the *Florida* captured the biggest prize of any raider during the entire war. Maffitt, should he have happened to remember it was Lincoln's birthday, would have appreciated the irony. (The president, reportedly restless about a coming naval assault on Charleston, was at the time conferring with Assistant Secretary of the Navy Gustavus Fox.)[26] At mid-morning, a look-out on the *Florida* sighted a large sail off the port beam. Extremely white sails were usually an indication that a ship was American, and this vessel's beautiful, clean canvas first suggested to Maffitt that the stranger was fair game for the raider. Maffitt, bringing the distant hull into view with his glasses, saw with mounting interest a magnificent Yankee clipper ship briskly plying the Antilles Current that runs northwestward from the equator. Getting steam up with the propeller down, crowding on sail, and hoisting the Stars and Stripes, Maffitt began the chase for the intended prize.[27]

The pursued was a clipper that had rounded the Horn from China, the famous *Jacob Bell*. On deck, its able Captain Charles Frisbie observed that the sail in his wake was gradually gaining, and he grew increasingly uneasy during the six hours Maffitt's chase continued. When Frisbie made the vessel out to be a steamer, he hoped it would prove to be a U.S. gunboat. His pursuer was directly in his track, with its outer studding sails deployed, and the telltale smoke of its funnels gave evidence that its machinery was in full operation. A day earlier, when the wind had been stronger, Frisbie could have kept out of range of the vessel's guns until dark and then eluded the stranger. But late in the afternoon, a shot from three miles astern struck the water just abaft and on the port side of the clipper. The *Jacob Bell* was doomed.[28]

When the victim rounded to, the Confederates observed its lines with awe. Midshipman Sinclair wrote: "As she lay thus, with black hull, gilt streak, scraped and varnished masts, and snow-white sails, there was a general exclamation of admiration, coupled with regret that such a thing of beauty must be destroyed."[29] Maffitt circled the clipper twice to ensure that it had no guns, then sent Lieutenant Read and a boarding party into a cutter that dropped down from the tackles to the water and over to the

Jacob Bell. The vessel was out of Foochow, China, bound for New York and laden with 1,380 tons of tea, 10,000 boxes of firecrackers, along with matting, camphor, cassia, fans, and carvings with an aggregate value of $1,500,000. Passengers and crew totaled forty-three persons. After the prisoners were aboard the *Florida*, Maffitt put a prize crew on the clipper under Lieutenant Hoole with orders to follow, while the raider steamed away in chase of a sail that escaped into the darkness.[30]

The next day, February 13, when the *Florida* was north of Puerto Rico, the prize caught up, and the Confederates transferred its crew's personal baggage and other spoils of war onto the *Florida*—items included a pig and chickens dressed on the deck of the clipper, fresh meat for Maffitt's passengers and crew. Maffitt's marauders then fired the *Jacob Bell*. They placed combustibles of melted butter and lard over a pile of fine upholstered chairs in the main cabin, and lightwood and whale oil in two other places on the clipper. The blaze created an unfolding spectacle in the gathering dusk as the *Florida* steamed away from the abandoned ship. Flames crept steadily up the *Jacob Bell*'s sails and rigging as the great clipper floated quietly on. The last that was seen of the vessel was a little before its masts fell, a display of melancholy grandeur. Long after dark, the fired vessel illuminated the distant horizon.[31]

The destruction of the *Jacob Bell* caused a tremendous popular outcry in the North. The *Florida* (and the *Alabama*) had seriously disrupted Union sea traffic. More of the same could deplete the blockade as ships would be needed to protect commerce—part of the strategy of the South. Hundreds of Union merchantmen had already gone under foreign registry, never to return to America's carrying trade. The Federal navy seemed ineffective. Shipowners and insurance executives called for action by Secretary Welles: Maffitt, the perpetrator of the deed against the legendary *Jacob Bell*, must be caught for the purpose of publicly adorning a yardarm.[32]

Sailing to the southeast in good weather with the *Florida*'s propeller hoisted, Maffitt relinquished his cabin and adjoining small stateroom to the passengers—one of whom, Mrs. Martha Williams, was a shrew. She and Frisbie were not on speaking terms, and the young officers of the raider learned to avoid her. Wrote Midshipman Sinclair: "We got in the habit of watching for her head, as it came up out of the cabin hatch, when there would be a general scamper; but the poor officer of the deck was compelled to stand and take her tongue-lashing." One deck officer, however, discovered a way to escape the woman's wrath. Lieutenant Stone climbed into the rigging, leaving Mrs. Williams to promenade the deck under her green umbrella, as was her habit, fretting over her tons of luggage and chastising Southern chivalry.[33]

The *Florida* cruised for several days without overtaking an American ship. Late in the afternoon of February 17, Maffitt halted the Danish brig *Morning Star* some two hundred miles north of the British island of Sombrero in the Leewards. The vessel was of recent U.S. registry and was bound from New York to the Island of St. Thomas in the Virgin Islands (which Lincoln unsuccessfully had sought to buy from Denmark). The captain of the *Morning Star* agreed to take the prisoners on board his vessel. Maffitt had treated them with great courtesy. "If they speak unkindly," he wrote, "such a thing as gratitude is a stranger to their abolition hearts." He was thankful to find relief from the overcrowded conditions on the *Florida* and happy to return to the captain's cabin from his sleeping quarters on deck between two guns. The Confederates set a course for the British Island of Barbados in the Windwards.[34]

Early on the morning of February 24, Barbados came into view, and soon the *Florida* entered Carlisle Bay and cast anchor before the city of Bridgetown. Maffitt immediately called upon Governor James Walker and requested permission to obtain coal. Walker demurred at first, probably because he knew Maffitt had coaled at Nassau less than three months ago, but finally asked for the request in writing. He then granted special permission under a loophole provision in British policy that gave a British governor authority to allow coaling at a British port more frequently under certain circumstances. Maffitt wrote: "Having been much injured in a recent gale of wind, and being entirely out of coal, expended in said gale, I have been forced into this port for repairs." Soon under special permission of stress of weather, the *Florida* began to refuel over the bitter protest of U.S. Consul Edward Trowbridge.[35]

The U.S. bark *Sarah A. Nichels* sailed that same day in search of Wilkes's fleet.[36] The *Florida* was therefore detained in port twenty-four hours in order to adhere to the British rule that belligerent vessels must not sail prior to that minimum interval. Meanwhile, Maffitt engaged in a festive exchange of hospitalities. He attended an official dinner of Governor Walker's where some twenty guests, mostly British officers from the Barbados garrisons, expressed warm Southern sentiments. The following evening, the officers called on him aboard the *Florida*. Wrote Maffitt: "I was lionized quite extensively—a kind of wondrous curiosity—a Rebel Pirate!!"[37]

Maffitt had first visited Barbados in 1841 while assigned to the *Macedonian*. "Then, the Stars and Stripes floated over my head and the Union seemed as firm as the Rock of Ages," he wrote; "Now, the Confederate flag, till this day a total stranger to Barbados, floated from our gaff." Why was this welcome much more enthusiastic? For one thing, the island had a strong seafaring tradition, and tales of Maffitt's exploits had preceded him. The planter class, for a generation growing sugar without slaves, perhaps looked on the South as a bygone golden era. Confederate fortunes were at a high-water mark, and the *Florida* and its captain represented, for the first time among them, an extension of the South.[38] "Secesh" was all the rage. Confederate songs filled the air. No excitement like the arrival of the *Florida* had occurred there in years.

It was noted in Bridgetown that Maffitt commanded a well-disciplined ship. The officers were described as very young, from eighteen to twenty-two years of age, and were polite and attentive, and the crewmen as well-behaved and orderly. They seemed to have great regard for their captain, who "runs the *Florida* any and everywhere as if she drew but one inch of water. The land or shoals didn't frighten him." Maffitt "was the observed of all observers. Even the negroes cheered him as he went up the wharf."[39]

Maffitt was delighted with the extra twenty-four hours, which gave him more time to ready his ship. He appointed Robert Gordon, of the local firm of Cavan and Company, as Confederate agent. According to Maffitt, Gordon was "a warm southern friend, a man of wealth and influence." Maffitt needed a business friend on shore to help furnish supplies for the *Florida*, including lumber for repairs.[40] He was also successful in recruiting new crew members. However, on advice of Assistant Engineer Quinn, who found the indifference to duty of Second Assistant Engineer William H. Jackson "very embarrassing," Maffitt sent Jackson home.[41]

On the evening of February 25, the delay-time having lapsed, the *Florida* stood due east out of Barbados. On its departure, a Northern journalist grudgingly observed: "She went out in splendid style. She is magnificently handled. This is the truth. I have written just as things are, not as I wish them. Facts are facts, however disagreeable."[42]

Chapter 11

First Cruise of the *Florida,* Barbados to Brest

Maffitt encountered heavy seas and strong eastern headwinds out of Barbados, so he turned toward the northeast.[1] According to one of his engineers, on March 4 the wind drove the raider through the water at eighteen knots under canvas alone. Maffitt's cruising ground would be an area through which ships passed to and from Asia by way of either Cape Horn or the Cape of Good Hope.[2]

Back in Barbados, Admiral Wilkes arrived on March 6 in his newly commandeered flagship, the *Vanderbilt.* Earlier, he had hunted the *Florida* off the northern coast of Cuba because he realized Maffitt was well acquainted with the locality, "having cruised here some time whilst in command of the *Crusader,* in looking for slave vessels a few years ago." Wilkes had then searched along Puerto Rico and put in at St. Thomas to better organize the search. He was still there when he learned that Maffitt had visited Barbados. He had reasoned that since Maffitt had coaled in Nassau, he could not, under British neutrality laws, refuel in any British port for three months. Wilkes had therefore expected Maffitt to have gone to the French island of Martinique. Having guessed wrong, he now learned from Consul Trowbridge the details of Maffitt's stay in Barbados. This information led to an acrimonious exchange between Wilkes and Governor Walker. International repercussions over the refueling of the *Florida* at Barbados began a paper trail that continued to the Alabama Claims.[3] Wilkes lost his professional poise at Barbados and acted more like a consul than a naval officer, a fact which contributed to the British sympathy for the South.[4]

Wilkes continued to search for Maffitt in the West Indies, where he could also back up the Union blockade. Maffitt, however, was cruising in the Atlantic east of the Virgin Islands, where on March 6 he captured the *Star of Peace.* When he sent a shot from three miles screeching across the bow of the clipper, its sails immediately furled. The 1,000-ton vessel was en route from Calcutta to Boston. The *Star of Peace* belied its name, for it carried 850 tons of saltpeter for Federal powder mills, as well as cow and

70

goat hides. The large quantity of nitrate was of national importance and a fortunate capture for the Confederacy. Maffitt paroled the vessel's master, Captain Francis Hickley, and the officers, and put the crew in irons because he considered them a threat to the *Florida*. At four o'clock that afternoon, after being stripped of provisions and valuables, the *Star of Peace* was fired.

Maffitt then ordered his crew to quarters and exercised his guns on the burning target at 850 yards. He wanted the practice for his men—the results of which, because of a heavy roll, Maffitt termed "not up to our expectations." There were a few excellent shots; of twenty-two rounds fired, six struck the victim. As the *Florida* moved away, the nitrate ignited on the *Star of Peace*. Wrote Maffitt: "A more beautiful panorama was never witnessed on the ocean. Although some twenty miles away from her, the flames were so high and so brilliant that the focal rays illumined our sails and the ship did not appear more than five miles distant."[5] Midshipman Bryan observed of the great inferno that one could have read very easily on the deck of the *Florida*.[6]

The *Aldebaran* was also named after a star, and for a moment, the vessel burned like one. The schooner came within Maffitt's view on March 13 when bound from New York to the vicinity of Sao Luis, Brazil, with a cargo of flour, a large assortment of food ("Yankee fixins"), and clocks. Its master, Captain Robert Hand, attempted to save his vessel (he and his father owned it) by saying he was a Democrat who voted for Stephen A. Douglas and did not support the Northern war effort. But Maffitt had his orders. The crewmen were clasp in irons as they came on board the *Florida,* and the Confederates took what they wanted of the cargo before setting the *Aldebaran* on fire. The vessel turned to ashes as it bobbled on the waves.[7] It was described as "a very pretty vessel and full 200 tons burden."[8]

Between captures, Maffitt chased sails, which he often found to be foreign. He also observed shipboard routine, which meant calling the men to quarters in practice drills. The men spent much time cleaning, scraping, and painting the vessel. On other occasions Maffitt would call all hands to muster, read the articles of war, and inspect the crew, as well as the ship "fore and aft." He would also, as a morale booster, allow a grog ration for the crew. After a drink of brandy, the crew sometimes sang (especially when Northern prisoners were on board) "I wish I had a Bowie knife to kill old Lincoln and his wife."[9]

Prisoners on board the *Florida* totaled forty—two captains, five mates, and thirty-three seamen. According to Quinn, the Confederates were "damn tired of them." On March 18, Maffitt was able to place eleven prisoners, including the officers, on a British brig, and later a few more were accepted by an Austrian bark. In both cases, Maffitt furnished them with water and provisions. On March 20, Maffitt made an example of a prisoner who struck another with a beef bone, and opened a severe gash, by lashing the aggressor spread-eagle to the rigging. The next day, a few prisoners signed on as crew members of the *Florida*. Prisoners were glad to gain the freedom of the ship after a few days in confinement. The hope of reward was high on the raider, and many of the men, not being Americans, had no loyalties in the war. Signing on prisoners was a first for Maffitt, although the idea was not new to him, and it must have been successful because he continued the practice for the remainder of the cruise.[10]

The *Florida* was now in mid-Atlantic, west of the Azores. On March 28, Maffitt captured the 590-ton bark *Lapwing*, bound from Boston to Jakarta, Indonesia. Its hold contained provisions, lumber, furniture, and, most importantly for Maffitt, 260 tons of anthracite coal. After transferring the crew and provisions, Maffitt sent Averett on board the prize as commander, along with three officers and fifteen men, two twelve-pound howitzers, a signal book, and flags. The *Lapwing* would be both tender and cruiser. Averett was to cruise six to eight miles away from, but on the same course southward, as the *Florida*, thus extending their view of the ocean. The two ships, if separated, were to rendezvous at 29° 30′ w on the equator. The next day, the sea was smooth, and Maffitt took on 10 tons of coal from the *Lapwing*. The two vessels then separated again. The prize apparently could not keep pace with the *Florida*, and the two ships lost contact.[11]

On March 30, Maffitt captured a "propaganda" ship, the *M. J. Colcord*. Northern businessmen, with Lincoln's blessing, were sending foreign aid to Britain's cotton-mill workers, who were unemployed because of the Union blockade. This enlightened self-interest on the part of Northerners helped cement support of the working class in England for the Union. A small portion of this aid went to Britain's Cape Colony at the southern tip of Africa. The bark *M. J. Colcord* was part of the latter effort, sailing from New York to Cape Town bulging with flour and bacon. A shot from the *Florida* brought the bark into the wind. Maffitt spent much of the next day transferring provisions from the prize and, at the same time, boarded a Danish ship whose master had agreed to take all the remaining prisoners. Maffitt sent them away with a liberal allowance of provisions. He then burned the *M. J. Colcord*.[12]

Continuing southward, the *Florida* frequently chased sails, but all proved to be neutral. On April 12, the raider arrived at St. Paul's Rocks, a jagged Brazilian mountain peak extending above water in the central Atlantic just above the equator. An attempt to land a boat to take sightings and check the chronometer failed because of dangerous rocks and heavy seas. The crew took advantage of a heavy rain the next day to scrub hammocks and wash clothes.

Maffitt was beginning to consider the disappearance of the *Lapwing* most unfortunate because of his need for coal. But on April 14 a sail came into view and, when chased, proved to be the tender. A strong southeast current had pushed both vessels thirty miles from the rendezvous. During coaling operations, Maffitt heard Averett's report. Averett had no captures and blamed that fact on the *Lapwing*'s lack of seaworthiness—it was leaky and sluggish. Maffitt sent Averett off again in the bark, which still contained some coal, to rendezvous on May 4 at Brazil's penal island of Fernando de Noronha.[13] (Maffitt disliked coaling at sea, when the coal was transferred by boats, because the loss of formality aboard ship produced a "general laxity.")

Resuming the cruise in the tropical zone after the coaling operation, which took two days, Maffitt entered a most fruitful period. On the morning of April 17, he captured the *Commonwealth*. A fine 1,300-ton clipper ship en route from New York to San Francisco, the vessel carried a large cargo of tobacco and provisions, $60,000 worth of Federal goods for troops in California. The ship and cargo went up in flames after Maffitt transferred what he needed to the *Florida*.

Maffitt continued to add to the heat of the tropical zone. The tall bark *Henrietta* next lit the ocean. Captured on April 23, it was bound from Baltimore to Rio de Janeiro with 3,250 barrels of flour and 600 kegs of lard. Among the passengers were a woman and her three children, whom Maffitt entertained in his cabin. He was amused by the *Henrietta*'s captain, George Brown, who was strong on states' rights. Maffitt was able to place some of his prisoners on neutral vessels and, in this way, avoided releasing a prize under bond in order to rid himself of them.

The *Oneida*, a clipper ship (not the blockader) from Shanghai, China, to New York was Maffitt's next seizure. Sighted on the morning of April 24, the vessel was aflame by noon. It had attempted to flee, but Maffitt added sail, and gongs rang in the engine room as a signal for the crew to stoke and feed the fires. Soon a shot from the *Florida* threw up water near the clipper's stern. Maffitt estimated the vessel and cargo of choice tea and silks were worth in the aggregate nearly a million dollars. Captain Jesse Potter of the *Oneida* was termed by Maffitt "an odd fish." Maffitt was happy to send him and fourteen other prisoners away that same day aboard a French bark. Potter had come on board the raider and proclaimed that the "pirates" would probably take the rings from his fingers. Wrote Maffitt: "I told him that we had the example but followed it not."[14]

On April 28 the *Florida* anchored off Fernando de Noronha, Brazil's

Bastille, a granite island located about five degrees below the equator off Cape St. Roque on the hump of Brazil. The ancient landmark had long been used by mariners to check their bearings. Maffitt learned that the *Alabama* had recently operated from this spot under a friendly local commandant. But now, higher Brazilian officials feared U.S. economic and naval reprisals and sent a new commandant to enforce strict neutrality. The steamer bearing the new commandant, Colonel Antonio Gomes Leal, arrived while the *Florida* was at the island. On May 1, Leal wrote Maffitt, protesting against the landing of thirty-two prisoners on the beach and notifying him to withdraw within twenty-four hours.[15] Maffitt decided against further offense and prepared to depart the island.

At daylight on May 2, the *Florida* stood out to sea and anchored twenty miles offshore to await the arrival of the *Lapwing*, which occurred the following day. Maffitt towed the vessel to a quiet spot and took on more coal. He detached Averett, who had no confidence in the vessel as a cruiser, and replaced him with Floyd. Since there was still coal aboard the tender after the refueling of the *Florida*, Maffitt directed Floyd to rendezvous at uninhabited Rocas Island, situated sixty miles west of Fernando de Noronha. At Rocas, Maffitt expected to take on the remaining coal in the *Lapwing*.[16]

Getting underway on a bearing west by southwest, the *Florida* on May 6 captured the brig *Clarence*. Bound from Rio de Janeiro to Baltimore, the vessel fell into Maffitt's hands off Cape St. Roque. In its hold were thousands of bags of coffee. But Read, who headed the boarding party, was not thinking of coffee. Instead, the daring lieutenant sent to Maffitt a bold plan to use the prize as a cruiser to raid ships in the Federal stronghold of Hampton Roads, Virginia. Maffitt undoubtedly recalled Read's background thus far in the war and his impatience to get out of Mobile. Maffitt decided to give the twenty-three-year-old lieutenant command of the *Clarence*: "I agree with your request and will not hamper you with instructions. Act for the best, and God speed you." He gave Read a twelve pound howitzer, small arms, provisions, and twenty men. Read, although a slight man with a boyish face, was the right man for the command, for he set out on one of the memorable raids of the war.[17]

Maffitt, after outfitting the *Clarence,* made his way southwesterly down the Brazilian coast without sighting an American vessel. The *Florida*'s engines began to knock on May 8, and he put in at Recife, capital of the state of Pernambucco. There he was able, after an initial rebuff, to persuade the governor of Pernambucco, Joao Silveira de Souza, to allow him three days beyond the twenty-four hour rule in order to repair his engines. Silveira granted the extension over the vigorous protest of the U.S. consul, Thomas Adamson. The governor insisted that he granted exactly the same conditions to U.S. and Confederate ships. He also, in the name of humanity and over Adamson's protest, allowed Maffitt to land prisoners. Silveira's dilemma was that he did not yet know which side would win the war.

During the four days at Recife, the *Florida* took on coal and provisions, and repairs were made to its engines. Maffitt allowed shore leave for the crew, and some of the men apparently sold captured goods. J. Watson Webb, U.S. minister to Brazil, echoed Adamson's charges and complained that selling goods captured at sea as part of a prize was a violation of international law. Silveira nervously informed Maffitt that Federal gunboats were on the way south and that protection of the *Florida* could not be guaranteed by Brazil. (In fact, one gunboat was cruising in that direction in search of the *Florida*—the U.S.S. *Mohican*.)[18] Maffitt, who had a personal interview with the governor in his palace, wrote: "I was very much impressed with his undisguised fear of the Federal government. . . . I could not but smile at his fears, and assured him that we did not require his protection."[19]

Maffitt departed Recife on May 12, over a week before the May 20 arrival of the *Mohican*.[20] Running to the southeast until out of sight of land, Maffitt ordered a northward course toward Rocas Island, the rendezvous point with the *Lapwing*. En route on May 13, the *Florida* captured the *Crown Point*, a ship of 1,100-tons burden, bound from New York to San Francisco and laden with assorted merchandise. After taking what they wanted, the Confederates burned the vessel. With prisoners aboard (nine of the captured crew joined the *Florida*), Maffitt resumed his course.

There was no sign of the *Lapwing* at Rocas Island. For two weeks Maffitt remained in the vicinity, waiting in vain for the tender. Chasing a sail on May 20, he found the ship to be a Danish brig, whose master agreed to take some of the prisoners. The prolonged inactivity at Rocas tested the morale of Maffitt's crew, and he kept them as busy as possible cleaning and painting the ship. The visit to the island proved unlucky. While there, three men were lost, one by illness and two by drowning. The most serious loss occurred when a cutter overturned in the rough sea near the beach and Joseph D. Grafton, ship's surgeon, drowned. Maffitt sent off boats to recover the body, but to no avail. On May 30, Maffitt, having concluded that the *Lapwing* had been captured or was otherwise unable to make the island, sent off a boat with orders to nail a signal to the beacon staff on the shore and leave the *Lapwing*'s orders nearby in a bottle. He then sailed westward. There would be no rendezvous with the *Lapwing*.[21]

On June 3, Maffitt gained permission from the governor Jose B. Da Cunha Figueirido to enter Fortaleza, capital of the Brazilian state of Ceara.

Here he disembarked his remaining eleven prisoners, and provisioned and coaled the ship. The presence of the *Florida* in these waters was now well-known to the Federals.[22] It was time for that delayed raid off New England. Departing Fortaleza the next day, the *Florida* would during the next few weeks traverse some fifty degrees of latitude. Cruising northward near the equator on June 6, the *Florida* captured the 1,000-ton ship *Southern Cross*, laden with logwood from the west coast of Mexico and bound for New York. Because Maffitt saw a woman on deck, he did not fire a shot. Captain Benjamin Howes, his wife,[23] three mates, and crew, a total of twenty people, were transferred to the deck of the raider. Then the prize was stripped and burned. Six days later, Maffitt sent the captain, his wife, and the clipper's officers away on board a French ship. He then ordered the prow of the raider toward the northeast.

Early in the morning of June 14, Maffitt lowered the propeller and gave chase to a ship off the starboard bow. After two hours, at 7° n 34° w, the clipper *Red Gauntlet* hove to. En route from Boston to Hong Kong, the vessel of 12,000 tons burden carried coal, ice, provisions, and musical instruments. After taking a full set of sails and some provisions, as well as twenty-eight prisoners, Maffitt sent a prize crew aboard for several days until he could transfer the coal.

Maffitt's next capture took place June 16 at 12° n 29° w. The prize was the clipper *Benjamin F. Hoxie*—bound from San Francisco to Falmouth, England, and carrying logwood, hides, and silver bars valued at $105,000. Maffitt, rejecting claims of neutral cargo as bogus, removed the silver and the prisoners, numbering thirty persons, and, on the following day, burned the vessel. It was the nearest thing to a treasure ship taken by a Confederate cruiser. Prisoners from the *Southern Cross*, the *Red Gauntlet*, and the *Benjamin F. Hoxie* now crowded the *Florida*—eleven of the men joining its crew. Captains and officers of the latter two prizes were sent off with provisions on an Italian brig on June 19, and the remainder of the prisoners, as usual, were kept in irons.[24] The silver bars might have constituted a prize if there had been a Confederate court available to condemn and apportion it; instead, Maffitt put it away for safekeeping.[25]

Maffitt set a northwest course with the *Red Gauntlet* still astern; the seas were too heavy to lower boats and receive the coal. For several days, no American ships were sighted. On June 27, he finished coaling from the *Red Gauntlet* and burned the ship. The next day, an American whaling schooner came into view at 30° n 48° 50′ w and became the next capture. It was the *Varnum H. Hill*, out of Providence, Rhode Island. The schooner was not a very valuable ship, and the raider was already crowded with fifty-four prisoners, so Maffitt bonded the vessel for $10,000. He put all his prisoners aboard it with provisions, to be landed at the nearest port of Bermuda.[26]

Unknown to the men on the *Florida,* the Southern war effort suffered twin blows at Gettysburg and Vicksburg during the next few days as the raider approached to within fifty miles of New York. On July 7, Maffitt captured the packet *Sunrise* that was en route from New York to Liverpool. Because of the neutral cargo and large number of passengers, he bonded the vessel for $60,000 and sent it on its way. From New York newspapers found on the *Sunrise,* he learned the latest war news, including the fate of Read, who before his capture in Portland had caused great alarm along the Northern seaboard. Because the Federals had numerous ships in the area looking for raiders, and because the poor quality of the coal taken from the *Red Gauntlet* would not produce a good head of steam, Maffitt reluctantly decided to abort his raid off New England.[27]

Indeed, at noon on July 8, one of the Federal gunboats came into view at 40° 28' n 69° 33' w and began to close on the *Florida.*[28] Maffitt immediately called his men to quarters, furled sails, and ran out the guns. He showed British colors until within range, then ran up the Confederate flag. Maffitt identified the stranger as the 900-ton U.S.S. *Ericsson,* a chartered side-wheel steamer with four funnels. Carrying a crew of twenty, the vessel had been armed by the Federals with three guns, a twenty-pound pivot, and two twelve-pounders on field carriages. Maffitt opened with a rifled shot from the fore pivot at twelve hundred yards. The shot screeched out and struck the water near the enemy vessel, ricocheted and struck its foretop. Then came a starboard broadside from the *Florida.* But at that moment, a patch of fog obscured the *Ericsson.*[29] Maffitt could easily have captured it and outfitted it as a cruiser, had not nature intervened. When Maffitt next saw the *Ericsson,* it was emerging from the fog four miles distant, beating a course for New York at maximum speed. He gave chase, but the poor quality of the coal and little favorable wind made the effort hopeless; besides, he was moving very close to New York. At five o'clock, Maffitt hauled off in pursuit of a brig, concluding his only offensive action against an enemy warship in the *Florida.*

The Confederate vessel would have the satisfaction of quickly taking two consolation prizes and lighting the waters while a Federal gunboat fled to safe harbor. The brig, captured at dusk, was the *William B. Nash,* out of New York and bound for Marseilles with lard and staves. After taking its crew on board, Maffitt fired the vessel. Nearby, the whaling schooner *Rienzi,* full of whale oil, was approaching its home port of Provincetown. When the crew of the *Rienzi* saw the fate of the *William B. Nash,* they rowed away in the small boats. Maffitt then fired the *Rienzi.* The lard in the brig and the oil in the whaling schooner created a tremendous pyrotechnic display. Flames shot hundreds of feet into the night sky. The red reflection could be seen just beyond the horizon in New York.[30]

Leaving the Northern coast, Maffitt set a course to the southeast. A few days later, on July 13, Assistant Paymaster Lynch died of consumption. Maffitt decided to put in at Bermuda to bury the officer, and to coal and repair the ship. On July 16, the vessel traversed the narrow channel and anchored at St. George's. To Maffitt's surprise and delight, Governor George Ord allowed a response in kind from the shore battery to a twenty-one gun salute from the *Florida*. This was a significant exchange in that it seems to have been the only time a foreign government ever saluted the Confederate flag.[31]

The exchange of salutes received much attention in the press. Many observers believed the exchange was an implicit recognition by the British of the independence of the South. A writer in a local paper, however, was probably more accurate. He considered the British salute "a mere act of courtesy shown by the authorities of the islands to a power acknowledged as a belligerent—a courtesy which they were willing to pay to the gallant representatives of that power, Captain Maffitt and his brave crew." The same writer continued: "The *Florida* was received with the utmost cordiality as well by the natives of these islands as by the Garrison, both being anxious to evince their sympathy for courage and patriotism."[32]

The hand of welcome was extended at every turn, and visitors swarmed to the craft. Maffitt and his fellow officers were honored guests at dinners ashore, including one given by Colonel William Munro, commander of the British garrison at Bermuda, who had returned the *Florida*'s salute gun for gun. Their demeanor was praised by the press—Maffitt and his officers were termed "gentlemen of great courtesy and manners." At age forty-four, Maffitt was at the zenith of his career, still the ladies' man, full of gallantry, wit, and glamour. His reputation for courage and patriotism was unquestioned; his recent captures and his brush with the *Ericsson* were simply his latest triumphs.[33] But underneath the extended celebration in Bermuda was a melancholy fact for Maffitt: the Southern cause was past its own zenith; after Gettysburg and Vicksburg, its downhill course could not be altered.

Bermuda was not meant to be a pleasure stop, and Maffitt had work to do. He at once engaged workers to caulk the *Florida*. But at the time, there was no private coal available, and Ord refused to release government coal. The governor, however, extended the vessel's stay in port until the arrival of a supply of coal from Halifax over a week later.[34] Maffitt entrusted to his colleague Captain John Wilkinson, of the blockade runner *Robert E. Lee,* three dozen chronometers and other captured items to be sent to the navy department in Richmond.[35] The *Robert E. Lee* also carried into the Confederacy from Bermuda sixteen bags of tea, nine bags of coffee, and a few boots and shoes for the soldiers in the Richmond hospitals as a present from the officers and crew of the *Florida*.[36] Maffitt landed prisoners and gave shore leave to the crew. The silver bullion, from the prize *Benjamin F. Hoxie,* he delivered to Confederate agent John T. Bourne. (It was subsequently learned that the silver did indeed belong to an English firm, and to placate the British government, the Confederacy shipped the silver to England, where it was returned to the claimants.)[37]

John Spidell, Maffitt's first engineer, resigned at Bermuda. There had been some difficulty between him and Assistant Engineer Quinn, who on July 14 had written in his journal: "Intend to leave *Florida* at Liverpool; unable to get along with Chief Engineer Spidell." While at Bermuda, Maffitt requested a group of officers, including Wilkinson, to investigate a charge of disloyalty brought by two assistant engineers of the *Florida* (other than Quinn) against Spidell. The board of inquiry reported on July 20: "We regard the charge as unsubstantiated and frivolous, if not malevolent." Yet the next day, Spidell resigned, citing ill health, and left the ship. Quinn then became the chief engineer of the *Florida*.[38]

At three o'clock in the afternoon of 25 July 1863, firemen activated the fireboxes preparatory to the departure of the *Florida*. Up the gangway went a group of women bearing flowers in a farewell visit to Maffitt. At 5:30 p.m.. the engineers started the engines, and the raider left the harbor amid great cheering from the residents on shore.[39] Maffitt headed eastward into the Atlantic, beyond the cruising range of most Federal gunboats. During the next several days, the Confederates sighted many ships—most flying English or French colors—and boarded a Russian ship. On August 6, at the mid-ocean coordinates of 40° 10′ n 44° 20′ w, Captain James T. Maloney of the packet ship *Francis B. Cutting,* Liverpool to New York, refused to hove to after a warning shot from the *Florida*. But Maffitt ended the chase with a second shot into the forward rigging. He sent over a boat and learned the packet had on board 230 passengers. Since this was too many to take on board the *Florida,* Maffitt released the *Francis B. Cutting* on $40,000 bond.[40]

Continuing across the Atlantic east by north, the *Florida* became unwieldy from the press of a long cruise. A report from the engineers revealed the propeller shaft out of line, the engine valves in need of resetting, and some of the copper sheathing on the hull in need of replacing. Such repairs called for dry-dock facilities. Maffitt considered either Liverpool or Brest, France. Because ninety days had not lapsed since he had entered a British port, and because Brest was difficult to blockade, Maffitt decided on Brest. Preparatory to entering the French port, however, Maffitt made his way to a point off Cork, Ireland and, on the night of August 18, sent ashore his executive officer. Averett's mission was to journey to Paris with an urgent message from Maffitt to the Confederate States commissioner to Paris, John Slidell. Maffitt asked Slidell to apply to the government of Napoleon III for use of the national dry dock, the only facility at Brest capable of effecting the extensive repairs needed by the *Florida.*[41]

The *Florida* created excitement for observers of its operations off the Irish coast.[42] Early in the morning of August 21, as the *Florida* was south-southeast of Cork, the Confederates sighted the sailing ship *Anglo-Saxon,* which was bound from Liverpool to New York with a cargo of coal. Maffitt captured the vessel and, after taking the crew of twenty-four and pilot on board the raider, burned the prize and used it for target practice.[43]

Plying southward from the coast of Ireland toward Brest on August 22, the Confederates captured in the English Channel the packet *Southern Rights.* Bound for New York, the prize was jammed with four hundred immigrants. Many of them were apparently Federal army enlistees. Maffitt must have caught the irony; the packet's name belied the true state of affairs. Southern rights were being trampled underfoot on American battlefields. He wanted to burn the vessel, but "as I had no way of disposing of her passengers," he wrote, "I bonded her for $40,000."[44] Maffitt then continued to Brest, arriving the next day, August 23, and here ended the first cruise of the *Florida.*

Maffitt's experiences in his guerilla warfare at sea were varied and exciting. A Southern newspaper rejoiced in his success:

> Like his father before him, he had to deal with some hardened sinners; but he generally manages to bring them to the anxious seat and make them howl for mercy. Between the Maffitts, father and son, the Devil has had a very uneasy time of it, both on land and water. One of the orator Maffitt's finest pulpit efforts was from the text, "Come thou and all thy house into the ark," an invitation which the son extends through the cannon of the *Florida* to all Yankee wayfarers upon the ocean.[45]

The effect of men like Maffitt was a disaster for the U.S. merchant fleet, more than half of which was lost during the war. The cruisers sank 110,000 tons of it, while 800,000 tons were sold abroad. The cruisers altogether captured 261 craft and destroyed nearly 200 of them. The direct losses in ships and cargoes may have reached $25,000,000—with indirect costs going much higher as insurance costs more than doubled. The raiders drove merchants to ship under foreign registry, and they never returned; the British alone received nearly a thousand vessels. Hence the American merchant flag was driven from the sea.[46]

The *Florida* not only destroyed Northern commerce but also weakened the blockade to some extent. That it was not further weakened was due to Welles, who refused to send more warships after the raiders and therefore sacrificed the merchant fleet in order to maintain the blockade. The raiders also increased the burden on influential Northern merchants (as well as their anxiety, since they thought they might be forced to pay for the bonded ships) and retarded U.S. preparations to attack vulnerable areas of the Southern coast.[47]

Maffitt's success had come against odds more overwhelming than those faced by the other cruiser commanders, especially his severe illness and necessity of running the blockade in and out of Mobile. He had damaged the enemy far beyond the cost of the *Florida,* making the cruiser one of the best investments made by the Confederacy. During its first cruise, the *Florida* captured twenty-three prizes, and her tenders took twenty-two (twenty-one by the *Clarence* and the *Tacony,* and one by the *Lapwing*) for a total of forty-five captures directly or indirectly under Maffitt's leadership. As a cruiser commander, he was closely identified with what was "certainly the most successful element of the Confederate navy."[48]

The Reverend John Newland Maffitt

Maffitt's father, John Newland Maffitt, Sr. (1794–1850), the famous Methodist revivalist, is depicted here (ca. 1825) in a steel engraving. (Moses Elsemore, *An
Impartial Account of the Life of the Rev. John N. Maffitt.*)

U.S.S. *Constitution*

John Newland Maffitt was a midshipman on the historic warship when grandly reflected in a painting by James G. Evans at Malta in 1837 during the celebration of Washington's birthday. It was also Maffitt's birthday. (U.S. Naval Academy Museum.)

Acting Lieutenant John N. Maffitt, U.S.N.

A handsome man, Maffitt is shown as he appeared in 1840, the year of his marriage in Mobile. (Emma Maffitt, *The Life and Services of John Newland Maffitt*.)

C.S.S. *Florida*

Maffitt is best known as commander of the famous Confederate raider during its first, and most successful, cruise. (Private collection of Charles Peery.)

Lieutenant John N. Maffitt, U.S.N.

Resplendent in his U.S. Navy uniform, Maffitt poses for the camera shortly before the Civil War. He was already known for capturing slave ships off the coast of Cuba. (Caldwell Delaney, *Confederate Mobile*.)

C.S.S. *Florida* at Brest

The arrival of the Florida in the French port in August 1863 marked the end of its first cruise, and here Maffitt resigned command. (*L'Illustration.*)

Florie Maffitt

Maffitt's daughter once ran the blockade with her father and had a blockade runner named after her—the *Florie*. (Emma Maffitt, *The Life and Services of John Newland Maffitt*.)

Midshipman Eugene Maffitt, C.S.N.

Maffitt's son was in the Battle of Port Royal Sound and served with Raphael Semmes on the C.S.S. *Alabama*. (Arthur Sinclair, *Two Years on the "Alabama."*)

On the Deck of the *Lilian*

Frank Vizetelly sketched the windswept deck of the blockade runner as it was chased in 1864 while steaming into Wilmington, North Carolina. Maffitt is to the left on the paddlebox. Vizetelly included himself nonchalantly leaning against the stack. (*Illustrated London News.*)

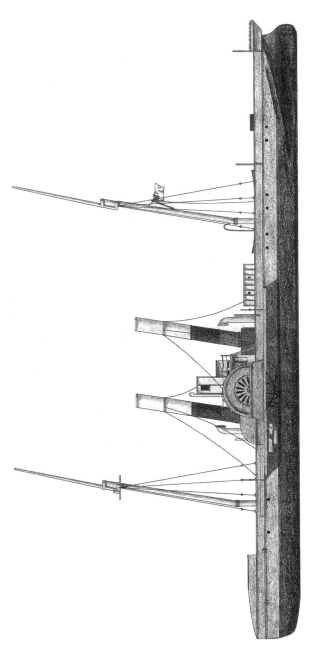

Blockade Runner *Owl*

Maffitt's last wartime command was a sleek vessel that outran all Federal blockaders. In it he delivered what was probably the last cargo of the war into the Confederacy. (Sketch by George Griffith. Private collection of the author.)

Commander John N. Maffitt, C.S.N.

Maffitt appears in the uniform of a Confederate commander. The rare photograph was probably taken near the end of the war. (Private collection of Charles Peery.)

Destruction of the *Jacob Bell*

The capture of the fine clipper ship by Maffitt was the most valuable nautical prize of the war claimed by any Confederate raider. (*Harper's Weekly.*)

Chapter 12

Maffitt Sets the Neutrality Standard

When the *Florida* put into Brest on 23 August 1863 for repairs, it was the first time a Confederate ship had touched at a French port. Without a precedent, French government officials in both Paris and Brest were in a quandary and equivocated for over a week.[1] It was a period of changing Confederate fortunes. A Northern victory in the war would threaten the French regime in Mexico, so French diplomats, in spite of the pro-Southern proclivities of Napoleon III, did not wish to antagonize Washington.[2]

Averett arrived in Paris from Cork to discover that Slidell was away on a visit to the seashore at Biarritz, France, the summer residence of Napoleon III on the Bay of Biscay. However, Slidell had left in charge his capable secretary, George Eustis.[3] Using the information imparted to him by Averett, Eustis wrote to French Minister of Foreign Affairs Drouyn de Lhuys, informing him that the damages to the *Florida* were of a serious and urgent character and called for prompt and immediate action. Maffitt in the meantime sent an emergency message to, then called upon, Vice Admiral Count de Gueyton, who was in charge of the port at Brest. Impressed with Maffitt, de Gueyton made clear that the *Florida* would be given the same rights as merchant ships. But in the critical question of the use of the government dry dock, all depended on the foreign minister, de Lhuys.[4]

While waiting for an answer from French officials, Maffitt discharged two-thirds of his crew, some sixty men. The reason for this action remains unclear, but according to Midshipman Sinclair, after Maffitt allowed his officers a short leave to visit Paris, an unfounded rumor circulated among the crew that only officers would be allowed to go ashore. This caused all the crew except about thirty to refuse duty. The thirty were retained, but the others were forced to leave, "notwithstanding their repentance when they found they had been deceived."[5] This was rare conduct for the crew of the *Florida,* and idleness must have been a factor. Fourteen crewmen at the time petitioned Maffitt to remain under his command even if he transferred to a new ship.[6]

In Paris, Eustis asked a judge, Pecquet du Belley, to go to Brest as a special Confederate agent and act as interpreter for Maffitt. When du Belley reached Brest, he found the locals greatly excited by false rumors that the *Florida* was a pirate ship filled with gold. They said that Maffitt was a sea wolf with a thirst for blood and that his crew were a set of cutthroats: "Before entering the roads, the *Florida* had been seen with several corpses hanging from her masts."[7] These rumors were carried in French newspapers opposed to Napoleon III. The U.S. minister to France, William L. Dayton, also charged that the raider was a pirate or a privateer.[8] One way Maffitt dispelled such claims was to invite visitors aboard for observation of the ship's regulation navy orientation. Further, he sent his officers to attend, first, the theater and, then, socials in Brest, where their modest and gentlemanly deportment won over the local inhabitants and French naval officers.

Among the international set of visitors to the *Florida* was a correspondent for the *London Times*. His group had been given cards by Lieutenant Hoole at the Hotel de Nates in Brest to assure admission on board. "I had no difficulty in making out this now celebrated vessel, as she lay at anchor among some of the giants of the French navy—a long, low, black, rakish looking craft," wrote the unnamed correspondent. They were immediately admitted on board, Maffitt coming to the top of the companionway to receive them and invite them to his cabin. The correspondent continued:

> Of the Captain himself I may say that he is a slight, middle-sized, well knit man, of about 42, a merry looking man, with a ready, determined air, full of life and business—apparently the sort of man who is equally ready for a fight or a jollification, and whom preference for the latter would by no means interfere with his creditable conduct of the former. His plainly furnished little stateroom looked as business-like as a merchant's office. The round table in the centre was strewn with books and innumerable manuscripts, and on the shelves were formidable looking rows of account books, charts, &c. I may observe of the cabin, as of every part of the Florida, that none of it appears to have been built for ornament—all for use. "You see," said the Captain, pointing to the heaps of papers, letters on file, account books, &c., which literally littered the table, "you see I've no sinecure of it."[9]

The long months of the cruise since leaving Mobile in January of 1863 had taken their toll on Maffitt. The exposure of the deck and the incessant wakefulness necessary to his command, combined with his earlier bout with yellow fever, seem to have affected his heart. He decided to resign command of the *Florida*. On September 5, Maffitt sent a reassignment request, along with a surgeon's certificate of ill health, to the ranking officer in France, Commander Matthew Fontaine Maury. The noted oceanographer, "grieved to learn" that Maffitt's health had given way under the severe trials of his command, wrote: "I am sure our countrymen will also learn with regret that they have to lose, even for a time, the services of an officer who has done so much to spread the fame of their flag over the seas."[10]

French Foreign Minister de Lhuys, after hearing the conflicting advice of Dayton and Eustis, eventually decided that the *Florida* was not a pirate nor a privateer. (The Congress of Paris in 1856 had attempted to abolish privateering, but the U.S. had declined to agree to the convention.)[11] The raider could use the government dry dock within the rules of French neutrality, a policy which meant no increase in armament. It was a momentous decision that opened French ports to all Confederate warships, a right used so extensively over the next year that Paris became the European headquarters of the Confederate navy. The *Florida* had caused the French to articulate their rules for belligerents' use of their port facilities, and the result was so much like that of the British ordinance that it became the standard for subsequent wars.[12] The *Florida* entered the dry dock at Brest on 11 September 1863.[13]

Hence, Maffitt had the honor of settling, with the aid of young Eustis, a vexing question in international law: Confederate cruisers were not privateers.[14] Writing to a Paris newspaper from Brest on 12 September 1863, Maffitt explained: "A privateer . . . is a vessel armed by a private individual with the authorization of the government." That standard was accepted in international law. The *Florida,* he pointed out, "has been built and armed by the government of the Confederate States of America, and her officers hold their commissions from that government." The raider carried the national flag and received instructions from the secretary of the navy of the Confederate States. European powers had recognized the Richmond government as a belligerent, with the right to form an army and fit out a navy. Concluded Maffitt: "I am at a loss to understand that the fact of my government not being yet officially acknowledged can take from it the rights inherent to every de facto government and placed in the category of a private individual fitting out a privateer."[15] No one could have said it better; the *Florida* was a man-of-war.

By now Maffitt would have learned that he had been promoted to the rank of commander in the navy effective 29 April 1863. The appointment (included with a letter from Mallory to Maffitt written in August) had been sent earlier to Nassau in May, but Maffitt had last visited that port in January. The promotion was "for gallant and meritorious conduct in command of the steam sloop *Florida* in running the blockade in and out of the port of Mobile against an overwhelming force of the enemy and under his fire, and since in actively cruising against and destroying the enemy's commerce." Mallory now added: "I congratulate you and the officers and men under your command upon the brilliant success of your cruise." While Mallory praised Maffitt for "skill, courage and coolness" as a seaman, the secretary complained that the only report of the cruise he had received from Maffitt was the list of articles sent from Bermuda on the *Robert E. Lee.* Maffitt had sent periodic reports, but dispatches both ways faced uncertain delivery. Mallory was annoyed because he was forced to rely on newspaper accounts for news of the exploits of the *Florida.*[16]

On September 17, Commander Joseph N. Barney, the same officer who was to relieve Maffitt in Mobile and a newcomer to Europe, arrived in Brest with orders from Maury, and Maffitt took his final leave of the *Florida.*[17] The raider eventually made a second, and less successful, cruise, capturing twelve more prizes, for a combined total for both cruises of thirty-five.[18] Since the *Florida*'s tenders from the first cruise totaled twenty-two, the grand total, directly or indirectly for both cruises, was fifty-seven prizes. Forty-three of the prizes were actually destroyed, for an estimated value of $4,051,000 in damages to U.S. shipping, compared to the *Alabama*'s fifty-eight prizes destroyed for an estimated value of $4,792,000 in tonnage sunk.[19] According to these figures, almost as much U.S. shipping tonnage was sunk by the *Florida* as by its sister ship.[20]

Had Maffitt retained command, he undoubtedly would have surpassed the record of Semmes, even though the *Florida* remained inactive for over four months at Mobile and over five months at Brest. The skillful, imaginative Maffitt would probably have mounted coastal raids during the second cruise to find Union prizes on a sea that admittedly held fewer of them. And had Maffitt been in command at Recife when the *Florida* was captured, he would hardly have left his ship with a dissipated crew in the harbor of a weak power where there lurked an enemy warship. He was usually found aboard ship, and had he been in command, there would have been a different ending to the saga. Indeed, the record of the two cruises of the *Florida* "illustrates the fact that commanders more than any other single element determined the ultimate success of the ship."[21]

Upon relinquishing command of the *Florida,* Maffitt went to Paris with his interpreter friend, Judge du Belley. In the City of Lights, Maffitt encountered another rumor—this one apparently spread by envious Confederate agents—that he used spirits too freely. Having helped Maffitt conquer adverse public opinion at Brest, du Belley now defended him on this score. The judge wrote that he was "invariably greeted" with such comments as "You are just from Brest. All is well with the *Florida*, I understand. Damned fine fellow that Maffitt. What a pity he should drink so as to render himself unfit for service! Of course you know that he has been discharged from duty." Such remarks, wrote du Belley, were "ridiculous" and "slanderous." He should have known, having been in company with Maffitt for over a month. Continued the judge: "I had never seen him drink one drop of liquor; and if he had ever indulged on board ship, the Federal officers who have pursued him with pertinacity can bear witness to the fact that it had no other effect than to sharpen his natural keenness and nautical abilities." Judge du Belley made reference to Lincoln's reply to stories of General U. S. Grant's drinking. If Maffitt possessed a nature that was prone to intemperance, the judge believed, it was "a pity that President Davis did not procure some of the same kind and send a barrel thereof to each and everyone of his European agents.[22]

Shortly after arriving in Paris, Maffitt and Judge du Belley dined at the Café de France, known for its delicious fare and excellent wines. They had nearly finished when two Englishmen entered, sat at a nearby table, and began to discuss the merits of Confederate heroes, including Lee, Jackson, Beauregard, and Longstreet. Having reached a certain state of happiness from their wine, the one opposite Maffitt suddenly exclaimed, "Well, I say, none of these chaps can compare with that fellow Maffitt! He's my man, by God! and he comes up precisely to my idea of a hero. I only wish I could see him. I am told he is in Paris." If he could meet him, the Englishman vowed, he would call for a bottle of the finest wine. The judge felt very much inclined to respond: "Call for that champagne, sir!" But he glanced at Maffitt, who was pale. Wrote du Belley: "His imploring countenance nailed my tongue. He called for the bill, and when we had left the room he looked as much relieved as though he had just run through a blockading squadron."[23] Amid rumors of his intemperance, Maffitt wanted no public display involving wine.

Leaving his interpreter friend to squelch the intemperance rumor, Maffitt attended to his health problem. He consulted one of the best physicians in Paris. Maffitt had mentioned in a letter home a few weeks earlier that he had heart trouble, and now the physician confirmed that his heart was "affected from tropical disease." He put Maffitt through a course of "severe" (but unidentified) treatment. Then, on his physician's orders, Maffitt traveled for his health in Sweden.[24]

Chapter 13

Return to Blockade Running

With his health on the mend by the end of 1863, Maffitt was in England conferring with Bulloch. Britain had ceased providing warships, but blockade runners especially designed to run the increasingly effective Federal blockade could be purchased, and on the River Clyde, in Scotland, a shipbuilding boom was in progress. Small size, shallow draft, and speed characterized this class of vessel. Southern individuals, firms, and state governments bought them to take advantage of the bonanza in the cotton trade.

The Clyde-built steamers, among the fastest in the world, were now needed to enter Wilmington.[1] As a letter from Maffitt expressed it: "The news from Bermuda runners is decidedly bad. Six of the last boats have recently been caught. . . . Nothing has entered Wilmington for one month." As if to emphasize the point, Maffitt's letter itself was captured by the blockaders.[2] More than ever, the Confederacy needed men like Maffitt, who refused to panic, were highly skilled, and knew the coastline.

The Clyde-built *Florie,* named for Maffitt's daredevil daughter, was chartered by the state of Georgia.[3] The vessel was an iron side-wheeler, 222 feet in length, 24 feet wide, 10 feet in depth, and registered at 215 tons, with a gross weight of 349 tons. The *Florie* and its sister ships, with turtle-back forecastles, slipped through as well as over the waves.[4] They could ply at speeds over 14 knots. Maffitt, carrying Confederate dispatches, took the *Florie* to Funchal, in the Portuguese islands of Madeira off the coast of Morocco, where he coaled and departed 4 January 1864 for Bermuda.[5] After reaching Bermuda, the *Florie* sustained damage at sea. Wrote Confederate agent John T. Bourne: "The steamer *Florie* returned into port yesterday in a sinking condition."[6] Maffitt was forced to take the *Florie* to Halifax, Nova Scotia, for repairs.[7]

Upon his return to Bermuda, Maffitt took command of the *Lilian* (sometimes referred to as *Lillian*).[8] It was a sister ship of the *Florie,* but slightly larger, with a registered weight of 246 tons and a gross weight of 630 tons,[9] and was also chartered by the state of Georgia.[10] Two engines of two boilers each drove the vessel. When the *Lilian* was loaded, its deck was only three or four feet above the waterline. "In heavy seas she labored so that she spent about as much time under the water as on top of it."[11]

When Maffitt ordered the *Lilian* out of St. George's on 1 June 1864, it was loaded to its marks with niter, lead, quinine, cloth, and other merchandise.[12] His reputation had attracted to the *Lilian* some notable British passengers. Among those on board was Frank Vizetelly, the celebrated sketch artist for the *Illustrated London News*. A friend described him as "charming, of great experience, capital narrator, and as for pencil of world-wide fame."[13] Also aboard was Francis C. Lawley, Vizetelly's traveling companion. Lawley, former private secretary to William Gladstone and former member of Parliament, visited the Confederacy as a correspondent for the *London Times*.[14] "I knew that Captain Maffitt was a favorite of General Lee, . . . and one glance at his resolute, straightforward face made me determined that I would go with him," wrote Lawley. "He was in truth a fine specimen of a sailor, and the more I saw of him during our short three days and four nights voyage, the more I liked him."[15]

Maffitt had a challenge ahead of him in addition to the Federal blockade—a race with the *Florie*. The *Lilian* and the *Florie*, painted leaden gray, simultaneously departed Bermuda. The well-matched vessels created intense rivalry among the respective crews and passengers, complete with betting, as to which would be the first to reach Wilmington. The "Lilianites" were impressed with their vessel, which had the graceful appearance of a racing yacht. "The celebrated John Newland Maffitt, no less, was, we thought, the man of all men to command her," wrote the young crew member James Sprunt.[16] The two blockade runners lost sight of each other after dark of the first day.

The next morning, the empty sea sparkled in glorious sunshine as flying fish emerged from the ocean in flights of over two hundred yards before disappearing again into the billowy depths. Soon Maffitt's quick eye picked up a sail off the port bow enveloped in smoke. Looking through his glasses, Maffitt decided the vessel might be on fire, but perhaps it was a Federal cruiser luring him into a trap. Timing was precious to a blockader runner— moons and tides and darkness had to be calculated. There was also the race with the *Florie*. But Maffitt believed that no ship captain could leave another vessel in distress at sea. He wore around toward the stranger, but upon making it out to be a Federal cruiser, he ordered the helmsman to resume course eastward for the coast of North Carolina.

Pressing on during the third day out of Bermuda, Maffitt hoped to reach Wilmington before dawn the next day. The *Lilian*'s sharp bow cleaved the waves like a razor at a speed that exhilarated those on board. Passengers and crew joined together in Confederate war songs. Maffitt silenced the mirth when night fell, ordering all lights extinguished and no smoking. The blockade runner blew off steam under water and used feathered paddles. As a means of further reducing the ship's low silhouette, no yards were on the two short masts, and only a small crow's nest maintained in the foremast. But in the gloom, the crew failed to find the light on the mound at Fort Fisher. At dawn, Maffitt ordered the engines stopped and lay to between the inner and outer cordon of blockaders. That afternoon, a large black steamer hove in sight, and Maffitt beat back to sea like a startled quail as shots fell around the *Lilian*.

A chase ensued that lasted over two hours. The beautiful little *Lilian* answered to the driving force within it, the paddles flying around at thirty-three revolutions a minute. The hull of the pursuer became invisible and its topgallant sails merely a speck on the far horizon. As the day began to wane, Maffitt circled into the sunset. He sighted the close-knit inner cordon of blockaders, forming a grim and forbidding barrier, just before dark. The Federals would soon sight the prey. "It is at such moments that you realize how paramount is the influence of a dauntless chief upon all around him; and it is felt more in so confined a space as a deck of a ship than in a great battle on land," wrote Lawley.

Although Lawley observed anxiety in Maffitt's face, the timing was perfect. Night fell before the *Lilian* was close enough to be seen by the Federals; the vessel approached while enemy crews were at evening meals. Tension mounted aboard the little craft as Maffitt slowly approached and slipped past the blockaders, expecting all the while a fatal broadside. Suddenly, just as they approached the bar, a dark hull loomed ahead, within easy range of the guns of Fort Fisher. The blockader, probably groping for secrets or sinking obstructions, pulled off just in time to avoid being rammed by Maffitt. The enemy vessel did not fire, either because its crew had been surprised or because they were within range of the fort's guns. Within minutes, Maffitt anchored near the mound. Exchanging news with Confederates on shore, the "Lilianites" were elated to hear they were ahead of the *Florie*.[17]

One Federal blockading officer, Commander Pierce Crosby, commander of the U.S.S. *Keystone State,* was outraged that Maffitt had again successfully breached the Federal blockade. He wanted "those blockade runners flaunting their secesh flags in our faces. . . entrapped, and Mr. Maffitt with the *Lilian* humbled."[18] But Maffitt was not easily humbled, and the *Lilian* would be remembered in poetry written by Sprunt:

> Freed from the lingering chase, in devious ways
> Upon the swelling tides
> Swiftly the *Lillian* glides

Through hostile shells and eager foemen past;
The lynx-eyed pilot, gazing through the haze,
His engines straining, "far hope dawns at last."

Now falls in billows deep the welcome night
    Upon white sands below;
    While signal lamps aglow
Seek out Fort Fisher's distant answering gleams,
The blockade runner's keen, supreme delight,—
Dear Dixie Land, the haven of our dreams![19]

Maffitt had extra reason for rejoicing on 5 June 1864. It was the first time he had touched upon Southern soil since, a year and a half ago, he left Mobile on the *Florida*. It had been even longer since he last ran the blockade from Wilmington. The city had become one of the most important in the South and was quickly becoming the last open port. It was rowdy. Fights between the crews of the steamers and the soldiers stationed there were frequent. Speculators from all over the South and abroad swarmed in, causing the old families to move away, or to stay off the streets. When a blockade runner arrived, people "rushed down to the wharves to see it, to buy, beg, or steal something."[20]

Maffitt spent little time in Wilmington. When he had resigned from the *Florida,* he received orders to report in person, when his health allowed, to the navy department. Maffitt traveled to Richmond, where he was the man of the hour. From all quarters of the capital came laurels: "Commander Maffitt has come to town and captured many a heart."[21] But the Confederacy needed every man at his post, and on June 8, Maffitt reported as he had been ordered. His new command was the C.S.S. *Albemarle,* located on the Roanoke River at Plymouth, North Carolina.[22] Commander James W. Cooke, who like Maffitt was a Tar Heel, had commanded the ironclad that spring when the vessel aided in the recapture of Plymouth and engaged enemy gunboats on Albemarle Sound. When Cooke's health failed under the strain, he requested a transfer and was placed in command of naval forces on the Roanoke, with headquarters upriver at Halifax.[23]

On 25 June 1864, Maffitt reported for duty at Plymouth. The *Albemarle*—patterned after, but an improvement over, the C.S.S. *Virginia*—carried 4 inches of armor. The screw steamer was 158 feet long, with a beam of 35 feet, and a depth of 8 feet; it carried 2 guns and had ramming capability.[24] Since no Federal ironclad had a shallow-enough draft to cross Hatteras bar and enter the sounds, the *Albemarle* was powerful enough to threaten Union naval supremacy in the sounds of North Carolina.[25] The

Confederate navy had great hopes for the vessel, just as they had had two years earlier for the C.S.S. *Virginia*.

A refugee from Plymouth carried the intelligence to the Federals that Maffitt was in command. This news lowered the morale of Union forces in eastern North Carolina at a time when the only remaining hope of the South was war weariness in the North.[26] Wrote Brigadier General Innis N. Palmer, commander of Federal forces at New Bern: "Captain Maffitt now commands the ram *Albemarle*, and we all know that he is not the man to sit down at Plymouth. He was ordered there to do something."[27]

It was in keeping with Maffitt's aggressive nature that he began to plan for another attack in Albermarle Sound. He informed Colonel George Wortham, commander at Plymouth, that Mallory had issued oral instructions to attack.[28] Wortham considered such action unwise. Brigadier General Lawrence S. Baker, district commander in Goldsboro, agreed with Wortham. On July 6, Baker wrote Maffitt to "beg that you will not make the movement unless you are *certain* of success."[29] Two day later, Baker requested that Secretary of War James A. Sedden "obtain an immediate revocation of the order to Captain Maffitt." Baker believed the ram would be lost if engaged, an occurrence which would probably necessitate the evacuation of Plymouth and, with it, the loss of the rich valley of the Roanoke.[30] He convinced authorities to delay until another ram could be completed to aid the *Albemarle*.

Under these circumstances, Maffitt's duty on the ram was that of river guard. To occupy his crew, Maffitt often sent the vessel on nighttime runs to the mouth of the river to sweep for mines, and perhaps to capture one of the Union picket boats or ram some unsuspecting Union vessel.[31] He also sent out a raiding party of some twenty men under one of his pilots, J. B. Hopkins—a group who, on the night of September 9, captured and burned the mail steamer *Fawn* plying the Dismal Swamp Canal between Elizabeth City, North Carolina, and Norfolk, Virginia.[32]

Maffitt learned or suspected that the Federals were planning to torpedo the *Albemarle*. To guard the ram against a raid, Maffitt surrounded the vessel with a shield of logs in the water, chained side by side and pointing outward.[33] There the *Albemarle* lay, by the wharf at Plymouth—a command that, because the Confederate army overruled the navy, was not suitable for Maffitt.

Events in Richmond now conspired to provide Maffitt a more exciting command. With blockade running becoming more hazardous, the government had recently contracted for eight fast blockade runners to serve the vital needs of the Confederacy. They would be under the direct control of the navy department. Mallory wanted his best commanders in charge of the sleek new vessels and, on September 9, ordered Maffitt detached from the *Albemarle*. He was to report to Wilmington and take command of the first one of the new vessels to arrive from England.[34] The *Albemarle's* new commander, Lieutenant Alexander F. Warley, having arrived in Plymouth, Maffitt relinquished his position on 20 September 1864.[35] As commander of the *Albemarle,* Maffitt had been too aggressive to suit local commanders. A victory over the Federal gunboats on Albemarle Sound would have been difficult, but Maffitt must have wondered what would have happened had he been allowed to attack.[36]

Chapter 14

Owl: The Last Blockade Runner

The first of the new class of blockade runners, the *Owl,* arrived in Wilmington about 19 September 1864.[1] The quarto of the *Owl* class, which included the *Bat,* the *Stag,* and the *Deer*—constructed in Liverpool under Bulloch's supervision, for initial consignment to Fraser, Trenholm and Company—were side-wheelers of 771-tons burden with long, low, molded steel hulls, 230 feet by 26 feet by 10½ feet. Their twin Watt engines drove them at speeds up to 16 knots. The entire cargo of the new ships was for the direct benefit of the government, a strategy that should have been adopted much earlier in the war. Their capacity was eight hundred bales of cotton, and oversized coal bunkers gave them extra range. Their silhouettes showed fore and aft schooner rigging and two funnels. The *Owl* was painted a light red color.[2] The ship was Maffitt's final command of the war as he served the Confederacy in its last desperate gamble.

Mallory sent instructions to Maffitt regarding the *Owl,* some of which help explain why Confederate naval officers on blockading-running duty were not captured. Mallory established command policy for all the new vessels, believing it was important that uniformity be observed in their management.[3] He telegraphed a "do not surrender" message to Maffitt on September 19: "As commanding officer of the *Owl,* you will please devise and adopt thorough and efficient means for saving all hands and destroying the vessel and cargo whenever these measures may become necessary to prevent capture."[4] This was followed by: "When capture, in your judgment, becomes inevitable, fire the vessel in several places and embark in the boats, making for the nearest land."[5] In Maffitt's case, not only were such instructions not needed; they contributed to the unnecessary loss of valuable papers, including Maffitt's log of the *Florida.*

To observe British neutrality laws, the *Owl*'s maiden voyage to Wilmington via Bermuda and Halifax was under British master Matthew J. Butcher.[6] Although Confederate naval officials attempted to take over the ship immediately, technical procedures involving a change of registry from a private "front" to government hands delayed possession until Butcher had steamed to Bermuda.[7] The *Owl* then steamed to Nassau to get a pilot, and Maffitt did not expect the ship until the next moon. He chafed at the setback caused by the registration embroglio, writing that "the delay was exceedingly annoying."[8] When the *Owl* returned to Wilmington on December 1 under Lieutenant John W. Dunninton, the navy department turned it over to Maffitt.[9]

On 21 December 1864, Maffitt finally cleared Wilmington in the *Owl*. With some eight hundred bales of cotton on board, Maffitt "ran clear of the Federal sentinels without the loss of a rope-yarn." As he departed, Union General Benjamin F. Butler was preparing for the first assault on Fort Fisher. Arriving in St. George's on December 27, Maffitt found several blockade runners awaiting word of the first attack on the fort. By this time, Butler had attempted in vain to annihilate the fort by exploding nearby a ship filled with powder. This effort was followed by an ineffective bombardment on Christmas Day. Hearing of Butler's failure, Maffitt headed for Wilmington. He had a valuable cargo aboard, probably consisting of clothing, blankets, shoes, and "articles for submarine purposes" as needed by the navy department.[10]

On the night of January 15, Maffitt approached Cape Fear. At this point, he made a most fateful decision to enter Old Inlet at the southern entrance to the river off Fort Caswell. After all, the Northern newspapers in Bermuda could have been wrong about Fort Fisher. He sighted only one blockader, which he easily eluded in the dark, and crossed the bar at high tide about 8:00 p.m., three hours before moonrise. Maffitt came to anchor off the wharf at Fort Caswell. A boat immediately pulled up containing Confederates who informed him that Fort Fisher had fallen that day as a result of a combined sea and land attack under Admiral David D. Porter and General Alfred H. Terry. Federal blockaders had already entered the Cape Fear River through New Inlet and cut off Fort Caswell. Confederate troops at Fort Caswell and outlying areas were moving to Southport for a retreat overland toward Wilmington.[11]

Gunboats were beginning to move in the direction of the *Owl*, and Maffitt was about to give the order to slip the chain, when his pilot requested permission to go ashore. "He represented the situation of his wife, whom he had left ill and without means of support, in such moving terms, that Maffitt granted permission, upon condition that he would return speedily."[12] Faithfully, in twenty minutes, the pilot was again on the deck. The crew hoisted the boat to the davits, and the fierce revolutions of the paddle wheel shot the *Owl* back to sea. There was no effort to evade the lone sentinel guarding the exit, and although that vessel began a furious chase, its cannonade, as with most night-firing at sea, did little damage to the *Owl*. Even the noise of the firing was smothered by the tremendous explosion heard on board the *Owl* as the Confederates blew up Fort Caswell. The overpowering noise "rumbled portentously from wave to wave in melancholy echoes." Watching the spectacle from the deck, Maffitt "in poignant distress . . . turned from the heartrending scene." The event foreshadowed the fate of Dixie.[13]

Maffitt returned to Bermuda, reaching there on January 21 with news of the fall of the Cape Fear forts, in time to stop five blockade runners from sailing.[14] Maffitt's information caused great dismay and nearly ended blockade running. The war was practically over, and the Confederates at sea were cut off from communication with home. Maffitt and his fellow officers, including John Wilkinson and John Low—who in 1862 had ferried the *Oreto* from Liverpool to Nassau—met to discuss strategy while enjoying the hospitality of Major Norman S. Walker, Confederate quartermaster agent, and his wife, Georgiana. The Walker's home became a rallying place for men who had to rely more than ever on their wits.[15]

Blockade running died hard for men like Maffitt. They had valuable cargoes that Confederates desperately needed: supplies for the Army of Northern Virginia in the trenches at Petersburg, and for the remnant of the Army of Tennessee falling back before Sherman in the Carolinas. When word came that Charleston had not fallen, Maffitt and several others sailed for that port. Maffitt, believing it was his duty to make an effort, cleared St. George's on January 26 with his original inbound cargo.[16] Moving along the coast, he saw the Federal ships inspecting the smallest inlets since the enemy was fully aware of the desperation of the blockade runners. A few chased Maffitt, but the *Owl* steamed away with superior speed.

Approaching Maffitt's Channel after dark, Maffitt placed the government mail, private correspondence, and his war journal—including his narrative of the entire cruise of the *Florida*—and other papers in two weighted bags, which were suspended over the side by a stout line. He ordered an intelligent quartermaster to stand by with a hatchet, and if capture became inevitable, he was to cut them free. Wrote Maffitt:

> When on the western tail-end of the Rattlesnake Shoal, we encountered streaks of mist and fog that enveloped stars and everything for a few moments, when it would become quite clear again. Running cautiously in one of those obscurations, a sudden lift in the haze disclosed that we were about to run into an anchored blockader. We had bare room with a hard-a-port helm to avoid him some fifteen or twenty feet, when their officer on deck called out, "Heave to, or I'll sink you!" The

order was unnoticed, and we received his entire broadside, that cut away turtle-back, perforated forecastle, and tore up bulwarks in front of our engine-room, wounding twelve men, some severely, some slightly. The quartermaster stationed by the mail-bags was so convinced that we were captured that he instantly used his hatchet, and sent them, well moored, to the bottom; hence my meager account of the cruise of the *Florida*.[17]

A swarm of blockaders were made visible by the rockets and drummond lights, and inexperienced volunteer officers ordered an indiscriminate discharge of guns. According to Maffitt, "this was attended with unfortunate results to the Federals."[18] He made his way out of the confused scene, his vessel so battered that he went for repairs to Nassau. The *Owl* entered Nassau on January 31 "with a shot through her funnel, several more through her hull, her standing rigging in rags and other indications of a hot time."[19]

While repairs were being made to the *Owl*, Charleston was evacuated on February 17, ending its potential as a destination for Maffitt. He was reluctant to end his blockade-running career while in command of a fast, fully loaded ship. Yet before Maffitt attempted to deliver another cargo, he engaged in some courier service. Maffitt had met Thomas Conolly in Nassau. Conolly, a wealthy pro-Southern Irishman and a member of parliament, had dispatches from James Mason in England for Confederate officials in Richmond.[20] With Conolly and two other passengers, Maffitt on February 23 was ready to depart for the coast of North Carolina, where he would put the men ashore. He dismissed the carpenters, although they had not completed repairs to the turtleback, and got underway at dark without a pilot.[21] A series of bumps into other ships so changed the course of the *Owl* that Maffitt was forced to exit the narrow entrance backwards. Conolly, who kept a diary, was impressed: "It was plucky! to go out backwards."[22] Once at sea, Maffitt assigned his passengers to quarters in the wheelhouse on the bridge. Then "with seamanlike cordiality and cocktails all around told us we must put up with 'rough and tumble' but he hoped to land us all safe in Dixie."

Arriving at the coast near Shallotte Inlet, North Carolina, at dawn of February 26, Maffitt, at Conolly's request, sent the three men ashore in a driving rain. After a rough landing, in which their boat was swamped by the heavy breakers, they made their way through the countryside to Maffitt's home town of Fayetteville. There, the wide muddy streets were filled with wagons and carts moving cotton bales to hiding places outside town. The bar at the Fayetteville Hotel was crowded with men in uniform talking about the approach of Sherman.

Conolly visited Ellerslie and had dinner with Florie. He "gave her intelligence of her good father" and described Florie as "very charming and retiring, exceedingly pretty and amiable, and very much delighted to hear of her papa." Conolly also complimented her upon her coming marriage to Joshua G. Wright. (Conolly went next to Raleigh, where he met Frank Vizetelly, and then journeyed on to Richmond. There, he met President Davis, dined with General Lee, and witnessed the fall of that city, afterwards making his way home to Castletown, his fine country estate outside Dublin.)[23]

Maffitt, his unconventional courier mission completed, steamed to Havana. There, he planned the war's last active blockade running venture with a run to Galveston. The city had been a rather minor port during the war: it was a long way from Havana, requiring much coal; the entrance was shallow and not well defended; and the stay in port was lengthy because not much cotton was stored in the exposed port. Nonetheless, Maffitt set off in the *Owl* for Galveston.[24]

Sixteen blockaders guarded the Texas port, and Maffitt ran the gauntlet, taking heavy fire. He was so hard pressed at the entrance to the harbor that he ran aground on Bird Island Shoals. Still under fire, Maffitt attempted to free the *Owl*. The scene became grand outdoor theater as the people of Galveston ascended to their housetops to view the action. Inside the harbor, a small Confederate fleet consisting of two gunboats and four transports could hardly offer protection, but one of the gunboats, the C.S.S. *Diana*, with a volunteer crew under Captain James H. McGarvey, steamed out into the spray of shot and shell to find Maffitt "at his exposed post on the bridge of the steamer, calmly directing his men and displaying . . . the greatest bravery." With the aid of the *Diana*, the *Owl* was soon floated and towed out of danger to the rejoicing of the housetop audience.[25]

The machinery of the *Owl* seems to have been damaged, since a few days after Maffitt's arrival in Galveston, the commanding general ordered the *Diana* to tow the *Owl* across Galveston Bay to Lynchburg, Texas.[26] The off-loaded cargo,[27] brought in by Maffitt, was undoubtedly the last major delivery to a Confederate port during the war, but it was too late to be of much service to the South. Maffitt was in Galveston after Lee surrendered, but the Stars and Bars still floated at Galveston. The far-southwest port did not surrender ("its fall may be regarded as the final act in the naval war"[28]) until 2 June 1865. By that time, Maffitt had run the blockade and had, on May 9, reached Havana.[29]

Shortly after the *Owl* departed Galveston, Lieutenant J. Pembroke Jones, assigned to special service, passed through Galveston from Richmond in search of Maffitt. Mallory had ordered Jones to make his way out of the Confederacy as best he could, report to Maffitt, purchase two steamers to take supplies to Lee on an urgent basis, one for a run up the York River and the other up the James River. Jones had with him money in specie checks and was accompanied by two pilots for the Virginia river trips, but when they reached the Mississippi headed for Texas, Jones heard of the end of the war in the East. He sent the pilots home, continued alone to Galveston, and conferred with General John B. Magruder, who informed him the war would not be continued in Texas. Jones decided to continue to Metamoras, where he took a steamer to Havana and found Maffitt.[30]

Jones probably brought with him the well-known 24 February 1865 letter from Mallory. It was the last from Mallory to Maffitt, and desperation was now apparent. Maffitt was the senior officer in the islands, and as such, he was to consult with Wilkinson. The two might enter shallow coastal waters with the *Chameleon* and the *Owl*. Or Maffitt might sell the *Chameleon*, purchase a smaller vessel, buy small arms, and run through the blockade to (or in the vicinity of) the small port of St Marks, Florida. Should the options seem impracticable, Maffitt could turn the vessels over to an agent of Fraser, Trenholm and Company. He almost surely received the letter too late to carry through with most of Mallory's suggestions.[31]

Maffitt decided to sail for Liverpool, but via Halifax for coal. En route, he was careful to elude blockaders. Jones accompanied him as far as Halifax, where they parted. Jones later remembered Maffitt: "He was the warmest-hearted and most generous friend and the most genial companion I ever knew. He was always the life of the mess, full of fun and tender sympathy for all around him. He was a born sailor and a splendid officer, and I have never known one more beloved."[32]

The *Owl* continued to Liverpool with a depleted crew, under sail much of the time, with Maffitt watching for trouble from Federal cruisers still trying to capture him for piracy. On 14 July 1865, the *Owl* steamed up the Mersey River and dropped anchor. The next day, Maffitt ordered his men piped to the stern for a farewell ceremony. He appeared in an immaculate uniform and addressed the men, saying it was the last time they would meet as Confederate sailors, and thanking them for their loyal service to him and the South. He paid them off and "spliced the mainbrace" one last time for the Confederacy. Then, to three cheers from the hands, Maffitt personally struck the colors.[33]

Chapter 15

The Moorings

After the war, Maffitt temporarily established residence in Liverpool with his son Eugene. He did not regret the end of the war, but he had hoped that the South would have enough success to gain liberal terms from the Federal government for Southerners. "As it is," he wrote, "we are truly at the mercy of despotism." The Northern government had stigmatized him as a pirate, although Federal naval officers recognized his excellence as a naval officer and his chivalrous bearing, as well as his humanity. Since he was uncertain what his reception might be in the United States, Maffitt waited for a possible general amnesty, intimated by President Andrew Johnson. Furthermore, he wrote, "My stomach is as yet too delicate to take the nauseous dose—or pardon asking pill."[1]

Meanwhile, Maffitt attended school to secure a master's license in order to enter the British merchant service and qualify for a ship. "I go to school like a good boy and do not play by the wayside," he wrote.[2] In the fall of 1865, Maffitt obtained his certificate and was assigned to command the British merchant steamer *Widgeon*.[3] His rank, for the first time in his career, was that of captain. The vessel plied between Liverpool and South American ports. In April 1866, he was in the Cape Verde Islands and wrote that he had "a most terrible time. . . . I believed that I had written you my last letter, but God in his mercy saved us."[4] He does not explain in that letter the nature of the trouble.

In January 1867, Maffitt was in Corrientes, on the Parana River in South America. The *Widgeon* had been chartered to the Brazilian government, one of the allies (Argentina, Uruguay, and Brazil) in the brutal War of the Triple Alliance (1865–1870) against Paraguay.[5] Brazil used the *Widgeon* as a transport vessel, and Maffitt moved soldiers, horses, provisions, and supplies up the Parana. He wrote home, amid the sting of mosquitoes, that as he transported soldiers to the war zone, smallpox broke out among the men. They refused to nurse the sick or bury the dead, so Maffitt had a fearful time—"sickening to the last degree." The soldiers were also mutinous. "Do not like the duty," wrote Maffitt, "but

99

as it pays well and enables me to support my family, I must not complain." He witnessed the great battle at Itapeva, where the allies lost 9,600 men.[6]

Maffitt retained command of the *Widgeon* for eighteen months. In March 1867, his contract period ended, and at the urging of his family, he resigned; the vessel was apparently sold to the government of Brazil.[7] Maffitt then took a steamer to New York and paid a visit to the Brooklyn Navy Yard. Apprehensive about how he might be received, he found that his old navy friends were delighted to see him. Inducing him to relate some of his war experiences, they kept him long, and he left encouraged by the warm reception.

Maffitt found the Federal government less cordial, however. Traveling to Washington, he attempted without success to effect restitution of his confiscated house and other property, estimated at $75,000, which represented the greatest financial loss of his life. Wrote Maffitt: "I, like hundreds of others, was left in the cold, to battle the exigencies of life, on a new departure."[8] In the short term, he especially missed his fine library in Washington, which had also been confiscated .[9] But later in life, it was clear that he would never recover from the magnitude of the total loss. "It has been an uphill business with me since the war," wrote Maffitt.[10] The confiscation acts of 1861 and 1862 were ways the North, along with the blockade and exchange of prisoners, treated the South as a belligerent without granting it belligerent status.[11] Thereby the North confiscated Southern assets without accepting liabilities—such as the ships bonded by Maffitt.

Maffitt continued southward to the home of his daughter Florie, who lived with her husband in Wilmington. Using the money he earned in the British merchant marine, Maffitt soon purchased a 212-acre farm six miles outside Wilmington, bordering upon Wrightsville Beach. He had fifty-one cleared acres, a seven-room house, a separate kitchen and other outbuildings, and five springs. A railroad ran through the property, enhancing its value as a truck farm.[12] Here, Maffitt gathered his family, including his son Eugene, and engaged in raising fruits, vegetables, flowers, and peanuts. He named his home "Moorings."[13]

With his new lifestyle, Maffitt retained some of his shipboard routine. For example, he continued to wear his old midshipman's cloak and kept buckets of water at certain points in case of fire. A visitor to the Moorings described him in 1868:

> I found the Captain a cultivated and gentlemanly man, small
> sized and spare in figure, but with a fine cast head, a dark keen
> eye, a strong tuft of black whiskers on his chin, and firm little
> mouth, that seemed to express the energy and determination

of his character. I remember very well his dignified appearance as he stepped about in his short military cloak, and with his keen and somewhat stern look. He was in reduced circumstances, having staked his whole fortune and position upon the lost cause; but like so many of his old military and naval associates, he was trying his hand at business, and striving to reconcile himself to the new order of things.[14]

But Maffitt was not entirely finished with sea duty. In October 1869, the *Hornet* (or *Cuba*) sailed into the Cape Fear River, and the ship's officers requested coal at Wilmington. The *Hornet* was a screw steamer of 1,800-ton register; having two pipes and two masts, it was brig-rigged, and pierced for eighteen guns. Most of its officers were former Confederates. The vessel's mission was to operate on behalf of the Cuban people under the aegis of the Cuban Junta in New York, an agency designed to further Cuban interests in the U.S. Cubans had long resented Spanish rule and, between 1868 and 1878, rebelled in what has been termed the Ten Years' War. The American people were sympathetic to the Cuban rebels, and the full power of the Grant Administration, prodded by Secretary of State Hamilton Fish, was required to quash a resolution in the House of Representatives to recognize Cuban belligerency.

The U.S. Treasury Department seized the *Hornet* on the grounds that the vessel intended to serve the people of Cuba against Spain, with which the U.S. was at peace, and that the vessel was fitted out in the U.S. Therefore, it was in violation of U.S. neutrality statutes of 20 April 1818. Nine months later, after two court cases, a Congressional investigation, and national press coverage, President Grant ordered the *Hornet* released and returned to its original purchaser (apparently connected with the Cuban Junta) in New York.

At this point, Maffitt received a letter from the Junta requesting him to inspect the vessel for seaworthiness and to estimate the cost of cruising to New York. When it became known that Maffitt was associated with the vessel, his name caused the impression that he intended to head an expedition to aid Cuba. He received applications from many daring souls who wanted to be a part of an operation led by Maffitt. The Junta was also well aware of Maffitt's reputation. J. W. Barron, on behalf of the Junta, wrote Maffitt in reference to an expedition which had at one time been proposed: "That project was never carried out, otherwise I would have written to you asking your advice."[15]

Maffitt agreed to convey the vessel to New York. There, he apparently entered into negotiations with representatives of the Junta, but the talks ended without an expedition by Maffitt. He wrote: "Am much troubled with business—not pleased with the Junta." Added Maffitt: "Captain Read [apparently Charles W. Read of the *Florida*] attends to me like a brother—and will not permit me to enter into any Cuban affair without his sanction."[16] The prospect of an expedition must have been thought-provoking for Maffitt, but the brief cruise of the *Hornet* from Wilmington to New York was his last command.

One reason Maffitt declined to lead an expedition to Cuba was that he had become keenly interested in Emma Martin, sister of Eugene's wife, Kate. Emma was the young and cheerful daughter of Alfred Martin of Wilmington. She possessed a literary bent and had already urged Maffitt to begin a book concerning his adventures at sea. They were married 23 November 1870 at the home of her father in Wilmington and settled at the Moorings. There, Maffitt devoted his early morning and late evening hours to literary pursuits.[17]

Life was pleasant at the Moorings. "Admired and beloved in that community where he was so well known and so justly esteemed, his life now became most agreeable in its tranquility. A charming conversational-ist, a man of lofty sentiments, and a gentleman distinguished for refine-ment and courtesy, he made the Moorings a resort where congenial spirits loved to assemble."[18] In summer, especially, the Moorings was filled with guests. Bathing, boating, sailing, rowing, fishing, and the annual regatta of the Carolina Yacht Club provided recreation.[19]

In 1872, Maffitt traveled to Washington to testify at Preble's Court of Inquiry on the latter's conduct at Mobile Bay. Maffitt's testimony aided greatly in Preble's subsequent rise to rear admiral. A friend wrote to Maffitt: "I think he is afraid of you a little yet as you beat him so very badly."[20] Maffitt also maintained a vigorous correspondence with old naval associates,[21] and his interest in naval matters continued. Years after the war, he wrote: "My interest in the service is as earnest as though I was still a member of the profession."[22]

Secretary of the Navy Mallory, however, does not appear among Maf-fitt's correspondents in the postwar period.[23] Maffitt disliked Mallory for several reasons. The rift began in 1857 when Mallory, as chairman of the Senate Committee on Naval Affairs, was involved in the naval retirement embroglio that affected Maffitt. Maffitt's alienation from Mallory escalated during the 1861 meeting in Montgomery, at which Mallory acted as if Maffitt had designs on his office. The list of reasons for the estrangement continues: Maffitt was critical of the preparations for the defense of Port Royal; Maffitt was convinced that Mallory failed to understand the needs of the Confederacy; and Mallory dismissed Maffitt as commander of the *Florida* in 1862 at Mobile (with Barney as the relief, and with Barney again as relief in Brest); and finally, Mallory apparently showed favoritism to a small circle of friends.[24]

In perceptive reflections, Maffitt summarized the important role of sea power in the war. He belonged essentially to what might be termed the "western theater school of thought." Particularly critical, as Maffitt now saw it, was the fall of New Orleans, which occurred in the spring of 1862, relatively early in the war, and which was the result of superior Union sea power. "The grand mistake of the South was neglecting her navy. All our army movements out west were baffled by the armed Federal steamers which swarmed on western waters, and which our government had provided nothing to meet." Maffitt—perhaps thinking of his dismay at the outcome of his discussion with Mallory in Montgomery—pointed out that prior to the capture of New Orleans, the South should have had a navy strong enough to prevent its capture and to hold the Mississippi River and its tributaries. Concluded Maffitt: "This would have prevented many disastrous battles; it would have made Sherman's march through the country impossible and Lee would have still been master of his lines . . . neglect of the navy proved irremediable and fatal."[25]

There were other factors contributing to the fall of New Orleans, such as general poverty in the South, and high water in the river that swept away obstructions, but Maffitt was essentially correct in his assessment of the role of sea power in the war. The setback at New Orleans, which Confederate Secretary of War James A. Seddon termed the "darkest hour of the struggle,"[26] had been foreshadowed at Port Royal, where Maffitt's suggestions were ignored just as they had been at Montgomery. Union success at Port Royal (and at Roanoke Island) prepared the way for more important operations against Confederate forts. It is doubtful if the Union would have risked its fleet at New Orleans without the precedent of Port Royal.[27]

Union sea power also had a telling effect in the blockade of the South. It ended privateering and denied raiders like the *Florida* the full advantages of their work, because prizes could not be taken into Southern ports, nor could they be taken into foreign ports because of neutrality laws. "If only," wrote Maffitt, "the old usage in regard to sea prizes in neutral ports had been still in vogue, we should have done more, and, the pecuniary gain to the officers and men and to the Confederate government would have been immense—but a Confederate cruiser out upon the ocean was a lonely knight-errant." The *Florida*'s facilities for supply and repairs had been far fewer than those for Union ships. "She had to do everything for herself, live upon the enemy, and contend friendless and alone in the world," concluded Maffitt.[28]

The Federal navy was also a strong argument against foreign intervention on behalf of the South.[29] Repeatedly, the diplomatic exchanges at high levels resulting from Maffitt's entry into neutral ports reflected concern by the neutrals regarding U.S. sea power. Union and Confederate armies were fairly well-matched throughout most of the war, but the difference was that the Union navy brought on the economic defeat of the South. As one writer concluded: "Mr. Lincoln's admirals, not his generals, broke the backbone of the Confederacy."[30]

During the early 1880s, Maffitt suffered a series of losses that combined to bring him physical and mental anguish. First, in 1881, he lost a thumb in an accident: "The injury was a wrenching off of the thumb by the very roots—a ligamentous disruption that was terrible." The wound did not mend well, causing Maffitt "a long period of suffering and mental debilitation."[31] It also reduced his writing ability. Then, on 28 September 1883, Florie died. Later, when Democrat Grover Cleveland became president, some of Maffitt's friends nominated him for a place in the Customs House at Wilmington. Cleveland refused to confirm the nomination, a fact which was a great shock to Maffitt, who by now was suffering from what his doctors diagnosed as Bright's disease.

Because Maffitt was now unable to supervise the farm, and because they wanted to give their children better access to school, the Maffitt's took a cottage in Wilmington in July 1885. His inability to care adequately for his family, together with his disease and personal blows, combined to drain Maffitt's fine mental powers. He declined rapidly that last year, spending three months in the state mental-health facility in Raleigh under the care of a specialist. While Maffitt was there, on 12 January 1886, Eugene died. Maffitt was brought home in February but could not rally from his illness. Confined to his home after February 10, he often quoted a poem, the first stanza of which is:

> Whether sailor or not, for a moment avast:
> Poor Jack's mizzentopsail is hove to the mast;
> He's now all a wreck, nor will sail shoot ahead;
> His cruise is done up: he'll no more heave the lead.[32]

A little later, Maffitt told his family: "The ship is ready, the sails are set and the wind is favorable . . . we will heave anchor and away on the billows." Confined to his bed after April 18, Maffitt continued to weaken. At the end, his mind turned to his father, the Reverend John Newland Maffitt, who had died in 1850: "He is to preach at New Market and we must be on time if we are to get seats."[33] On Saturday afternoon, 15 May 1886, Maffitt, as he would have put it, "slipped the mortal cable."[34]

Appendix

Captures by Maffitt During First Cruise
of the C.S.S. *Florida*

No.	Date (1863)	Vessel	Place	Cargo	Estimated Value	Disposition
1	19 JAN	*Estelle*	off Tortugas	sugar, honey, molasses	$130,000	burned
2	22 JAN	*Windward*	off Matanzas	sugar, molasses	unknown	burned
3	22 JAN	*Corris Ann*	off Cardenas	timber, barrel staves	unknown	burned
4	12 FEB	*Jacob Bell*	24° n 65°20' w	tea, firecrackers, assorted cargo	$1,500,000	burned
5	6 MAR	*Star of Peace*	15°13' n 54°38' w	nitrate, hides	$580,000	burned
6	13 MAR	*Aldebaran*	29°15' n 51°04' w	flour, other provisions, clocks	$23,000	burned
7	28 MAR	*Lapwing*	31° n 33°30' w	coal	$77,000	tender and burned
8	30 MAR	*M. J. Colcord*	29°30' n 31°33' w	flour, bacon	unknown	burned
9	17 APR	*Commonwealth*	below St. Paul's Rocks	tobacco, provisions	$370,000	burned

No.	Date (1863)	Vessel	Place	Cargo	Estimated Value	Disposition
10	23 APR	*Henrietta*	1°40' s 29°10' w	flour, lard	$57,000	burned
11	24 APR	*Oneida*	1°40' s 29°10' w	tea, silk	$760,000	burned
12	6 MAY	*Clarence*	6° s 34°30' w	coffee	unknown	tender and burned
13	13 MAY	*Crown Point*	below Rocas Island	assorted merchandise	unknown	burned
14	6 JUN	*Southern Cross*	1°15' s 36° w	logwood	unknown	burned
15	14 JUN	*Red Gauntlet*	7° n 34° w	coal, ice, musical instruments	unknown	burned
16	16 JUN	*Benjamin F. Hoxie*	12° n 29° w	silver, hides, logwood, lead, ore	unknown	burned
17	28 JUN	*Varnum H. Hill*	30° n 48°50' w	whale oil	$10,000	bonded
18	7 JUL	*Sunrise*	off New York	passengers	$60,000	bonded
19	8 JUL	*William B. Nash*	off New York	lard, staves	$80,000	burned
20	8 JUL	*Rienzi*	off New York	whale oil	unknown	burned
21	6 AUG	*Francis B. Cutting*	40°10' n 44°20' w	passengers	$40,000	bonded
22	21 AUG	*Anglo-Saxon*	off Cork	coal	unknown	burned
23	22 AUG	*Southern Rights*	in English Channel	passengers	$40,000	bonded

Notes

Chapter 1: To the Sea Born

1. John Newland Maffitt, "Blockade Running," *United Service* 7 (July 1882): 20–21; Frank L. Owsley, Jr., "The C.S.S. *Florida*'s Tour de Force at Mobile Bay," *Alabama Review* 15 (October 1962): 266–70.
2. Alexander D. Bache, superintendent of the United States Coastal Survey, cited in James Sprunt, "Running the Blockade," in *Southern Historical Society Papers,* 52 vols. (Richmond: Southern Historical Society, 1896), 24:164.
3. *New York Herald,* 23 March 1863.
4. Edward Boykin, *Sea Devil of the Confederacy: The Story of the "Florida" and Her Captain, John Newland Maffitt* (New York: Funk and Wagnalls, 1959), 44–45, 64, 69.
5. *New York Herald,* 28 January 1863.
6. John Newland Maffitt, Sr., *Tears of Contrition, or Sketches of the Life of John N. Maffitt* (New London, Conn.: Samuel Green, 1821), 9, 111, 136.
7. Moses Elsemore, *An Impartial Account of the Life of the Rev. John N. Maffitt* (New York: John F. Feeks, 1848), 4–6. Maffitt, Sr., sailed with his physician brother William. They departed 1 February 1819 from Dublin aboard the brig *Standard* and, sailing under canvas, arrived in New York on April 21. Since Maffitt, Jr., was born at sea on February 22, his mother, Ann, must have sailed with her husband or shortly thereafter (Maffitt, Sr., *Tears of Contrition,* 212–34). See also Charles B. Davenport, *Naval Officers: Their Heredity and Development* (Washington: Carnegie Institution, 1919), 124.
8. *Atlanta Constitution,* 1 November 1891; Thomas O. Summers, *Biographical Sketches of Eminent Itinerant Ministers* (Nashville: Methodist Episcopal Church, South, 1858), 78–79. The junior Maffitt's sisters—Eliza, Matilda Caroline, and Henrietta (the latter, twins)—became well-known for their beauty and intellect. Eliza, called "Belle of the Brazos," married (the second time) a Texas doctor, Matilda married a Texas judge, and Henrietta became the second wife of the second president of the Republic of Texas, Mirabeau

B. Lamar. (See *Dictionary of American Biography*, s.v. "Lamar, Mirabeau B.") A brother, Frederic, married in Mobile, and another, William, married in St. Louis. Emma Martin Maffitt, *The Life and Services of John Newland Maffitt* (New York: Neale Publishing, 1906), 27–30.

9. Grover C. Loud, *Evangelized America* (New York: Dial Press, 1928), 210.

10. Richard Carwardine, *Trans-Atlantic Revivalism: Popular Evangelicalism in Britain and America, 1790–1865* (Westport, Conn.: Greenwood Press, 1978), 21–22, 25.

11. Loud, *Evangelized America*, 211. Concerning personal appearance, Loud was the Reverend Maffitt's harshest critic, terming him "the cross-eyed, bow-legged Beau Brummel Methodist incongruity from Ireland" (198).

12. Unidentified newspaper, clipping, in John Newland Maffitt Papers, Southern Historical Collection, University of North Carolina, Chapel Hill.

13. Loud, *Evangelized America*, 212.

14. Unidentified newspaper (clipping, in Maffit Papers).

15. *Raleigh Christian Advocate*, 27 September 1882.

16. Benjamin F. Tefft, *Methodism Successful, and the Internal Causes of Its Success* (New York: Derby and Jackson, 1860), 153–55. The senior Maffitt was strong on dramatic entrances. During an appearance in New York, he "ran a ladder up against the rear wall of the church and crawled in through an opening above the pulpit to the enthusiastic response of his audience" (Carwardine, *Trans-Atlantic Revivalism*, 22). This, however, was perhaps not altogether the antic of a master showman. The junior Maffitt, who heard his father preach once in Baltimore and again in Washington, D.C., noted that in the nation's capital, the house was so packed "his father had to be lifted into the building through a window over the heads of the waiting crowd" (Emma Maffitt, *Life of Maffitt*, 21).

17. Ormsby M. Mitchell to William B. Sprague, 12 January 1861, in William B. Sprague, ed., *Annals of the American Pulpit*, 9 vols. (New York: Robert Carter and Brothers, 1857–1869), vol. 7, *Methodism*, 838–41.

18. A. C. Cook to John N. Maffitt, Jr., 26 November 1884 (in Maffitt Papers); Emma Maffitt, *Life of Maffitt*, 22–25; *The South in the Building of the Nation*, 12 vols. (Richmond: Southern Historical Publication Society, 1909–1913), vol. 12, *Southern Biography*, ed. Walter L. Fleming, 149.

19. Elsemore, *Impartial Account of the Rev. John N. Maffitt*, 15.

20. *Brooklyn Advertiser*, n.d. (clipping, in Maffitt Papers); Carwardine, *Trans-Atlantic Revivalism*, 22; Emma Maffitt, *Life of Maffitt*, 26. In addition to his autobiography, *Tears of Contrition* (which contains forty pages of poetry), the senior Maffitt wrote a volume of pulpit sketches, a book of Irish poems, and an oratorical dictionary. See Fleming, ed., *Southern Biography*, 150.

Chapter 2: Midshipman Maffitt

1. Duncan Rose, *The Romantic Career of a Naval Officer, Federal and Confederate: Captain Maffitt of the U.S.S. "Crusader" and the C.S.S. "Florida"* (Spray, N.C., 1935), 1–3.

2. Hugh T. Lefler and Albert R. Newsome, *The History of a Southern State: North Carolina* (Chapel Hill: University of North Carolina Press, 1973), 79–80, 259, 315, 382.

3. No mention of Dr. Maffitt's wife is made in the literature. However, he had married Margaret Adam, who was still alive as late as December 1824; see Will of Robert Adam (1801) and Will of Janet Mumford (1824), North Carolina State Archives, Division of Archives and History, Raleigh.

4. Rose, *The Romantic Career of a Naval Officer*, 2–6.

5. Lefler and Newsome, *North Carolina*, 456.

6. Cited in *Dictionary of American Biography*, s.v. "McRae, Duncan Kirkland."

7. Cited in Rose, *The Romantic Career of a Naval Officer*, 7.

8. *Fayetteville Observer*, 24 February and 10 March 1825; Auguste Tevasseur, *Lafayette in America in 1824 and 1825*, trans. John D. Godman (Philadelphia: Carey and Lea, 1829), 34–36.

9. *Weekly North Carolina State*, 10 April 1943.

10. Cited in Olivier Bernier, *Lafayette: Hero of Two Worlds* (New York: E. P. Dutton, 1983), 296. Lafayette was somewhat familiar with Fayetteville prior to his visit, having on a wall in his French home a drawing of the town that depicted two long streets in the shape of a cross (*Weekly North Carolina State*, 10 April 1943).

11. Maffitt to Eliza Maffitt, 26 April 1833, in John Newland Maffitt Papers, Southern Historical Collection, University of North Carolina, Chapel Hill.

12. Emma Martin Maffitt, *The Life and Services of John Newland Maffitt* (New York: Neale Publishing, 1906), 30–31.

13. Maffitt to Dr. Maffitt, 7 January 1833 (in Maffitt Papers).

14. Rose, *The Romantic Career of a Naval Officer*, 3.

15. Renoda Hoffman, *It Happened in Old White Plains* (White Plains, N.Y.: Efficiency Printing, 1989), 40–41, 44; John Rosch, *Historic White Plains* (White Plains, N.Y.: Balletto-Sweetman, 1939), 312. Civic-minded Prof. John M. Swinburne, who served as principal from 1832 to 1841, apparently made a positive impact on Maffitt (Renoda Hoffman, official historian of White Plains, personal communication, 16 June 1991). See also Emma Maffitt, *Life of Maffitt*, 31. Maffitt has been described as "hyperkinetic"; see Charles B. Davenport, *Naval Officers: Their Heredity and Development* (Washington: Carnegie Institution, 1919), 122.

16. "Record of Service of John Newland Maffitt in the United States Navy," compiled by the Navy Department (in Maffitt Papers); *American State Papers*, 38 vols. (Washington: Gales and Seaton, 1832–1861), 26:256; Edward Boykin, *Sea Devil of the Confederacy: The Story of the "Florida" and Her Captain, John Newland Maffitt* (New York: Funk and Wagnalls, 1959), 58. Maffitt's father, who was in the New York state area, seems to have been playing a part in the rearing of his son, including the naval appointment; see J. Thomas Scharf, *History of Westchester County*, 2 vols. (Philadelphia: L. W. Preston, 1886), 2:692.

17. *The Naval Magazine* 1, no. 111 (May 1836): 218; Elmer B. Potter, *Illus-*

trated History of the U.S. Navy (New York: Galahad Books, 1971), 65. One of the most persistent advocates of naval education was Commodore Matthew C. Perry. See Samuel Eliot Morrison, *"Old Bruin," Commodore Matthew C. Perry, 1794–1858* (Boston: Little Brown, 1967), 132–34; and Charles L. Lewis, *Famous American Naval Officers* (Freeport, N.Y.: Books for Libraries Press, 1971), 196–97. Perry also advocated higher ranks for naval officers to reward the competent, but until 1862, when the ranks of commodore and rear admiral were established, the highest official rank was that of captain, equivalent to colonel in the army. Prior to 1862, a captain commanding a squadron often received the courtesy title "commodore" (Morrison, *"Old Bruin,"* 135).

18. "Record of Service of John Newland Maffitt" (in Maffitt Papers); *American State Papers* 26:256.
19. "Statistical Data of U.S. Ships," *Official Records of the Union and Confederate Navies in the War of the Rebellion,* 33 vols. (Washington: U.S. Government Printing Office, 1894–1922), 1st ser., 28:198.
20. Ira N. Hollis, *The Frigate Constitution: The Central Figure of the Navy Under Sail* (Boston: Houghton Mifflin, 1931), 5.
21. Boykin, *Sea Devil of the Confederacy,* 61–62.
22. Maffitt to Dr. Maffitt, 7 January 1833 (in Maffitt Papers).
23. "Record of Service of John Newland Maffitt" (in Maffitt Papers). Meanwhile, on 25 July 1833, Maffitt's status changed from that of acting midshipman to midshipman.
24. Maffitt to Eliza Maffitt, 26 April 1833 (in Maffitt Papers).
25. "Record of Service of John Newland Maffitt" (in Maffitt Papers); *American State Papers* 26:662.
26. Alexander Laing, *Seafaring America* (New York: American Heritage, 1974), 145–46.
27. "Statistical Data of U.S. Ships" (in *Official Records of the Navies,* 1st ser., 28:66); Hollis, *The Frigate Constitution,* 6, 38–40.
28. The U.S. eschewed the ships of the line, or line-of-battle ships, which formed the largest class of other navies' vessels, in favor of specially designed frigates that were faster, more maneuverable, and more heavily armed than European frigates (Hollis, *The Frigate Constitution,* 40).
29. Elliott was also engaged in a longer-running controversy with Commodore Oliver H. Perry. As the ranking officer under Perry, Elliott had received criticism for his slowness in bringing his gunboat into action at the 1813 Battle of Lake Erie. See *Dictionary of American Biography,* s.v. "Elliott, Jesse Duncan"; and Charles J. Peterson, *The American Navy* (Philadelphia: James B. Smith, 1859), 404–7.
30. Elliott Snow and H. Allen Gosnell, *On the Decks of "Old Ironsides"* (New York: McMillan, 1932), 183–84; Hollis, *The Frigate Constitution,* 220–26.
31. "Record of Service of John Newland Maffitt" (in Maffitt Papers); *American State Papers* 26:789; Hollis, *The Frigate Constitution,* 226–27; Laing, *Seafaring America,* 146; Snow and Gosnell, *On the Decks of "Old Ironsides,"*

189–90. President Jackson qualified in one way for the honor of having his likeness adorn America's favorite ship: he left the presidency advocating a larger navy. See John H. Schroeder, *Shaping a Maritime Empire: The Commercial and Diplomatic Role of the Navy, 1829–1861* (Westport, Conn.: Greenwood Press, 1985), 36.

32. Peterson, *The American Navy*, 409.
33. Snow and Gosnell, *On the Decks of "Old Ironsides,"* 190.
34. Alexander DeConde, *A History of American Foreign Policy* (New York: Charles Scribner's Sons, 1971), 149.
35. Snow and Gosnell, *On the Decks of "Old Ironsides,"* 190–96.
36. Hollis, *The Frigate Constitution*, 228.
37. Snow and Gosnell, *On the Decks of "Old Ironsides,"* 197–201.
38. Hollis, *The Frigate Constitution*, 228. The period of testiness between France and America finally gave way to conciliation as President Jackson softened his language toward France, and France began to pay the installments on the claims (DeConde, *American Foreign Policy*, 150).

Chapter 3: Acting Lieutenant Maffitt

1. Edward Boykin, *Sea Devil of the Confederacy: The Story of the "Florida" and Her Captain, John Newland Maffitt* (New York: Funk and Wagnalls, 1959), 60–61; Nathan Miller, *The U.S. Navy: An Illustrated History* (Annapolis: United States Naval Institute Press, 1977), 118.
2. Elliott Snow and H. Allen Gosnell, *On the Decks of "Old Ironsides"* (New York: McMillan, 1932), 204–6, 297–99.
3. *On the Decks of "Old Ironsides,"* 206.
4. "Naval Intelligence," in *The Naval Magazine* 2, no. 4 (July 1837): 406, and in 2, no. 5 (September 1837): 513. See also David F. Long, *Gold Braid and Foreign Relations: Diplomatic Activities of U.S. Naval Officers, 1798–1883* (Annapolis: Naval Institute Press, 1988), 202–3; and *Dictionary of American Biography*, s.v. "Cass, Lewis."
5. Boykin, *Sea Devil of the Confederacy*, 62–63.
6. Speech of Commodore Elliott, Hagerstown, Maryland, 14 November 1843, in John Newland Maffitt Papers, Southern Historical Collection, University of North Carolina, Chapel Hill.
7. Snow and Gosnell, *On the Decks of "Old Ironsides,"* 206–7, 298–99.
8. The *Constitution* returned several months later, anchoring at Hampton Roads 31 July 1838. Unfortunately for Elliott, he was court-martialed for his harshness in discipline and for his having loaded the berth-deck on the return trip with blooded livestock. See Charles J. Peterson, *The American Navy* (Philadelphia: James B. Smith, 1859), 409; Snow and Gosnell, *On the Decks of "Old Ironsides,"* 208–11; Hollis, *The Frigate Constitution*, 229; *Dictionary of American Biography*, s.v. "Elliott, Jesse D."
9. Testimony of Lieutenant J. R. Madison Mullany, "The Case of Lieutenant John Newland Maffitt," U.S. Naval Court of Inquiry, Washington, D.C., July

1857, cited in Emma Martin Maffitt, *The Life and Services of John Newland Maffitt* (New York: Neale Publishing, 1906), 144–45, 147–48.

10. "Record of Service of John Newland Maffitt in the United States Navy," compiled by the Navy Department (in Maffitt Papers); Boykin, *Sea Devil of the Confederacy,* 64.

11. Maffitt to Eliza Maffitt, 3 January 1839 (in Maffitt Papers). Both the Reverend Maffitt and Dr. Maffitt had daughters named Eliza, and Maffitt's letters preserved in the Maffitt Papers are to his cousin.

12. Abstract of Lieutenant Maffitt's Sea Service and Coast Survey Service taken from the Official Register, "Case of Maffitt," cited in Emma Maffitt, *Life of Maffitt,* 137–38, 153.

13. Maffitt to Eliza, 3 May 1839 (in Maffitt Papers); Commander Uriah P. Levy—commanding officer of the *Vandalia,* who wrote out Maffitt's promotion at sea—to Maffitt, 11 March 1839, "Case of Maffitt," cited in Emma Maffitt, *Life of Maffitt,* 138.

14. Maffitt to George H. Preble, 13 June 1882, in George H. Preble Papers, Massachusetts Historical Society, Boston.

15. Maffitt to Eliza, 1 June 1840 (in Maffitt Papers);"Statistical Data of U.S. Ships," *Official Records of the Union and Confederate Navies in the War of the Rebellion,* 33 vols. (Washington: U.S. Government Printing Office, 1894–1922), 1st ser., 28:130; Abstract of Maffitt's Service, "Case of Maffitt," cited in Emma Maffitt, *Life of Maffitt,* 137.

16. Maffitt to Eliza, 3 May 1839 (in Maffitt Papers).

17. "Record of Service of John Newland Maffitt" (in Maffitt Papers); *The Naval Magazine* 2, no. 3 (May 1837): 58; Emma Maffitt, *Life of Maffitt,* 56–57.

Chapter 4: With the U.S. Coast Survey

1. "Record of Service of John Newland Maffitt in the United States Navy," compiled by the Navy Department, in John Newland Maffitt Papers, Southern Historical Collection, University of North Carolina, Chapel Hill. President Thomas Jefferson recommended to Congress in 1807 the creation of the Coast Survey, yet when Maffitt assumed his duties, the survey extended only somewhat northward and southward from New York. See Joseph Henry, "Memoir of Alexander Dallas Bache (1806–1867)," *National Academy of Sciences Biographical Memoirs* (Washington: The Home Secretary, 1877), 194–96.

2. Department of Commerce, *Centennial Celebration of the United States Coast and Geodetic Survey* (Washington: U.S. Government Printing Office, 1916), 175.

3. "Record of Service of John Newland Maffitt" (in Maffitt Papers); Emma Martin Maffitt, *The Life and Services of John Newland Maffitt* (New York: Neale Publishing, 1906), 64. Edward Boykin wrote of Maffitt's marital problems that "the catastrophe seems to have involved Mary Florence Maffitt and this unidentified individual," i.e., the Irishman; see Boykin, *Sea Devil of the Confederacy: The Story of the "Florida" and Her Captain, John Newland Maffitt*

(New York: Funk and Wagnalls, 1959), 65. Maffitt ultimately gained control of the children, although as late as December 1850, his eight-year-old daughter Florie was in school in Mobile (Seventh Census of the United States, 1850. Population).

4. "Record of Service of John Newland Maffitt" (in Maffitt Papers).

5. Maffitt to George Bancroft, 18 May 1846, "Case of Maffitt," cited in Emma Maffitt, *Life of Maffitt,* 146.

6. At age eighteen, Bache graduated from West Point at the head of his class and without a single demerit. After three years in the army, he enjoyed wide experience in public service, and researched magnetism and electricity; he received several awards from foreign governments, and his scientific papers are innumerable. See Henry, "Memoir of Alexander Dallas Bache," 201, 203, 205–12; Department of Commerce, *U.S. Coast and Geodetic Survey,* 136–37; *Dictionary of American Biography,* s.v. "Bache, Alexander D."

7. Testimony of Bache, "Case of Maffitt," cited in Emma Maffitt, *Life of Maffitt,* 163.

8. "Record of Service of John Newland Maffitt" (in Maffitt Papers).

9. Boykin, *Sea Devil of the Confederacy,* 65.

10. Testimony of Bache, "Case of Maffitt," cited in Emma Maffitt, *Life of Maffitt,* 162.

11. See series of letters and reports of Bache and Maffitt (1847–1851), cited in Emma Maffitt, *Life of Maffitt,* 65–84.

12. Report of the Superintendent of the Coast Survey (1850), cited in Emma Maffitt, *Life of Maffitt,* 75,

13. "Recollection of Life at Smithville During the Sojourn of . . . John N. Maffitt While in the U.S. Coast Survey" (in Maffitt Papers).

14. Emma Maffitt, *Life of Maffitt,* 85–87.

15. *Wilmington Herald,* 30 August 1851, cited in Emma Maffitt, *Life of Maffitt,* 89–95. The owner of Orton, a rice plantation, was Dr. Frederick Hill. See James Sprunt, *The Story of Orton Plantation, with References to Other Places of Interest on the Cape Fear River* (Wilmington: Privately printed, 1958), 10.

16. Report of the Superintendent of the Coast Survey (1852), cited in Emma Maffitt, *Life of Maffitt,* 98. By this time, there were eleven field sections of the Coast Survey. Six were along the Atlantic coast, three were in the Gulf of Mexico, and two were on the Pacific coast. See Peter J. Guthorn, *United States Coastal Charts, 1783–1861* (Exton, Pa.: Schiffer Publishing, 1984), 19.

17. *Wilmington Herald,* 18 August 1852, cited in Emma Maffitt, *Life of Maffitt,* 99; Boykin, *Sea Devil of the Confederacy,* 66. Caroline Laurens Read Maffitt was the great-granddaughter of Henry Laurens (1724–1792), a Charleston merchant, planter, and Revolutionary War patriot. See *South Carolina Genealogies: Articles From The South Carolina Historical (and Genealogical) Magazine,* 4 vols. (Spartanburg, S.C.: Reprint Co., 1983), 4:137. Caroline was the mother of three children by her first husband—Mary, Laurens, and Caroline. Young Caroline accidentally burned to death when she ran too

near a fire in the yard at Ellerslie and her dress became inflamed. Two children resulted from Maffitt's second marriage—John and Colden (Emma Maffitt, *Life of Maffitt,* 99).

18. "Record of Service of John Newland Maffitt" (in Maffitt Papers). On one occasion, Maffitt was almost lost on the steamer. According to Bache, the *Legare* was "in a most perilous condition in the Gulf Stream" but was brought into port "mainly by the energy, knowledge, and promptness of Lieutenant Commanding Maffitt" (Testimony of Bache, "Case of Maffitt," cited in Emma Maffitt, *Life of Maffitt,* 162–63).

19. Emma Maffitt, *Life of Maffitt,* 204.

20. Report of Maffitt (1854), cited in Emma Maffitt, *Life of Maffitt,* 109.

21. Report of the Superintendent of the Coast Survey (1854), cited in Emma Maffitt, *Life of Maffitt,* 108.

22. Unidentified newspaper (clipping, in Maffitt Papers).

23. Report of the Superintendent of the Coast Survey (1855), cited in Emma Maffitt, *Life of Maffitt,* 115.

24. Unidentified newspaper (clipping, in Maffitt Papers).

25. "Record of Service of John Newland Maffitt" (in Maffitt Papers). Detached from the *Legare* on 26 August 1854, Maffitt had been briefly assigned to command of the schooner U.S.S. *J. Y. Mason.*

26. Report of the Superintendent of the Coast Survey (1855), cited in Emma Maffitt, *Life of Maffitt,* 115.

27. Rear Admiral Stephen B. Luce to Emma Maffitt, 29 September 1906, cited in Emma Maffitt, *Life of Maffitt,* 122.

28. "Record of Service of John Newland Maffitt" (in Maffitt Papers).

29. While under the threat of retirement, Maffitt continued surveys and resurveys, including ones of the coast of South Carolina, Maffitt's Channel, Beaufort, the Cape Fear entrance, and the James River. See series of reports of Bache and Maffitt (1856–1857), cited in Emma Maffitt, *Life of Maffitt,* 124–35.

30. Unidentified newspaper (clipping, in Maffitt Papers).

31. Testimony of Lieutenant Charles H. Cushman, "Case of Maffitt," cited in Emma Maffitt, *Life of Maffitt,* 193.

32. Testimony of naval officers, "Case of Maffitt," cited in Emma Maffitt, *Life of Maffitt,* 139–96. See also Roy F. Nichols, *Franklin Pierce: Young Hickory of the Granite Hills* (Philadelphia: University of Pennsylvania Press, 1969), 384–85; and Paolo E. Coletta, ed., *American Secretaries of the Navy,* 2 vols. (Annapolis: Naval Institute Press, 1980), 1:291. Bache testified that Maffitt had applied for transfer to Secretaries of the Navy George Bancroft, John Y. Mason, and William B. Preston, as well as Dobbin, but each time, Bache intervened to prevent it (Testimony of Bache, "Case of Maffitt," cited in Emma Maffitt, *Life of Maffitt,* 161–66).

33. Maffitt's defense statement, "Case of Maffitt," cited in Emma Maffitt, *Life of Maffitt,* 173–78. Maffitt's case, the transcripts of which were printed in pamphlet form, became a *cause celebre* in the navy. See Emma Maffitt, *Life of*

Maffitt, 198; and Duncan Rose, *The Romantic Career of a Naval Officer, Federal and Confederate: Captain Maffitt of the U.S.S. "Crusader" and the C.S.S. "Florida"* (Spray, N.C., 1935), 12. Commander Samuel Francis Du Pont, more than any other, bore the onus of the board, called the "star chamber" (no records were kept), which recommended that 49 officers be retired, 81 be furloughed on half pay—Maffitt was on this list—and that 71 be dropped without pay, for a total of 201 of the navy's 712 officers. Pressure on Congress brought about a second law that established the Courts of Inquiry. The enactment of the new law forced the navy to review 108 dismissals, and a majority of these were reversed. See John D. Hayes, ed., *Samuel Francis Du Pont: A Selection from His Civil War Letters,* 3 vols. (New York: Cornell University Press, 1969), 1:lxii–lxiii; and Samuel Eliot Morrison, *"Old Bruin," Commodore Matthew C. Perry, 1794–1858* (Boston: Little Brown, 1967), 416. U.S. Senator Stephen R. Mallory, chairman of the Committee on Naval Affairs, also played an active role in the affair; see *Dictionary of American Biography,* s.v. "Mallory, Stephen Russell."

34. "Record of Service of John Newland Maffitt" (in Maffitt Papers); Report of the Superintendent of the Coast Survey (1858), cited in Emma Maffitt, *Life of Maffitt,* 135.

Chapter 5: Suppression of the Slave Trade

1. "Record of Service of John Newland Maffitt in the United States Navy," compiled by the Navy Department, in John Newland Maffitt Papers, Southern Historical Collection, University of North Carolina, Chapel Hill.; "Statistical Data of U.S. Ships," *Official Records of the Union and Confederate Navies in the War of the Rebellion,* 33 vols. (Washington: U.S. Government Printing Office, 1894–1922), 1st ser. 28:74; David M. Cooney, *A Chronology of the U.S. Navy: 1775–1965* (New York: Franklin Watts, 1965), 69, 74.

2. *Suppression of the African Slave Trade and Negro Colonization, 1854–72* (Washington: U.S. Government Printing Office, 1961), 1; Henry Steele Commager, ed., *Documents of American History* (New York: Appleton-Century-Crofts, 1973), 298–300; Carroll S. Alden and Allan Westcott, *The United States Navy: A History* (Chicago: J. B. Lippincott, 1943), 114, 117; W. E. B. DuBois, *The Suppression of the African Slave-Trade to the United States of America, 1638–1870* (New York: Dover, 1970), 178; Alexander DeConde, *A History of American Foreign Policy* (New York: Charles Scribner's Sons, 1971), 160–61; Charles L. Lewis, *Famous American Naval Officers* (Freeport, N.Y.: Books for Libraries Press, 1971), 190; Elmer B. Potter, *Illustrated History of the U.S. Navy* (New York: Galahad Books, 1971), 59.

3. J. Laurens Read to Florie and Eugene Maffitt and Mary Read, 2 July 1858 (in Maffitt Papers). Young Read, Maffitt's stepson, was on the *Dolphin.* He says in this letter that during a stopover in Havana, when Maffitt went ashore for an official visit with Spanish authorities, "he was in full togs—and looked as fine as a peacock."

4. Maffitt to Secretary of the Navy Isaac Toucey, 21 August 1858, cited in the

New York Herald, 1 September 1858; *The Federal Cases, 1789–1880,* 30 vols.
(St. Paul: West Publishing, 1894–1897), 2:1016; "Extract of a Decree of the
United States District Court for South Carolina," 16 December 1858, in the
Case of the United States vs. the Brig *Echo,* cited in Emma Martin Maffitt,
The Life and Services of John Newland Maffitt (New York: Neale Publishing,
1906), 199–201; Maffitt to George H. Preble, 23 September 1882 (in
Maffitt Papers); Cooney, *Chronology of the U.S. Navy,* 74. No defense of the
Echo was made in the case, and the court declared the ship forfeited. Sold at
public auction, the brig during the war became the famous privateer *Jefferson
Davis.* See William M. Robinson, *The Confederate Privateers* (New Haven:
Yale University Press, 1928), 59–61; and Navy Department, Naval History
Division, *Civil War Naval Chronology, 1861–1865,* 6 parts (Washington: U.S.
Government Printing Office, 1971), 6:256. The rescued Africans sailed in
the frigate U.S.S. *Niagara* for the rehabilitation colony of Liberia, although
seventy-two of them died en route (*New York Herald,* 27 September 1858).

5. *New York Herald,* 29 and 30 August, and 5 September 1858. In Charleston,
   local press coverage of the capture of the *Echo* was extensive—e.g., *Charleston
   Daily Courier,* 28, 30, 31 August; 2, 4, 10, 13, 15 September; 1 October
   1858.

6. "Record of Service of John Newland Maffitt" (in Maffitt Papers).

7. Maffitt to "Josh"—Joshua G. Wright, Florie's husband—18 August 1867 (in
   Maffitt Papers).

8. Florie Maffitt to "Maggie" (?), 31 March 1859 (in Maffitt Papers). Florie
   Maffitt and Mary Read were boarded at Kingford's Seminary in Washington;
   Eugene Maffitt and Laurens Read were tutored in Georgetown, and the
   younger children were sent to live with Eliza Maffitt Hybart, now married
   but still at Ellerslie (Emma Maffitt, *Life of Maffitt,* 205–6).

9. "Record of Service of John Newland Maffitt" (in Maffitt Papers).

10. "Statistical Data of U.S. Ships" (in *Official Records of the Navies,* 1st ser.,
    28:68); *Harper's Weekly,* 20 April 1861.

11. Maffitt to Florie Maffitt and Mary Read, 22 May 1860 (in Maffitt Papers);
    Unidentified newspaper (clipping, in Maffitt Papers).

12. Maffitt to "My Dear Girls"—Florie Maffitt and Mary Read—4 November
    1859 (in Maffitt Papers). See also Merritt P. Allen, *William Walker: Filibuster*
    (New York: Harper and Brothers, 1932), 171; Thomas A. Bailey, *A
    Diplomatic History of the American People* (New York: Appleton-Century-
    Crofts, 1958), 277–78. An added duty for Maffitt was acting as his own
    purser aboard the *Crusader* ("Record of Service of John Newland Maffitt," in
    Maffitt Papers).

13. Norman C. DeLaney, *John McIntosh Kell of the Raider Alabama* (University,
    Ala.: University of Alabama Press, 1973), 102–3. Maffitt was in Pensacola
    on two occasions during the winter of 1859–1860, once in November
    for coal, and sometime after that to have a new deck laid on the *Crusader*—
    which took a month (Maffitt to "My Dear Girls," 4 November 1859; and
    unidentified newspaper, clipping, in Maffitt Papers).

14. The *Crusader* carried two inclined cylinders twenty-three inches in diameter ("Statistical Data of U.S. Ships," *Official Records of the Navies,* 1st ser., 28:66).

15. Maffitt to Florie Maffitt, 9 May 1860; and Maffitt to Florie Maffitt and Mary Read, 22 May 1860 (in Maffitt Papers).

16. *New York Herald,* 5 June 1860; *Charleston Daily Courier,* 8 June 1860. These accounts were posted from Key West, by unnamed eyewitnesses on board the *Crusader.* See also *U.S. vs. Bark Name Unknown [Bogata],* Southern District of Florida Admiralty Final Record Books, Record Group 21, Records of District Courts of the U.S., Regional Branch of the National Archives, Atlanta, Ga.

17. *Key of the Gulf* newspaper, quoted in an unidentified New Orleans newspaper (clipping, in Maffitt Papers); *New York Herald,* 4 June 1860; James S. Olson, ed., *Historical Dictionary of European Imperialism* (New York: Greenwood Press, 1991), 165; Cooney, *Chronology of the U.S. Navy,* 75. Africans rescued by Maffitt were commingled with others at Key West (*New York Herald,* 4 June 1860). During 1860–1861, 4,500 Africans recaptured on the high seas by the U.S. Navy eventually found sanctuary in Liberia with the aid of the American Colonization Society (*Suppression of the African Slave Trade and Negro Colonization,* 2). Those engaged in the slave trade usually lost their ships and human cargoes, but were seldom found guilty on the basis of the act passed on 15 May 1820 that made the slave trade "piracy on the high seas" and punishable by death. Only in the case of *U.S. vs. Gordon* (1861) was a person found guilty: Nathaniel Gordon, of the slaver *Erie,* was sentenced to death and executed on 21 February 1862. See Charles H. Wesley and Patricia W. Romero, *Negro Americans in the Civil War: From Slavery to Citizenship* (New York: Publishers Co., 1969), 7; George F. Dow, *Slave Ships and Slaving* (Salem, Mass.: Marine Research Society, 1927), 279; DuBois, *Suppression of the African Slave-Trade to the United States,* 185.

18. *Wilmington Daily Journal,* 25 September 1863; Edward Boykin, *Sea Devil of the Confederacy: The Story of the "Florida" and Her Captain, John Newland Maffitt* (New York: Funk and Wagnalls, 1959), 68–69.

19. Maffitt to Florie Maffitt, 7 and 30 August 1860 (in Maffitt Papers). See also Cooney, *Chronology of the U.S. Navy,* 75–76; Cooney refers to the *Young Antonio* as an "unarmed slave brig."

20. Maffitt to "My Dear Coz"—his cousin Eliza—21 August 1860 (in Maffitt Papers). Maffitt calculated that he rescued the following numbers of slaves: *Echo,* 360; *Bogata,* 426; *William R. Kirby,* 3 (list of rescued slaves in Maffitt's handwriting, in Maffitt Papers).

21. *Charleston Mercury,* n.d. (clipping, in Maffitt Papers).

22. *Charleston Daily Courier,* 26 November 1860; "Events Between the Presidential Election and the Declaration of War," *Confederate Annals: A Semi-Monthly Magazine, Reciting Facts and Incidents of the War in the South* 1 (June 1883): 26.

23. Lieutenant T. Augustus Craven to Florie Maffitt, 11 January 1861, cited in Emma Maffitt, *Life of Maffitt,* 217.

24. Commodore James Armstrong, commandant of Pensacola Navy Yard, to Isaac Toucey, 3 January 1861 (in *Official Records of the Navies,* 1st ser., 4:5).
25. Memorandum of Maffitt for Emma Maffitt, n.d., cited in Emma Maffitt, *Life of Maffitt,* 215–16. To prevent the guns of Fort Morgan, which were guarding the entrance of Mobile Bay, from joining the Alabama navy in an attack on the *Crusader,* Maffitt reportedly said: "I may be overpowered, but, in that event, what will be left of the *Crusader* will not be worth taking"; cited in Virgil C. Jones, *The Civil War at Sea,* 3 vols. (New York: Holt, Rinehart, and Winston, 1960–1962), 1:40–41.
26. Armstrong to Toucey, 12 January 1861; Toucey to Maffitt, 5 January 1861; Toucey to Armstrong, 5 and 10 January 1861; and Maffitt to Toucey, 9 January 1861 (in *Official Records of the Navies,* 1st ser., 4:7, 10, 14).
27. Meigs to Major Lewis G. Arnold, commandant of Fort Jefferson, 23 January 1861 (in *Official Records of the Navies,* 1st ser., 1:347); Meigs to Brigadier General Joseph G. Totten, chief engineer, Washington, D.C., 25 January 1861; and Totten to Toucey, 13 February 1861 (in *Official Records of the Navies,* 1st ser., 4:83–84); Richard S. West, Jr., *Mr. Lincoln's Navy* (New York: Longmans, Green, and Co., 1957), 13.
28. Jefferson B. Browne, *Key West: The Old and the New* (Gainesville: University of Florida Press, 1973), 92.

Chapter 6: From Navy Blue to Navy Gray

1. "Record of Service of John Newland Maffitt in the United States Navy," compiled by the Navy Department, in John Newland Maffitt Papers, Southern Historical Collection, University of North Carolina, Chapel Hill; Toucey to Maffitt, 18 January 1861, in *Official Records of the Union and Confederate Navies in the War of the Rebellion,* 33 vols. (Washington: U.S. Government Printing Office, 1894–1922), 1st ser., 4:64; memorandum of Maffitt for Emma Maffitt, n.d., cited in Emma Martin Maffitt, *The Life and Services of John Newland Maffitt* (New York: Neale Publishing, 1906), 216.
2. Private Journal of John Newland Maffitt (in Maffitt Papers).
3. Maffitt to George H. Preble, 8 January 1879, in George H. Preble Papers, Massachusetts Historical Society, Boston. Maffitt here defends secession, pointing out that the states entered the Union piecemeal (only nine were necessary to create the Union, and some drifted in later), so that "it is absurd to claim that the people of the U.S. in the aggregate—as one nation—ordained and established the Constitution."
4. Private Journal of John Newland Maffitt (in Maffitt Papers).
5. "Record of Service of John Newland Maffitt" (in Maffitt Papers); Maffitt to George H. Preble, 8 January 1879 (in Preble Papers). Maffitt later told editor R. Barnwell Rhett of the *Charleston Mercury* that while in Washington he was "caressed and offered a command in the Pacific"; see Rhett, "The Confederate Government at Montgomery," in *Battles and Leaders of the Civil War,* ed. Robert U. Johnson and Clarence C. Buel, 4 vols. (New York: Castle Books, 1956), 1:107.

6. Private Journal of John Newland Maffitt (in Maffitt Papers).
7. John Newland Maffitt, "Reminiscences of the Confederate Navy," *United Service* 3 (October 1880): 495.
8. See James R. Soley, "The Union and Confederate Navies," in *Battles and Leaders of the Civil War,* ed. Robert U. Johnson and Clarence C. Buel, 1:631; and David C. Roller and Robert W. Twyman, *The Encyclopedia of Southern History* (Baton Rouge: Louisiana State University Press, 1979), 278. The number of enlisted men in the Confederate navy at any given time was probably less than 4,000; foreign sailors chiefly manned the commerce-destroyers (Soley, "The Union and Confederate Navies," 631).
9. Maffitt, "Reminiscences of the Confederate Navy," *United Service* 3 (October 1880): 496.
10. Private Journal of John Newland Maffitt (in Maffitt Papers). During the war, the Confederate press almost never had praise for Mallory. See J. Cutler Andrews, *The South Reports the Civil War* (Princeton: Princeton University Press, 1970), 512; and Joseph T. Durkin, *Stephen R. Mallory: Confederate Navy Chief* (Chapel Hill: University of North Carolina Press, 1954), 292–93.
11. Jefferson Davis, *Rise and Fall of the Confederate Government,* 2 vols. (New York: Thomas Yoseloff, 1958), 1:314.
12. Durkin, *Stephen R. Mallory,* 133–36. Durkin details that the Confederate Navy Department which emerged consisted of the secretary, four clerks, and a messenger; subordinate to this department were four operational bureaus.
13. Cited in Rhett, "The Confederate Government at Montgomery," 107. See also Durkin, *Stephen R. Mallory,* 72–77. Confederate foreign purchasing agent Major Edward C. Anderson, a former naval officer who had been a midshipman with Maffitt on the *Constitution,* suggested the formation of a naval squadron under Maffitt to convoy blockade runners into Southern ports, but Mallory refused. This refusal was ultimately to deal a blow to the government's foreign supply operations. See Stephen R. Wise, *Lifeline of the Confederacy: Blockade Running During the Civil War* (Columbia: University of South Carolina Press, 1988), 50–55.
14. Private Journal of John Newland Maffitt (in Maffitt Papers).
15. *Register of Officers of the Confederate States Navy, 1861–1865* (Washington: U.S. Government Printing Office, 1931), 126.
16. Cited in Private Journal of John Newland Maffitt (in Maffitt Papers). See also "Statistical Data of Confederate Ships" (in *Official Records of the Navies,* 1st ser., 28:266) and Navy Department, Naval History Division, *Civil War Naval Chronology, 1861–1865,* 6 parts (Washington: U.S. Government Printing Office, 1971), 6:298. In addition to the *Savannah,* only three other vessels (armed tugs) at the time made up the mosquito fleet—the C.S.S. *Resolute,* the C.S.S. *Sampson,* and the C.S.S. *Lady Davis;* see J. Thomas Scharf, *History of the Confederate States Navy* (n.p.: Fairfax Press, 1977), 664.
17. Private Journal of John Newland Maffitt; and Maffitt to Florie Maffitt, 11 June 1861 (in Maffitt Papers). On May 27, Maffitt shipped from Norfolk

twelve forty-two-pound guns and twelve thirty-two-pound guns to Beauregard in Charleston; see Maffitt to Beauregard, 27 May 1861, in *Official Records of the Union and Confederate Armies in the War of the Rebellion,* 128 vols. (Washington: U.S. Government Printing Office, 1880–1901), 1st ser., 5.2.114.

18. David D. Porter, *The Naval History of the Civil War* (New York: Sherman Publishing, 1886), 62.

19. Private Journal of John Newland Maffitt (in Maffitt Papers).

20. Daniel Ammen, "Du Pont and the Port Royal Expedition," in *Battles and Leaders of the Civil War,* ed. Robert U. Johnson and Clarence C. Buel, 1:674–75; Charles B. Boynton, *The History of the Navy During the Rebellion,* 2 vols. (New York: D. Appleton, 1868), 1:432; David Stick, *Graveyard of the Atlantic: Shipwrecks of the North Carolina Coast* (Chapel Hill: University of North Carolina Press, 1952), 50–51.

21. Maffitt, "Reminiscences of the Confederate Navy," *United Service* 3 (October 1880): 498–99; *Charleston Mercury,* 6 November 1861; John D. Hayes, ed., *Samuel Francis Du Pont: A Selection from His Civil War Letters,* 3 vols. (New York: Cornell University Press, 1969), 1:165n; Porter, *The Naval History of the Civil War,* 55–59.

22. Statement of Isaac Tattnall, a black pilot who witnessed the action (in *Official Records of the Navies,* 1st ser., 12:487); *Savannah Republican,* 12 November 1861; Virgil C. Jones, *The Civil War at Sea,* 3 vols. (New York: Holt, Rinehart, and Winston, 1960–1962), 1:274; Ammen, "Du Pont and the Port Royal Expedition," 678–79; Charles C. Jones, Jr., *The Life and Services of Commodore Josiah Tattnall* (Savannah: Morning News, 1878), 133.

23. *Charleston Mercury,* 8 November 1861. The mosquito squadron perhaps had intended to skirt the Federal men-of-war and sink the transports, a prospect that concerned Du Pont. See Elbridge J. Copp, *Reminiscences of the War of the Rebellion, 1861–1865* (Nashua, N.H.: Telegraph Publishing, 1911), 60; and Ammen, "Du Pont and the Port Royal Expedition," 681.

24. *Savannah Republican,* 12 November 1861; *Wilmington Daily Journal,* 8 and 9 November 1861. The *Lady Davis* and the C.S.S. *Huntress*—an insignificant recent addition to the mosquito squadron—had been sent to Beaufort for boats to block Skull Creek, but they returned too late, burned the boats, and retreated to Beaufort. See Maxwell C. Orvin, *In South Carolina Waters, 1861–1865* (Charleston, S.C.: Southern Printing and Publishing, 1961), 28.

25. Maffitt to Florie Maffitt, 5 December 1861 (in Maffitt Papers). Maffitt confided to his daughter regarding Tattnall: "The commander is a kind, brave, and generous man, but impulsive, passionate, and ambitious—we had not got on well together and I had tried for some time to get to some other station." A member of the Maffitt family remained a while longer on the *Savannah,* however—Maffitt's son, Midshipman Eugene Maffitt, who had served with honor at Fort Beauregard during the battle of Port Royal (Captain Stephen Elliott, Jr. to Lieutenant William H. Talley, 13 November 1861, in *Official Records of the Navies,* 1st ser., 12:317–19).

26. Lee to Secretary of War Judah P. Benjamin, 9 and 29 November 1861 (in *Official Records of the Navies,* 1st ser., 12:299–300, 327–28); Alden and Westcott, *United States Navy,* 179.

27. Private Journal of John Newland Maffitt (in Maffitt Papers).

28. "Officers of General R. E. Lee's Staff," in *Southern Historical Society Papers,* 52 vols. (Richmond: Southern Historical Society, 1896), 35:25; Douglas Southall Freeman, *R. E. Lee: A Biography,* 4 vols. (New York: Charles Scribner's Sons, 1946), 1:640.

29. Maffitt to Florie Maffitt, 5 December 1861 (in Maffitt Papers). Later, when Maffitt was running the blockade, he brought in a sword belt for Lee, who responded: "It is very handsome, and I appreciate it highly as a token of your remembrance. I recall with great pleasure the days of our association in Carolina—with equal admiration your brilliant career since, in defense of your country." Cited in Samuel A. Ashe, "John Newland Maffitt," *Biographical History of North Carolina,* ed. Samuel A. Ashe, 8 vols. (Greensboro, N.C.: Charles L. Van Noppen, 1906), 5:207.

30. Inspecting a fortification at Fernandino, Florida, Maffitt met the tall, weathered Floridian, now well-off, who formerly owned the *Mary Ann.* Maffitt recalled the occasion in 1839 when he had rescued the *Mary Ann,* the schooner driven by a storm upon St. Rosa's beach near Pensacola (Maffitt to Preble, 13 June 1882, in Preble Papers). Ironically, the incident foreshadowed the greatest role reversal the war would bring to Maffitt—from protecting to destroying commercial vessels.

31. Private Journal of John Newland Maffitt; and Maffitt to "My Dear Girls," 20 December 1861 (in Maffitt Papers).

32. In December, Maffitt, assisting with ferry operations for troops between Pages's Point and Port Royal Island during a cotton-burning operation on the island by Confederates, reported amphibious enemy troop movements at night in the vicinity. Although Maffitt looked forward to "a chance for the first fair fight on shore," there was no major battle (Maffitt to Florie Maffitt, 5 December 1861, in Maffitt Papers; Colonel James Jones to Captain Thornton A. Washington, 8 December 1861; and Colonel William Martin to Lee, 9 December 1861, in *Official Records of the Armies,* 1st ser., 6:36–38, 341).

33. Lee to Benjamin, 16 December 1861 (in *Official Records of the Navies,* 1st ser., 12:833–34).

34. Lee to Benjamin, 20 December 1861 (in *Official Records of the Navies,* 1st ser., 12:423); Hayes, ed., *Du Pont Letters,* 319.

35. Orvin, *In South Carolina Waters,* 45, 48, 57, 59.

Chapter 7: Running the Blockade

1. Stephen R. Wise, *Lifeline of the Confederacy: Blockade Running During the Civil War* (Columbia: University of South Carolina Press, 1988), 58–59.

2. Maffitt to "My Dear Girls," 20 December 1861, in John Newland Maffitt Papers, Southern Historical Collection, University of North Carolina, Chapel

Hill. On December 11, the "Great Fire" of Charleston swept through 145 acres. Consumed in the flames was the home of Maffitt's brother-in-law, John Laurens. The Laurens family saved nothing, and Maffitt says in this letter that he himself lost much—"clothes, books, important papers, accounts" that were in the Laurens' home. See also Walter J. Fraser, Jr., *Charleston! Charleston! The History of a Southern City* (Columbia: University of South Carolina Press, 1989), 253–55; and Robert Molloy, *Charleston: A Gracious Heritage* (New York: D. Appleton-Century, 1947), 162.

3. Wise, *Lifeline of the Confederacy*, 58–59.
4. "Blockade Running," speech delivered by Maffitt in Wilmington, 8 May 1879 (in Maffitt Papers).
5. Trenholm to Benjamin, 2 January 1862, in *Official Records of the Union and Confederate Armies in the War of the Rebellion,* 128 vols. (Washington: U.S. Government Printing Office, 1888–1901), 4th ser., 1:828–29. See also Wise, *Lifeline of the Confederacy,* 60.
6. Dave Horner, *The Blockade-Runners: True Tales of Running the Yankee Blockade of the Confederate Coast* (New York: Dodd, Mead and Co., 1968), 189; Wise, *Lifeline of the Confederacy,* 292. Wise says that Trenholm offered Maffitt command of the *Cecile,* but maintains that, on the first trip at least, Charleston Master Ferdinand Peck commanded the vessel (*Lifeline of the Confederacy,* 59, 337n.). Peck registered the vessel in Charleston, listing himself as the sole owner, on 11 February 1862 (*Cecile* File, Vessel Papers, Record Group 109, Confederate Records, Military Reference Branch, National Archives, Washington, D.C.).
7. Trenholm to Benjamin, 7 January 1862; and Benjamin to Louis Heyliger, Confederate agent in Nassau, 22 March 1862 (in *Official Records of the Armies,* 4th ser., 1:835–36, 1017–18); Wise, *Lifeline of the Confederacy,* 60, 255, 260–61. In England, Confederate agent James D. Bulloch praised the new system of transshipment: "Maffitt has a fine, fast little steamer in which he will ply regularly between the West Indies and the southern coast, varying the place of arrival to distract the blockaders"; see Bulloch to Lieutenant James H. North, 14 March 1862, in *Official Records of the Union and Confederate Navies in the War of the Rebellion,* 33 vols. (Washington, D.C.: Government Printing Office, 1894–1922), 2d ser., 2:166.
8. Private Journal of John Newland Maffitt (in Maffitt Papers); Randolph to Maffitt, Trenholm to Randolph, and Randolph to Heyliger, 11 April 1862 (in *Official Records of the Armies,* 4th ser., 1:1055–57).
9. Wise, *Lifeline of the Confederacy,* 59, 323. Early in the war, the *Nassau,* then named the *Gordon,* had been a privateer. In October 1861, as the *Theodora,* the vessel had carried James Mason and John Slidell, Confederate commissioners to England and France respectively and principals in the "*Trent* Affair," on the first leg of their trans-Atlantic trip through the blockade from Charleston to Cuba (*Lifeline of the Confederacy,* 323; James Mason to Secretary of State R. M. T. Hunter, in *Official Records of the Navies,* 1st ser., 1:151–52).

10. Maffitt had been renovating the *Nassau* and informing General Lee of the arrival of munitions and stores in Wilmington. See Robert E. Lee to Chief of Ordnance Bureau Josiah Gorgas, 26 April 1862 (in *Official Records of the Armies*, 1st ser., 1.2.547); and Wise, *Lifeline of the Confederacy*, 62. After Maffitt invited his family to Wilmington for a visit, Florie "by hard begging" received his consent to accompany him to Nassau (Florie to "Mr. Hinsdale," a family friend, 4 July 1862, in Hinsdale Family Papers, William R. Perkins Library, Duke University, Durham, N.C.).

11. Stewart Sifakis, *Who Was Who in the Civil War* (New York: Facts on File Publications, 1988), 177.

12. Florie to "Mr. Hinsdale," 4 July 1862 (in Hinsdale Family Papers). Florie wrote of the storm: "I felt so happy, because if my father was in danger, with him I could share it, his fate could be mine."

13. *Nassau Guardian*, 15 March 1862.

14. Private Journal of John Newland Maffitt (in Maffitt Papers).

15. Bulloch to Maffitt, 21 March 1862 (in *Official Records of the Navies*, 1st ser., 1:753). Bulloch respected Maffitt and hoped he would command the *Oreto*: "I know of no officer whose tact and management could so well overcome the difficulties of equipping her or who could make better use of her when in cruising order."

16. Frank L. Owsley, Jr., *The C.S.S. Florida: Her Building and Operations* (Philadelphia: University of Pennsylvania Press, 1965), 18–19. This edition of Owsley's book contains a diagram of the screw-lift device, as well as an inboard and deck profile of the *Florida*.

17. Certificate of British Registry, 3 March 1862, in FO5/1314, British Foreign Office Papers, Public Record Office, London; "Statistical Data of Confederate Ships" (in *Official Records of the Navies*, 1st ser., 28:252); *Conway's All the World's Fighting Ships, 1860–1905* (New York: Mayflower Books, 1979), 135. Most accounts give a weight in excess of 700 tons for the *Florida*. The original weight of 410 tons did not include the ship's armaments, which were added later, and various modifications.

18. Certificate of British Registry, 3 March 1862 (in FO5/1314, British Foreign Office Papers); Owsley, *C.S.S. Florida*, 20; Warren F. Spencer, *The Confederate Navy in Europe* (University, Ala.: University of Alabama Press, 1983), 41; J. Roger Fredland et al., *American Sea Power Since 1775* (Chicago: J. B. Lippincott, 1947), 194–95.

19. The law in question was the British Foreign Enlistment Act, already in place by the time of the Civil War. In addition, Queen Victoria, on 14 May 1861, proclaimed neutrality, chiefly to protect British ships and cargoes from both North and South. Britain led the way among maritime nations in according the Confederacy belligerent status. The reasoning was that a nation does not blockade its own ports, that President Abraham Lincoln himself had therefore recognized the belligerency of the Confederacy, and that a foreign government was justified in following suit. The U.S. Supreme Court upheld this line of thought in 1863. Nonetheless, Union Secretary

of the Navy Gideon Welles characterized Confederate cruisers as "piratical British wolves." See George W. Dalzell, *The Flight from the Flag: The Continuing Effect of the Civil War Upon the American Carrying Trade* (Chapel Hill: University of North Carolina Press, 1940), 10–11; and Spencer, *The Confederate Navy in Europe*, 43.

20. Dudley to Charles Francis Adams, U.S. Minister to the Court of St. James, 17 February 1862; Adams to British Foreign Secretary Lord John Russell, 18 February 1862; and Adams to Russell, 25 March 1862 (in FO5/1313, British Foreign Office Papers). Russell promised to detain the *Oreto* if it were equipped to war on the U.S. (Russell to Adams, 27 March 1862, in FO5/ 1313, British Foreign Office Papers). But British customs officials in Liverpool uncovered nothing that would justify interference with the *Oreto* (Thomas F. Fremantle and Grenville C. Berkeley to the Lords Commissioners of Her Majesty's Treasury, 4 April 1862 and 1 May 1862, in FO5/ 1313, British Foreign Office Papers). Meanwhile, Dudley informed U.S. Secretary of State William H. Seward that the *Oreto* would be "when fully armed and equipped, . . . a formidable and dangerous craft" (Dudley to Seward, 12 February 1862, in *Official Records of the Navies,* 1st ser., 6:683– 84). Seward forwarded this information to Secretary of the Navy Gideon Welles, who in turn passed it on to commanders of the Union blockading squadrons (Welles to blockade flag officers, 6 March 1862, in *Official Records of the Navies,* 1st ser., 6:683). Adams notified Washington and alerted American consulates in the transshipment ports such as Bermuda and Nassau; see Philip Van Doren Stern, *Secret Missions of the Civil War* (Chicago: Rand McNally, 1959), 137.

21. S. Price Edwards, collector of customs in Liverpool, to "Honorable Sir," 28 March 1862 (in FO5/1313, British Foreign Office Papers); *Register of Officers of the Confederate States Navy, 1861–1865* (Washington: U.S. Government Printing Office, 1931), 117; William S. Hoole, *Four Years in the Confederate Navy: The Career of Captain John Low* (Athens: University of Georgia Press, 1964), 27; Charles C. Beaman, Jr., *The National and Private Alabama Claims* (Washington: W. H. Moore, 1871), 49–53; Spencer, *The Confederate Navy in Europe*, 43; Owsley, *C.S.S. Florida*, 24. Maffitt's son Eugene had recently arrived in England with other officers aboard the *Annie Childs,* and Dudley suspected they were assigned to the *Oreto.* He reported that the *Oreto* dipped its ensign in salute as the *Annie Childs* came into Liverpool, and that the next evening the newly arrived officers dined aboard the *Oreto* (Dudley to Adams, 22 March 1862, in FO5/1313, British Foreign Office Papers). Midshipman Maffitt, however, was destined for the C.S.S. *Alabama.*

22. Private Journal of John Newland Maffitt (in Maffitt Papers); Hoole, *Four Years in the Confederate Navy,* 32. Maffitt privately assumed command of the *Oreto* from Henry Adderley and Company, Nassau agents for Fraser, Trenholm and Company; see Richard I. Lester, *Confederate Finance and Purchasing in Great Britain* (Charlottesville: University Press of Virginia), 69.

23. Whiting to Charles J. Bayley, British colonial governor of the Bahamas, 9 May 1862 (in FO5/1313, British Foreign Office Papers). To Confederate Secretary of War George W. Randolph, Maffitt gave a report on his recent activities as Confederate agent: "I have judiciously dispatched arms . . . in all the steamers." In regard to his new command, the seasoned forty-three-year-old Maffitt reflected the spirit of the Confederate navy: "My difficulties are great, my ambition greater" (Maffitt to Randolph, 21 May 1862, in *Official Records of the Navies,* 1st ser., 1:758).

24. Private Journal of John Newland Maffitt (in Maffitt Papers). Maffitt's daughter Florie departed in the *Nassau,* commanded by Captain George Walker, on 24 May 1862. When the vessel came under fire off Wilmington, Florie sat on the open deck and watched in amusement the fire from enemy ships. The U.S.S. *State of Georgia* captured the *Nassau,* and Florie landed in Fortress Monroe. She presented a letter from Maffitt requesting that she be treated well if captured. Detained only two days, she journeyed · under a flag of truce to City Point and, from there, to Petersburg. Wrote Florie: "Once on the Confederate side, you can imagine our joy, the rough uniforms of our soldiers seemed sacred" (Florie Maffitt to "Mr. Hinsdale," 4 July 1862, in Hinsdale Family Papers; unidentified newspaper, clipping, in Maffitt Papers).

25. Private Journal of John Newland Maffitt (in Maffitt Papers). When North (promoted to commander) failed to board the *Bahama* for Nassau and assume command of the *Oreto,* Mallory became disenchanted and recalled him from England (Mallory to North, 12 July 1862, in *Official Records of the Navies,* 2d ser., 2:215).

26. Private Journal of John Newland Maffitt (in Maffitt Papers); Commander Henry D. Hickley, of the H.M.S. *Greyhound,* to Bayley, 15 June 1862 (in FO5/1313, British Foreign Office Papers).

27. Boatswain Edward Jones, formerly third officer of the *Oreto,* gave a statement to Whiting from Nassau Prison, where he was held for refusing duty. Jones wrote that the vessel had ports and bolts for guns: "Everything is rigged and ready for mounting—even all the articles necessary for seamen, such as hammocks, bedding, kettles and pans—with three years' provisions. In short, she is a perfect man of war" (Statement of Edward Jones, June 1862, which Whiting sent to Bayley on 4 June 1862, in FO5/1313, British Foreign Office Papers). Maffitt described Jones as "an excellent rascal, a low, dirty, Liverpool dock-rat" (cited in Hoole, *Four Years in the Confederate Navy,* 31).

28. Private Journal of John Newland Maffitt (in Maffitt Papers).

29. Captain Henry McKillop, of the H.M.S. *Bulldog,* to Bayley, 28 May 1862; Bayley to McKillop, 2 June 1862; Whiting to Bayley, 12 June 1862; Hickley to Bayley, 13 and 16 June 1862; Bayley to Hickley, 16 and 17 June 1862; Bayley to the Duke of Newcastle (Henry P. F. P. Clinton, British Secretary of State for the Colonies), 21 June 1862; Whiting to Hickley, 24 June 1862; Hickley to Whiting, 25 June 1862; and Bayley to Newcastle, 26 June 1862 (in FO5/1313, British Foreign Office Papers).

30. Raphael Semmes, *Service Afloat: The Remarkable Career of the Confederate Cruisers "Sumter" and "Alabama"* (New York: P. J. Kenedy and Sons, 1903), 354. The layover of *"Sumter* Semmes" in Nassau served to confuse British and American officials concerning the intended commander of the *Oreto* (Hoole, *Four Years in the Confederate Navy,* 31).

31. James Sprunt, *Derelicts: An Account of Ships Lost at Sea in General Commercial Traffic and a Brief History of Blockade Runners Stranded Along the North Carolina Coast, 1861–1865* (Baltimore: Lord Baltimore Press, 1920), 213–16. Whiting was not particularly effective at Nassau; Governor Bayley had even requested, without immediate success, his recall (Owsley, *C.S.S. Florida,* 28).

32. Decree of John Campbell Lees, Judge of the Vice Admiralty Court of the Bahamas, in the Case of the British Steamship *Oreto,* 2 August 1862 (in FO5/1313, British Foreign Office Papers).

Chapter 8: Audacity at Mobile Bay

1. Maffitt to Mallory, 1 August 1862, in John Newland Maffitt Papers, Southern Historical Collection, University of North Carolina, Chapel Hill. The armament for the *Oreto* had been secretly removed from the *Bahama* and stored in a warehouse at dockside. See William S. Hoole, *Four Years in the Confederate Navy: The Career of Captain John Low* (Athens: University of Georgia Press, 1964), 31.

2. Private Journal of John Newland Maffitt (in Maffitt Papers). This was Maffitt's first open connection with the *Oreto.* See Maffitt to Bulloch, 20 August 1862, in *Official Records of the Union and Confederate Navies in the War of the Rebellion,* 33 vols. (Washington: U.S. Government Printing Office, 1894–1922), 1st ser., 1:760. Maffitt, known to the Federals as a blockade-running captain, had been working undercover to persuade leading merchants in Nassau to testify at the trial of the *Oreto* that it was nothing more than a commercial vessel; he also spent personal funds for boat hire, bribes to police, and runners during the trial. See Gideon Welles to Commander Francis Winslow, of the U.S.S. *R. R. Cuyler,* 1 July 1862 (in *Official Records of the Navies,* 1st ser., 1:398); and Hoole, *Four Years in the Confederate Navy,* 34.

3. Stribling had been with Semmes on the C.S.S. *Sumter* and, passing through Nassau on his way home, relinquished his leave and volunteered to sail with Maffitt (Private Journal of John Newland Maffitt, in Maffitt Papers). See also *Register of Officers of the Confederate States Navy, 1861–1865* (Washington: U.S. Government Printing Office, 1931), 189. Other officers included Master Otey Bradford, as acting lieutenant, and Midshipmen George D. Bryan, Richard S. Floyd, and G. Terry Sinclair; aboard were also three engineers, a lieutenant of marines, a captain's clerk, and a paymaster's clerk. Maffitt made his stepson, Laurens Read, acting assistant paymaster and surgeon. See Abstract of the Log of the C.S.S. *Florida,* 17 August 1862 to

31 May 1863 (kept by Bryan), Record Group 45, Records Collection of the Office of Naval Records and Library, National Archives, Washington, D.C.

4. Maffitt, "Blockade Running," *United Service* 7 (July 1882): 16; Raphael Semmes, *Service Afloat: The Remarkable Career of the Confederate Cruisers "Sumter" and "Alabama"* (New York: P. J. Kenedy and Sons, 1903), 356.

5. Winslow to Welles, 12 August 1862 (in *Official Records of the Navies,* 1st ser., 1:416).

6. Private Journal of John Newland Maffitt (in Maffitt Papers); Depositions of Peter Crawley, James Lockyer, and Andrew Hagen—seamen lately from various British vessels in Nassau who helped with the transfer of munitions and stores—in FO5/1314, British Foreign Office Papers, Public Record Office, London; *New York Herald,* 25 September 1862; James R. Soley, "The Confederate Cruisers," in *Battles and Leaders of the Civil War,* ed. Robert U. Johnson and Clarence C. Buel, 4 vols. (New York: Castle Books, 1956), 4:595.

7. Jim Dan Hill, *Sea Dogs of the Sixties: Farragut and Seven Contemporaries* (Minneapolis: University of Minnesota Press, 1935), 74. Fawcett, Preston and Company, the Liverpool firm that built the engines for the *Florida,* also manufactured Blakely rifles; see Warren Ripley, *Artillery and Ammunition of the Civil War* (New York: Van Nostrand Reinhold, 1970), 365. According to a history of the company, "there is not much doubt that [the guns of the *Florida*] were of Fawcett manufacture"; see Horace White, *"Fossets": A Record of Two Centuries of Engineering* (N.p.: Fawcett, Preston and Co., 1958), 48.

8. Private Journal of John Newland Maffitt (in Maffitt Papers); Abstract of the Log of the *Florida,* Records Collection of the Office of Naval Records and Library, National Archives.

9. Mallory to Maffitt, 14 July 1862 (in Maffitt Papers).

10. Maffitt, "Blockade Running," *United Service* 7 (July 1882): 16–17; See also G. Terry Sinclair, "The Eventful Cruise of the *Florida,*" *Century Magazine* 56 (1898): 418; Charles L. Lewis, *Famous American Naval Officers* (Freeport, N.Y.: Books for Libraries Press, 1971), 197.

11. Maffitt to Bulloch, 20 August 1862 (in *Official Records of the Navies,* 1st ser., 1:760).

12. Private Journal of John Newland Maffitt (in Maffitt Papers); John D. Hayes, ed., *Samuel Francis Du Pont: A Selection from His Civil War Letters,* 3 vols. (New York: Cornell University Press, 1969), 2:205n.

13. Maffitt, "Blockade Running," *United Service* 7 (July 1882): 17.

14. Private Journal of John Newland Maffitt (in Maffitt Papers).

15. Semmes, *Service Afloat,* 357.

16. Maffitt, "Blockade Running," *United Service* 7 (July 1882): 18–19. Maffitt writes here that upon becoming conscious again, he learned that his sixteen-year-old stepson, Laurens Read, who had nursed Maffitt earlier, had died and was buried on shore, along with several others from the *Florida.*

17. Charles J. Helm, Confederate agent in Havana, to Judah P. Benjamin, 3 September 1862 (in *Official Records of the Navies,* 1st ser., 1:760–61).

18. Private Journal of John Newland Maffitt (in Maffitt Papers).
19. Du Pont, writing to his wife from the South Atlantic Blockading Squadron, took some pride in Maffitt's choice to sail for Mobile instead of Charleston: "Maffitt's going to Mobile was showing some respect to the Charleston blockade, of which ground he knows every foot; the channel most resorted to is one discovered by him when making the survey of the harbor" (Du Pont to "My precious Sophie," 23 September 1862, cited in Hayes, ed., *Du Pont Letters,* 2:232–35).
20. Private Journal of John Newland Maffitt (in Maffitt Papers).
21. Maffitt to Preble, 11 June 1867 (in Maffitt Papers)—Maffitt and Preble, wartime enemies, were prewar and postwar friends; Farragut to Welles, 8 September 1862 (in *Official Records of the Navies,* 1st ser., 1:431); "List of United States Vessels of War" (in *Official Records of the Navies,* 1st ser., 18:xvi). See William H. Brantley, *Unparalleled Audacity Off Mobile Bay* (Birmingham [?]: A. H. Cather, 1954), n.p.
22. Farragut to Preble, 14 October 1862 (in *Official Records of the Navies,* 1st ser., 1:441). See also Frank L. Owsley, Jr., "The C.S.S. *Florida*'s Tour de Force at Mobile Bay," *Alabama Review* 15 (October 1962): 265–66.
23. The second and third shots by the *Oneida* across the bow of the *Florida* were Preble's mistake. His commander, Farragut, wrote: "You should have fired but one blank cartridge or shot to heave the vessel to; the others should have been fired into her" (Farragut to Preble, 5 September 1862, in *Official Records of the Navies,* 1st ser., 1:433).
24. Private Journal of John Newland Maffitt (in Maffitt Papers); "Abstract of the Log of the U.S.S. *Oneida*" (in *Official Records of the Navies,* 1st ser., 1:432–33). Maffitt struck the British colors and gave the order to hoist the Confederate flag. The latter order apparently was not carried out during the run in because of damage to the signal halliards and injury to the man attempting to raise the colors. See Maffitt, "Blockade Running," *United Service* 7 (July 1882): 21; and Farragut to Welles, 8 September 1862 (in *Official Records of the Navies,* 1st ser., 1:431).
25. Testimony of Commander James S. Thornton, Court of Inquiry of Captain George H. Preble, 20 April 1872 (in *Official Records of the Navies,* 1st ser., 1:460).
26. Private Journal of John Newland Maffitt (in Maffitt Papers). One of the men at the helm during the bombardment was William Sharkey, who kept up a lively commentary as the shells burst over the *Florida.* To the blockaders Sharkey proclaimed: "And sure ye are a parcel of cowards; thray [three] upon one poor *sick man* is hathenish"; cited in *Charleston Mercury,* 3 September 1862.
27. Maffitt, "Blockade Running," *United Service* 7 (July 1882): 21–22.
28. *Punch,* cited in Richard S. West, Jr., *Gideon Welles: Lincoln's Navy Department* (Indianapolis: Bobbs-Merrill, 1943), 252.
29. Preble to Farragut, 4 September 1862 (in *Official Records of the Navies,* 1st ser., 1:432).

30. Farragut to Welles, 8 September 1862 (in *Official Records of the Navies,* 1st ser., 1:431).

31. Preble's punishment came in the form of a general order of 20 September 1862, signed by Welles. To insure proper humiliation in this object lesson, Welles mandated that the order be read on the quarterdeck of each war vessel at general muster and be spread upon the log of each ship (*New York Herald,* 22 September 1862; *Charleston Mercury,* 4 October 1862; West, *Gideon Welles,* 196). The Preble name was an illustrious one in the navy. Preble's uncle, Commodore Edward Preble, had commanded a squadron in the Tripolitan War in 1803 with the U.S.S. *Constitution* as his flagship. See *Dictionary of American Biography,* s.v. "Preble, Edward." Powerful friends of the family exerted pressure on the Lincoln administration in the form of petitions. See Petitions to Abraham Lincoln, 23–24 September, and 19 November 1862, cited in *The Chase of the Rebel Steamer of War "Oreto"* (Cambridge: Allen and Farnham, 1862), 44–48; Welles to Lincoln, 10 February 1862; and Lincoln to the U.S. Senate, 12 February 1862 (in *Official Records of the Navies,* 1st ser., 1:58–59). Although soon reinstated in the navy, Preble was not fully exonerated until a hearing in 1872, at which Maffitt testified. Testimony of Maffitt, Court of Inquiry of Captain George H. Preble, 20 April 1872 (in *Official Records of the Navies,* 1st ser., 1:464–68).

32. Preble to Farragut, 6 September 1862 and 8 October 1862 (in *Official Records of the Navies,* 1st ser., 1:433–36).

33. Maffitt to Preble, 11 June 1867 (in Maffitt Papers). See also Virgil C. Jones, *The Civil War at Sea,* 3 vols. (New York: Holt, Rinehart, and Winston, 1960–1962), 2:269.

Chapter 9: Escape of the *Florida*

1. Maffitt, "Blockade Running," *United Service* 7 (July 1882): 22.

2. Private Journal of John Newland Maffitt, in John Newland Maffitt Papers, Southern Historical Collection, University of North Carolina, Chapel Hill.

3. Buchanan to Maffitt, 7 September 1862 (in Maffitt Papers). Farragut seems to have used Maffitt's exploit as a model for his alleged 1864 "damn the torpedoes" utterance at Mobile Bay. Edward Boykin even maintained that Maffitt was lashed to the railing—much as Farragut later would be tied to the rigging; see Boykin, *Sea Devil of the Confederacy: The Story of the "Florida" and Her Captain, John Newland Maffitt* (New York: Funk and Wagnalls, 1959), 122.

4. Mallory to Maffitt, 8 October 1862, in *Official Records of the Union and Confederate Navies in the War of the Rebellion,* 1st ser., 33 vols. (Washington: U.S. Government Printing Office, 1894–1922), 1:761. At the time, the Naval Investigating Committee of the Confederate Congress was examining Mallory's administration of naval affairs. The Committee began work the day Maffitt entered Mobile Bay, and its final report was favorable to Mallory. See Navy Department, Naval History Division, *Civil War Naval Chronology,*

1861–1865, 6 parts (Washington: U.S. Government Printing Office, 1971), 2:95.

5. Raphael Semmes, *Service Afloat: The Remarkable Career of the Confederate Cruisers "Sumter" and "Alabama"* (New York: P. J. Kenedy and Sons, 1903), 360. Historian James Russell Soley agreed with Semmes, writing of Maffitt's exploit at Mobile Bay that "as a bold dash, it was hardly paralleled during the war"; see Soley, "Gulf Operations in 1862 and 1863," in *Battles and Leaders of the Civil War,* ed. Robert U. Johnson and Clarence C. Buel, 4 vols. (New York: Castle Books, 1956), 3:571.

6. Shufeldt to Farragut, 1 December 1862 (in *Official Records of the Navies,* 1st ser., 19:386–87).

7. Maffitt to Florie, 8 September 1862 (in Maffitt Papers). Over a week later, Maffitt wrote to Florie of the ravages of yellow fever upon him, saying he was so "pale, cadaverous and thin, you would not know me" (Maffitt to Florie, 19 September 1862, in Maffitt Papers).

8. Private Journal of John Newland Maffitt (in Maffitt Papers); *Charleston Mercury,* 9 September 1862.

9. Charles Lee Lewis, *Admiral Franklin Buchanan: Fearless Man of Action* (Baltimore: Norman, Remington Co., 1929), 203.

10. Private Journal of John Newland Maffitt (in Maffitt Papers); *Register of Officers of the Confederate States Navy, 1861–1865* (Washington: U.S. Government Printing Office, 1931), 7, 161. The officers of the *Florida* assembled by Maffitt at Mobile were: Lieutenants Samuel W. Averett, James L. Hoole (who had been badly wounded in the head at Roanoke Island), Charles W. Read, and Sardine G. Stone, Jr.; Midshipmen Richard S. Floyd, George D. Bryan, James H. Dyke, George Terry Sinclair, Jr. (who later wrote an article on the cruise), William B. Sinclair, Jr., and Robert Scott; Engineers John Spidell (whom Maffitt commended), Charles W. Quinn (who kept a diary of the cruise), William H. Jackson (whom Maffitt ultimately detached as incompetent), and Eugene H. Brown; Surgeons Frederick Garretson and Joseph D. Grafton; Paymaster Junius J. Lynch; and Captain's Clerk Lionel Vogel. See Averett et al. to Maffitt, 23 January 1863 (in *Official Records of the Navies,* 1st ser., 2:640); *Register of Officers of the Confederate States Navy,* 6–7, 24, 53, 61, 73, 98, 118, 158, 161, 186, 189, 201; and Clement A. Evans, ed., *Confederate Military History,* Extended Edition, 17 vols. (Wilmington, N.C.: Broadfoot Publishing, 1989), 2:218–19. To Maffitt's relief, Lieutenant Otey Bradford, who had signed on at Nassau, was detached. According to Maffitt, Bradford meant well, but was shallow and erratic—"the most perfect weathercock who ever lived" (Log of the *Florida,* in Maffitt Papers).

11. Private Journal of John Newland Maffitt (in Maffitt Papers). See also G. Terry Sinclair, "The Eventful Cruise of the *Florida,*" *Century Magazine* 56 (1898): 419; and Frank L. Owsley, Jr., *The C.S.S. Florida: Her Building and Operations* (Philadelphia: University of Pennsylvania Press, 1965), 45–46.

12. Maffitt to Averett, 5 December 1862 (in *Official Records of the Navies,* 1st ser., 19:810).

13. Mallory to Maffitt, 25 October 1862 (in Maffitt Papers).
14. Maffitt to John Maffitt, 15 November 1862; Robert W. Smith, a friend of Maffitt in Mobile, to Maffitt, 19 November 1862 (in Maffitt Papers). Smith was to invest 450 pounds in Bank of England notes for Florie.
15. U.S. Vessels of War in the West Gulf Blockading Squadron (in *Official Records of the Navies*, 1st ser., 18:xvi); J. Thomas Scharf, *History of the Confederate States Navy* (n.p.: Fairfax Press, 1977), 537. Spectators reported the *Florida*'s guns were "admirably served, the practice being excellent, placing the shot and shell all around the mark, so close in many instances, as to apparently dash the water upon the Lincolnites' decks" (*Mobile Evening News*, 26 December 1862).
16. Log of the *Florida* (in Maffitt Papers).
17. Private Journal of John Newland Maffitt (in Maffitt Papers).
18. Owsley, *C.S.S. Florida*, 45. Barney had commanded the C.S.S. *Jamestown* and participated in the battle of Hampton Roads; he was also in the engagement at Drewry's Bluff (*Register of Officers of the Confederate States Navy*, 10).
19. Private Journal of John Newland Maffitt, and Log of the *Florida* (in Maffitt Papers). Owsley wrote that "Mallory's sudden decision is a mystery and cannot be documented," but offered the opinion that Mallory believed Maffitt simply was unwilling to leave the safety of Mobile (*C.S.S. Florida*, 44–45).
20. Davis to Mallory, 31 December 1862 (in *Official Records of the Navies*, 1st ser., 19:827).
21. Maffitt to Florie, 11 January 1862 (in Maffitt Papers).
22. Buchanan to Maffitt, 6 January 1862 (in Maffitt Papers).
23. As a precaution against Federal attack at night, Maffitt kept on deck one gun's crew at a time (Farragut to Commodore Henry H. Bell, commander off Mobile, 31 October 1862, in *Official Records of the Navies*, 1st ser., 19:325–26).
24. Maffitt to Florie, 11 January 1863 (in Maffitt Papers).
25. Private Journal of John Newland Maffitt (in Maffitt Papers); Owsley, *C.S.S. Florida*, 47–48; Sinclair, "The Eventful Cruise of the *Florida*," *Century Magazine* 56 (1898): 420.
26. Captain Thornton A. Jenkins, commander of the U.S.S. *Oneida*, to commanding officers of blockading vessels off Mobile, 14 November 1862 (in *Official Records of the Navies*, 1st ser., 19:344–45); Charles B. Boynton, *The History of the Navy During the Rebellion*, 2 vols. (New York: D. Appleton, 1868), 2:367.
27. Private Journal of John Newland Maffitt (in Maffitt Papers).
28. Bell to Emmons, 5 December 1862 (in *Official Records of the Navies*, 1st ser., 19:391); Virgil C. Jones, *The Civil War at Sea*, 3 vols. (New York: Holt, Rinehart, and Winston, 1960–1962), 2:347. According to Emmons, the blockading force off Mobile on 15 January 1863 consisted of U.S. steamers *Susquehaunna, Oneida, R. R. Cuyler, Pembina, Aroostook, Kennebec,* and *Pinola*

(Emmons to Commodore Robert B. Hitchcock, new senior officer off Mobile, 12 March 1862, in *Official Records of the Navies,* 1st ser., 2:30–31).

29. Abstract of the Log of the C.S.S. *Florida,* 17 August 1862 to 31 May 1863, Record Group 45, Records Collection of the Office of Naval Records and Library, National Archives, Washington, D.C.

30. Sinclair, "The Eventful Cruise of the *Florida,*" *Century Magazine* 56 (1898): 421.

31. Hitchcock to Farragut, 16 January 1863 (in *Official Records of the Navies,* 1st ser., 2:27–28). Hazard saw the signal from the *Cuyler,* which he described as "signal No. 3, white and green (steamer running out)"; he then beat to quarters, stationed extra lookouts, and made ready to slip the cable, but "everything being quiet, not hearing the report of guns, and the *Cuyler* appearing to be in her berth by the bearings taken at sunset, induced me and the other officers to think it a mistake or false alarm" (Hazard to Hitchcock, 17 January 1863, in *Official Records of the Navies,* 1st ser., 2:28).

32. Temple to Hitchcock, 16 January 1863 (in *Official Records of the Navies,* 1st ser., 2:33–34). The *Florida* passed under the guns of a Federal sloop of war (identity unknown) just before day, causing Maffitt to comment: "A broadside would have sunk us." He thought it looked like the U.S.S. *Brooklyn* and that it took the raider for one of the numerous Union vessels in the locality (Private Journal of John Newland Maffitt, in Maffitt Papers).

33. "List of United States Vessels of War" (in *Official Records of the Navies,* 1st ser., 4:xv).

34. Private Journal of John Newland Maffitt (in Maffitt Papers); Maffitt, "Blockade Running," *United Service* 7 (July 1882): 24–27; Emmons to Farragut, 21 January 1863; and Emmons to Hitchcock, 12 March 1863 (in *Official Records of the Navies,* 1st ser., 2:28–29, 30–31). A court of inquiry excoriated the commanding officers off Mobile, including Flag Officer Hitchcock (Boykin, *Sea Devil of the Confederacy,* 139). No officer was treated as harshly as Preble had been, probably because the *Florida* ran in during the day and out at night.

35. Unidentified officer of the *Cuyler,* at the time searching for the *Florida* off the coast of Yucatan, 21 January 1863, cited in Maffitt, "Blockade Running," *United Service* 7 (July 1882): 26. The officer also noted that the episode was another of "the too numerous instances in which we have been foiled by the superior daring and neck-or-nothing pluck of the 'dashing buccaneers' of Jeff. Davis" ("Blockade Running," 25).

36. Extracts from the Journal of Commander Semmes, 5 January 1863 to 31 March 1864 (in *Official Records of the Navies,* 1st ser., 2:731).

37. Cited in *Wilmington Daily Journal,* 2 February 1863.

Chapter 10: First Cruise of the *Florida,* Tortugas to Barbados

1. Journal of Charles W. Quinn, 7 September 1862 through 13 September 1863, Museum of the Confederacy, Richmond, Va.; Statement of John

Brown, 21 January 1863, in *Official Records of the Union and Confederate Navies in the War of the Rebellion,* 33 vols. (Washington: U.S. Government Printing Office, 1894–1922), 1st ser., 2:48–49.

2. Master John Brown, cited in *New York Herald,* 1 February 1863. The crew of the raider were mostly Irish and English, with a few Northern men (the boatswain was from Portland, Maine) and one Chinese. Many had been prisoners of war in the North. They were adept at using the guns and well-disciplined. No profane or insulting language was allowed on board, and any offender was severely punished (Statement of Zenrow M. Fickett, first mate of the *Estelle,* cited in *New York Herald,* 31 January 1863).

3. Private Journal of John Newland Maffitt, in John Newland Maffitt Papers, Southern Historical Collection, University of North Carolina, Chapel Hill; Edward Boykin, *Sea Devil of the Confederacy: The Story of the "Florida" and Her Captain, John Newland Maffitt* (New York: Funk and Wagnalls, 1959), 148–49.

4. W. Adolphe Roberts, *Havana: The Portrait of a City* (New York: Coward-McCann, 1953), 95.

5. Cited in Raphael Semmes, *Service Afloat: The Remarkable Career of the Confederate Cruisers "Sumter" and "Alabama"* (New York: P. J. Kenedy and Sons, 1903), 360.

6. *New York Herald,* 28 January 1863.

7. Welles to Wilkes, 15 December 1862 (in *Official Records of the Navies,* 1st ser., 1:587–88); William W. Jeffries, "The Civil War Career of Charles Wilkes," *The Journal of Southern History* 11 (February-November 1945): 324; Richard S. West, Jr., *Gideon Welles: Lincoln's Navy Department* (Indianapolis: Bobbs-Merrill, 1943), 255–61.

8. Private Journal of John Newland Maffitt (in Maffitt Papers). Shufeldt attempted without success to portray the express steamer to Governor Servano as a warship in order to delay for twenty-four hours the sailing of the *Florida;* see Helm to Benjamin, 26 January 1863 (in *Official Records of the Navies,* 2d ser., 3:670).

9. Shufeldt to Farragut, 29 January 1863 (in *Official Records of the Navies,* 1st ser., 19:598).

10. Maffitt to Mallory, 27 January 1863 (in *Official Records of the Navies,* 1st ser., 2:639–40); Journal of Charles W. Quinn, Museum of the Confederacy; *New York Herald,* 1 and 2 February 1863; *Charleston Mercury,* 5 February 1863.

11. Private Journal of John Newland Maffitt, and Log of the *Florida* (in Maffitt Papers). The coal at Nassau had been selected by Assistant Engineer Quinn. Maffitt ordered a formal inquiry by his officers at sea, who condemned the coal and spurred his decision to set a course for Nassau (Averett et al. to Maffitt, 23 January 1863, in *Official Records of the Navies,* 1st ser., 2:640).

12. Journal of Charles W. Quinn, Museum of the Confederacy.

13. *Liverpool Journal of Commerce,* 27 February 1863, cited in Charles C. Beaman, Jr., *The National and Private Alabama Claims* (Washington: W. H. Moore, 1871), 64.

14. Whiting to Welles, 26 January 1863, in FO5/1313, British Foreign Office Papers, Public Record Office, London.
15. Bayley to Lyons, 11 March 1863 (in FO5/1313, British Foreign Office Papers).
16. Whiting to Welles, 26 January 1863 (in *Official Records of the Navies,* 1st ser., 2:59–60). Consul Whiting explains in this letter that he sent "a trusty confidential man, Samuel T. Smith, to visit the *Florida* and glean what information he could, but they would not allow him alongside." The consul then engaged Smith to alert Union cruisers near Abaco Light.
17. Log of the *Florida* (in Maffitt Papers).
18. Private Journal of John Newland Maffitt (in Maffitt Papers); Journal of Charles W. Quinn, Museum of the Confederacy.
19. Boykin, *Sea Devil of the Confederacy,* 154–55. Boykin details that the new crewmen were brought out in a tugboat under the guise of a deep-sea fishing expedition. Midshipman Bryan wrote that only two of the deserters were of much service, whereas the six replacements were good seamen (Abstract of the Log of the C.S.S. *Florida,* 17 August 1862 to 31 May 1863, Record Group 45, Records Collection of the Office of Naval Records and Library, National Archives, Washington, D.C.).
20. Log of the *Florida* (in Maffitt Papers); Journal of Charles W. Quinn, Museum of the Confederacy; *New York Herald,* 11 March 1863.
21. Private Journal of John Newland Maffitt (in Maffitt Papers); Stevens to Welles, 3 February 1863 and 9 February 1863; and Abstract of the Log of U.S.S. *Sonoma,* 1 and 2 February 1863 (in *Official Records of the Navies,* 1st ser., 2:68–70); "List of United States Vessels of War" (in *Official Records of the Navies,* 1st ser., 7:xvi); Journal of Charles W. Quinn, Museum of the Confederacy.
22. Maffitt to Mallory, 27 January 1863 (in Maffitt Papers). While in Nassau, officers of the *Florida* said openly that they were bound for the equator (*New York Herald,* 12 February 1863).
23. Log of the *Florida* (in Maffitt Papers); "List of United States Vessels of War" (in *Official Records of the Navies,* 1st ser., 7:xvi); Frank L. Owsley, Jr., *The C.S.S. Florida: Her Building and Operations* (Philadelphia: University of Pennsylvania Press, 1965), 54.
24. Private Journal of John Newland Maffitt, and Log of the *Florida* (in Maffitt Papers); Abstract of the Log of the *Florida,* Office of Naval Records and Library, National Archives.
25. Don Higginbotham, "A Raider Refuels: Diplomatic Repercussions," *Civil War History* 4 (June 1958): 131.
26. Navy Department, Naval History Division, *Civil War Naval Chronology, 1861–1865,* 6 parts (Washington: U.S. Government Printing Office, 1971), 3:27.
27. Abstract of the Log of the *Florida,* Office of Naval Records and Library, National Archives; Boykin, *Sea Devil of the Confederacy,* 157–58.
28. Martha Noyes (Mrs. H. Dwight) Williams, *A Year in China: And a Narrative*

of Capture and Imprisonment, When Homeward Bound, on Board the Rebel Pirate Florida (New York: Hurd and Houghton, 1864), 303–4.

29. G. Terry Sinclair, "The Eventful Cruise of the *Florida,*" *Century Magazine* 56 (1898): 421.

30. Abstract of the Log of the *Florida,* Office of Naval Records and Library, National Archives; Journal of Charles W. Quinn, Museum of the Confederacy. The passengers of the *Jacob Bell* consisted of Mrs. Charles Frisbie, wife of the captain, and their son Louis; Martha Noyes Williams, wife of a customs commissioner at Swartow, China; and a lad, Charlie Johnson, son of a missionary in Swartow (Private Journal of John Newland Maffitt, in Maffitt Papers; *New York Herald,* 11 March 1863).

31. Boykin, *Sea Devil of the Confederacy,* 168; Williams, *A Year in China,* 321.

32. *New York Herald,* 3 and 6 March 1863; *Harper's Weekly,* 21 March 1863; Boykin, *Sea Devil of the Confederacy,* 170–71.

33. Sinclair, "The Eventful Cruise of the *Florida,*" *Century Magazine* 56 (1898): 424. Mrs. Williams, in her controversial book, *A Year in China,* published in 1864, attacked the "notorious Maffitt" with biting invective. She became an instant celebrity and was reportedly invited to Washington to give an account of her war adventure to Lincoln. See Boykin, *Sea Devil of the Confederacy,* 169–70; and Emma Martin Maffitt, *The Life and Services of John Newland Maffitt* (New York: Neale Publishing, 1906), 275. Mrs. Williams was cordial to Maffitt while she was on board the *Florida;* the book was an afterthought for propaganda and pecuniary purposes. The "libelous twaddle" depicted Maffitt "as the Piratical Nero of her brandy soaked brain" (Maffitt to Preble, 11 April 1880, in George H. Preble Papers, Massachusetts Historical Society, Boston). One of the petty officers aboard the *Florida,* Surgeon's Steward Tennie Matthews, Jr., wrote that Mrs. Williams was an "ungrateful spit-fire" whose book was a "lying narrative" (Matthews to Maffitt, 27 January 1875, 17 February and 4 May 1876, in Maffitt Papers). Maffitt and Frisbie were on "excellent terms—he made me a present of a beautiful painting of the *Jacob Bell* and I gave him a pocket sextant that he earnestly coveted" (Maffitt to Preble, 24 May 1882, in Maffitt Papers).

34. Private Journal of John Newland Maffitt; and Maffitt to Florie, Mary, John, and Colie, 13 March 1863 (in Maffitt Papers); Journal of Charles W. Quinn, Museum of the Confederacy.

35. Maffitt to Walker, 24 February 1863; and Maffitt to Mallory, 26 February 1863 (in Maffitt Papers).

36. Higginbotham, "A Raider Refuels," *Civil War History* 4 (June 1958): 133.

37. Maffitt to Florie, Mary, John, and Colie, 13 March 1863 (in Maffitt Papers). Maffitt said concerning his incapacity for alcohol: "I have found myself on several occasions excited by one glass—my sense of propriety and duty to the position I occupy induces a positive prohibition hereafter" (Private Journal of John Newland Maffitt, in Maffitt Papers).

38. Private Journal of John Newland Maffitt (in Maffitt Papers); Boykin, *Sea Devil of the Confederacy,* 174–75.

39. *New York Herald,* 23 March 1863.
40. Private Journal of John Newland Maffitt; Proclamation of John Newland Maffitt; and Maffitt to Walker, 24 February 1863 (in Maffitt Papers). A Northern correspondent commented on the crew of the *Florida:* "I only hope that ere forty days are passed every man of them may be hung from the highest trees in Pennsylvania, my native state" (*New York Herald,* 23 March 1863).
41. Quinn to Maffitt, 14 February 1863 (in Maffitt Papers). Jackson had complained of a liver ailment since leaving Mobile; Maffitt relieved him of duty at sea and sent him ashore at Barbados (Jackson to Maffitt, and Maffitt to Jackson, 21 February 1863, in Maffitt Papers). Quinn wrote that Jackson was "entirely ignorant of his profession. . . . Mr. Jackson so fooled with the feed valve of the forward boiler before coming out of Mobile, as to make it perfectly useless, and sir, had I not by chance found it out, and set it to rights, the *Florida* would have been lost had she went out the night of the 15th of January" (Quinn to Maffitt, 30 August 1863, in Maffitt Papers).
42. *New York Herald,* 23 March 1863.

Chapter 11: First Cruise of the *Florida,* Barbados to Brest

1. Abstract of the Log of the C.S.S. *Florida,* 17 August 1862 to 31 May 1863, Record Group 45, Records Collection of the Office of Naval Records and Library, National Archives, Washington, D.C.
2. Journal of Charles W. Quinn, Museum of the Confederacy, Richmond, Va.; George W. Dalzell, *The Flight from the Flag: The Continuing Effect of the Civil War Upon the American Carrying Trade* (Chapel Hill: University of North Carolina Press, 1940), 103.
3. Wilkes to Walker, 6 March 1863; Wilkes to Welles, 13 and 26 February, and 7 March 1863; and Walker to Wilkes, 7 March 1863, in *Official Records of the Union and Confederate Navies in the War of the Rebellion,* 33 vols. (Washington: U.S. Government Printing Office, 1894–1922), 1st ser., 2:83, 113–17; *Bermuda Royal Gazette,* 24 March 1863; Walker to Russell and the Duke of Newcastle, 25 February 1863; Trowbridge to Walker, 24 February 1863; Trowbridge to the Duke of Newcastle, 7 March 1863; Seward to Lyons, 13 April 1863; Lyons to Seward, 16 April 1863; and Lyons to Russell, 17 April 1863, in FO5/1313, British Foreign Office Papers, Public Record Office, London. The refueling of the *Florida* at Barbados was the only instance during the war that could be considered a violation of British neutrality laws, and that of doubtful application because of Maffitt's claim of stress of weather. See James D. Bulloch, *The Secret Service of the Confederate Agents in Europe* (New York: G. P. Putnam's Sons, 1884), 182.
4. Bulloch, *The Secret Service,* 318.
5. Private Journal of John Newland Maffitt; Maffitt to Mallory, 11 May 1863;

and Log of the *Florida,* in John Newland Maffitt Papers, Southern Historical Collection, University of North Carolina, Chapel Hill.

6. Abstract of the Log of the *Florida,* Office of Naval Records and Library, National Archives.

7. Edward Boykin, *Sea Devil of the Confederacy: The Story of the "Florida" and Her Captain, John Newland Maffitt* (New York: Funk and Wagnalls, 1959), 178–79.

8. *Bermuda Royal Gazette,* 31 March 1863. On the same day that Maffitt captured the *Aldebaran,* he stopped the British schooner *Laura Ann,* whose captain arrived in Bermuda and reported the capture of the *Aldebaran.* The captain noted that the crew of the *Florida* could crowd on canvas "so quickly indeed that one might fancy it was the 'Flying Dutchman.' "

9. Abstract of the Log of the *Florida,* Office of Naval Records and Library, National Archives; Journal of Charles W. Quinn, Museum of the Confederacy.

10. Journal of Charles W. Quinn, Museum of the Confederacy; Frank L. Owsley, Jr., *The C.S.S. Florida: Her Building and Operations* (Philadelphia: University of Pennsylvania Press, 1965), 61.

11. Maffitt to Averett, 28 March 1863 (in *Official Records of the Navies,* 1st ser., 2:643); Dalzell, *Flight from the Flag,* 104. After the first day, Bryan transferred to the *Lapwing* (C.S. Bark *Oreto*) and continued his journal from that vessel until May 3, when he returned to the *Florida* (Abstract of the Log of the *Florida,* Office of Naval Records and Library, National Archives).

12. Private Journal of John Newland Maffitt (in Maffitt Papers); Boykin, *Sea Devil of the Confederacy,* 180–81.

13. Maffitt to Mallory, 11 May 1863 (in Maffitt Papers); Journal of Charles W. Quinn, Museum of the Confederacy.

14. Private Journal of John Newland Maffitt; and Maffitt to Mallory, 11 May 1863 (in Maffitt Papers); Statement of George Brown, 2 May 1863; and Private Journal of Jessee Potter (in *Official Records of the Navies,* 1st ser., 2:204–6); Dalzell, *Flight from the Flag,* 105.

15. Leal to Maffitt, 1 May 1863 (in *Official Records of the Navies,* 1st ser., 2:643–44). At Fernando de Noronha, Maffitt learned that the *Alabama* had departed on April 20, causing him to miss by a week a visit with his midshipman son, Eugene.

16. Owsley, *C.S.S. Florida,* 63. The *Lapwing* had taken one prize, the *Kate Dyer.* The 1,278-ton vessel was twice the size of its captor (with its small twelve-pound guns), but the Confederates had fashioned a "Quaker" gun, a sawed-off wooden spar mounted on a set of carriage wheels found on deck. The deception suggested a major piece of ordnance (Dalzell, *Flight from the Flag,* 104). The *Kate Dyer,* because of its neutral cargo, had been bonded by Averett. The term "bonded," or ransomed, means the captured vessel was released, provided that its captain signed a bond on behalf of the owners to pay a stipulated sum to the Confederacy after the war. (None of these shipowners ever paid.) Ships were bonded for two reasons: to release a

neutral cargo, and to carry away prisoners. See J. Thomas Scharf, *History of the Confederate States Navy* (n.p.: Fairfax Press, 1977), 792n.

17. Read to Maffitt, 6 May 1863; and Maffitt to Read, 6 May 1863 (in *Official Records of the Navies*, 1st ser., 2:644–45). Read learned that raiding Hampton Roads was impracticable because of tight Federal security, so he raided along the eastern seaboard, changing in the process from the *Clarence* to a better captured vessel, the *Tacony*, and eventually, for the purpose of disguise, to the 90-ton fishing schooner *Archer*. Read captured twenty vessels, eight of them fishing schooners, before entering the harbor of Portland, Maine. Before dawn on June 27, he cut out the revenue cutter *Caleb Cushing*. Caught by pursuers before getting to sea, Read fought to the end of his ammunition and then was captured, but not before burning the *Caleb Cushing*. See Read to Mallory, 19 October 1864 (in *Official Records of the Navies*, 1st ser., 2:655–57); *Leslie's Weekly*, 18 July 1863; and Jim Dan Hill, *Sea Dogs of the Sixties: Farragut and Seven Contemporaries* (Minneapolis: University of Minnesota Press, 1935), 178–84.

18. Maffitt to Silveira, 8 May 1863; Silveira to Maffitt, 8 May 1863; Maffitt to Silveira, 8 May 1863; and Silveira to Maffitt, 9 May 1863 (in *Official Records of the Navies*, 1st ser., 2:645–48); Adamson to Seward, 27 May 1863 (in *Official Records of the Navies*, 1st ser., 2:217–21); Captain Oliver S. Glisson, commander of the *Mohican*, to Seward, 9 May 1863 (in *Official Records of the Navies*, 1st ser., 2:182); Owsley, *C.S.S. Florida*, 66–77.

19. Maffitt to Mallory, 11 May 1863 (in Maffitt Papers).

20. Glisson to Welles, 20 May 1863; and Adamson to Glisson, 20 May 1863 (in *Official Records of the Navies*, 1st ser., 2:201–3). Glisson took the *Mohican* southward the next day, May 21, for Salvador, the capital of the Brazilian state of Bahia. From there, he wrote that he would continue to cruise the coast, but he failed to find the *Florida* (Glisson to Welles, 26 May 1863, in *Official Records of the Navies*, 1st ser., 2:216).

21. Private Journal of John Newland Maffitt (in Maffitt Papers); Adamson to Seward, 10 June 1863 (in *Official Records of the Navies*, 1st ser., 2:263–64); Journal of Charles W. Quinn, Museum of the Confederacy. Floyd had sailed the *Lapwing* to what he thought was the place of rendezvous, and waited a month. Wind and currents perhaps carried him northward. Running low on supplies, he sailed to Barbados, where on 20 June 1863, he burned the *Lapwing* offshore and landed the crew in a boat. Received with cheering hospitality, they later boarded a British ship for Ireland and, from there, rejoined the *Florida* at Brest, France (Owsley, *C.S.S. Florida*, 69).

22. On June 1, Welles relieved Wilkes of command, mainly because Wilkes detained the *Vanderbilt* from other duty, and appointed Commodore James L. Lardner commander of the West India Squadron (Welles to Lardner, 1 June 1863, in *Official Records of the Navies*, 1st ser., 2:253–54).

23. Of the captain's wife, Quinn noted: "She seems to take it very cool, notwithstanding her husband's loss, but this is the way the Yankee women act" (Journal of Charles W. Quinn, Museum of the Confederacy).

24. *Bermuda Royal Gazette,* 7 July 1863; *Leslie's Weekly,* 1 August 1863.
25. Dalzell, *Flight from the Flag,* 115–16.
26. *Bermuda Royal Gazette,* 7 July 1863.
27. Maffitt to Mallory, 27 July 1863 (in *Official Records of the Navies,* 1st ser., 2:653).
28. Welles to Commodore John B. Montgomery, commandant of the Boston Navy Yard, 10 July 1863 (in *Official Records of the Navies,* 1st ser., 2:385). Welles was busily dispatching gunboats in search of the *Florida;* he was in possession of a journal captured from a *Tacony* crew member and, from it, deduced that Read had expected to meet the *Florida* off Nantucket.
29. Commander Joseph N. Miller, commander of the *Ericsson,* to Welles, 9 July 1863 (in *Official Records of the Navies,* 1st ser., 2:383–84).
30. Maffitt to Mallory, 27 July 1863 (in *Official Records of the Navies,* 1st ser., 2:653).
31. Maffitt to Mallory, 27 July 1863 (in *Official Records of the Navies,* 1st ser., 2:653); Journal of Charles W. Quinn, Museum of the Confederacy. The salute of the Confederate flag by the British at Bermuda created keen interest in the North, and eventually found its way into the Alabama Claims. See Lyons to Ord, 7 August 1863; and Ord to the Duke of Newcastle, 27 August 1863 (in FO5/1313, British Foreign Office Papers).
32. *Bermuda Royal Gazette,* 21 July 1863.
33. Munro to Maffitt, 15 July 1863 (in *Official Records of the Navies,* 1st ser., 2:650); *South Carolinian,* n.d. (clipping, in Maffitt Papers); *Bermuda Royal Gazette,* 21 July 1863; Boykin, *Sea Devil of the Confederacy,* 228–29.
34. Ord to the Duke of Newcastle, 3 August 1863 (in FO5/1313, British Foreign Office Papers).
35. The captured articles consisted of twenty-one chronometers, fourteen quadrants, four sextants, fifteen lamps, twenty-five compasses, eight barometers, eight spy glasses, four bags of charts, three bags of flags and signals, and three thermometers (George D. Bryan, acting master of the *Florida,* to Maffitt, 22 July 1863, in *Official Records of the Navies,* 1st ser., 2:652).
36. Maffitt to Mallory, 27 July 1863 (in *Official Records of the Navies,* 1st ser., 2:653); unidentified newspaper (clipping, in Maffitt Papers). Wilkinson observed the crew of the *Florida* at meals: "It was a curious scene; the plain fare of the sailors being served in costly china." The men had also become "fastidious in their taste about tea." See John Wilkinson, *The Narrative of a Blockade Runner* (New York: Sheldon, 1877), 161.
37. John Slidell to Fraser, Trenholm and Company, 4 December 1863 (in *Official Records of the Navies,* 2d ser., 3:980); Owsley, *C.S.S. Florida,* 71.
38. Journal of Charles W. Quinn, Museum of the Confederacy; Wilkinson et al. to Spidell, 20 July 1863; and Spidell to Maffitt, 21 July 1863 (in Maffitt Papers).
39. Journal of Charles W. Quinn, Museum of the Confederacy; Boykin, *Sea Devil of the Confederacy,* 228.
40. Unidentified newspaper (clipping, in Maffitt Papers); *Leslie's Weekly,* 12 September 1863.

41. Maffitt to Mallory, (?) September 1863 (in *Official Records of the Navies,* 1st ser., 2:659–60); Maffitt to Slidell, 18 August 1863 (in *Official Records of the Navies,* 1st ser., 2:658–59).
42. *Cork Herald,* 20 August 1863, and *Liverpool Times,* 21 August 1863, cited in *Charleston Mercury,* 1 September 1863; *Dublin Freeman's Journal,* 24 August 1863, cited in *Charleston Mercury,* 18 September 1863.
43. Maffitt to Mallory, (?) September 1863 (in *Official Records of the Navies,* 1st ser., 2:659–60); Evan Evans, the British pilot of the *Anglo-Saxon,* to the British consul in Brest, Anthony Perrier, 25 August 1863, and Perrier to Lord Russell, 26 August 1863 (in FO5/1313, British Foreign Office Papers).
44. Maffitt to Mallory, (?) September 1863 (in *Official Records of the Navies,* 1st ser., 2:659).
45. *Wilmington Daily Journal,* 11 August 1863.
46. David C. Roller and Robert W. Twyman, eds., *The Encyclopedia of Southern History* (Baton Rougue: Louisiana State University Press, 1979), 278; Dalzell, *Flight from the Flag,* 247; Carroll S. Alden and Allan Westcott, *The United States Navy: A History* (Chicago: J. B. Lippincott, 1943), 255.
47. Bulloch, *The Secret Service,* 197–98.
48. Owsley, *C.S.S. Florida,* 156–63. Lists of captures vary somewhat from source to source. Lieutenant Charles Read reports his twenty-one captures in the *Clarence* and *Tacony* in his report of his raid (Read to Mallory, 19 October 1864, in *Official Records of the Navies,* 1st ser., 2:655–57).

Chapter 12: Maffitt Sets the Neutrality Standard

1. Warren F. Spencer, *The Confederate Navy in Europe* (University, Ala.: University of Alabama Press, 1983), 162, 165.
2. Napoleon III had issued a Proclamation of Neutrality in 1861, but he favored the South because of his Mexican venture, which violated the U.S. Monroe Doctrine. See James D. Bulloch, *The Secret Service of the Confederate Agents in Europe* (New York: G. P. Putnam's Sons, 1884), 21–23.
3. Slidell to Secretary of State Judah P. Benjamin, 29 August 1863, in *Official Records of the Union and Confederate Navies in the War of the Rebellion,* 33 vols. (Washington: U.S. Government Printing Office, 1894–1922), 2d ser., 3:881–82.
4. Eustis to Maffitt, 2 September 1863; and Maffitt to de Gueyton, (?) August 1863, in John Newland Maffitt Papers, Southern Historical Collection, University of North Carolina, Chapel Hill; Spencer, *The Confederate Navy in Europe,* 166.
5. G. Terry Sinclair, "The Eventful Cruise of the *Florida,*" *Century Magazine* 56 (1898): 423. Although Sinclair wrote this over thirty years later, another officer gives credence to him by noting that the crew began refusing duty on September 1 and, over the next two days, were put ashore; see Journal of Charles W. Quinn, Museum of the Confederacy, Richmond, Va. A crewman who had refused duty wrote that the incident was not against Maffitt: "It was

against Mr. Averett, and through him the mutiny began and took shape. . . . That ship's crew admired you, respected you, as a scholar, a gentleman, and a soldier, and sailor" (Frank Rivers to Maffitt, 20 April 1883, in Maffitt Papers).

6. William Boynton et al. to Maffitt, 16 September 1863 (in Maffitt Papers).

7. "Narrative of Monsieur du Belley," cited in Emma Martin Maffitt, *The Life and Services of John Newland Maffitt* (New York: Neale Publishing, 1906), 312–15. Judge du Belley wrote that the presence of the *Florida* "resounded in Paris as a thunderstorm" (313).

8. Dayton protested that since the *Florida* had sails as well as steam power, it could put to sea without repairs. To this, Napoleon III is reported to have responded: "Because a duck can swim is no reason why his wings should be cut"; cited in Sinclair, "The Eventful Cruise of the *Florida*," *Century Magazine* 56 (1898): 423.

9. Cited in *Wilmington Daily Journal,* 25 September 1863.

10. Maury to Maffitt, 9 September 1863, in *Official Records of the Union and Confederate Navies in the War of the Rebellion,* 33 vols. (Washington: U.S. Government Printing Office, 1894–1922), 1st ser., 2:660.

11. *Wilmington Daily Journal,* 1 October 1863; Bulloch, *The Secret Service,* 115.

12. Spencer, *The Confederate Navy in Europe,* 166, 168.

13. Private Journal of Charles W. Quinn, Museum of the Confederacy.

14. George W. Dalzell, *The Flight from the Flag: The Continuing Effect of the Civil War Upon the American Carrying Trade* (Chapel Hill: University of North Carolina Press, 1940), 10.

15. *La Patrie,* 14 September 1863, cited in *Wilmington Daily Journal,* 11 October 1863. By establishing a blockade and exchanging prisoners, the North acknowledged the South as a belligerent, and not simply a rebellious faction.

16. See Mallory to Maffitt, 6 May 1863 and 7 August 1863 (in Maffitt Papers); Mallory to Captain Samuel Barron, 24 October 1863 (in *Official Records of the Navies,* 2d ser., 2:514); *Journal of the Congress of the Confederate States of America,* 7 vols. (Washington: U.S. Government Printing Office, 1904–1905), 4:144. Maffitt's daughter Florie had been concerned about his lack of promotion. She wrote Confederate Senator James L. Orr, who knew Maffitt well. Orr called on Mallory, who spoke in "very commendatory terms" of Maffitt's performance at Mobile, "but as the service was rather civil than military—not having his guns mounted—he had concluded to await a suitable occasion when he might promote him in the legitimate performance of his duty" (Orr to Florie, 2 April 1863, in Maffitt Papers).

17. Maury to Maffitt, 11 September 1863 (in *Official Records of the Navies,* 2d ser., 2:660–61). This letter, which relieved Maffitt of command of the *Florida,* also ordered him to report, as soon as his health would allow, to Mallory in Richmond.

18. Captures of the *Florida* under C. M. Morris (in Maffitt Papers). Barney was also taken ill, but on 10 February 1864, Lieutenant Charles M. Morris took

the *Florida* out on its second cruise. The vessel was finally rammed and captured in Recife, Brazil, in flagrant violation of international law and, despite Brazil's protests, towed to Hampton Roads. There, under mysterious circumstances, the *Florida* was sunk by the Federals.

19. *Mobile Daily Register,* 4 May 1886. According to this account, the C.S.S. *Shenandoah* destroyed twenty-seven prizes with an estimated value of $2,041,000. Only the damages of the *Florida* (and its tenders), the *Alabama,* and the *Shenandoah* (after it left Melbourne) were accepted by the Geneva Tribunal of Arbitration against Britain. The $15,500,000 awarded the U.S. in damages included losses of ships, cargoes, and interest. See also Adrian Cook, *The Alabama Claims: American Politics and Anglo-American Relations, 1865–1872* (Ithaca: Cornell University Press, 1975), 238–39.

20. After the war, two Union officers, both of whom rose to the rank of admiral, depicted the contrasting styles of Confederates Maffitt and Semmes. Wrote David D. Porter: "Maffitt was a different kind of man from Semmes. . . . He made no enemies among those officers who had once known him and who now missed his genial humor in their messes. He was never inhumane to those whom the fortunes of war threw into his hands." See Porter, *The Naval History of the Civil War* (New York: Sherman Publishing, 1886), 623–24. And George H. Preble wrote: "I fell in during my cruise in the *St. Louis* with navy officers and men of merchantmen who had been captured by Semmes and yourself—not *one* of whom spoke well of Semmes. While all I met with spoke well of you and your treatment of them" (Preble to Maffitt, 1 June 1882, in Maffitt Papers).

21. Frank L. Owsley, Jr., *The C.S.S. Florida: Her Building and Operations* (Philadelphia: University of Pennsylvania Press, 1965), 158–59.

22. "Narrative of Monsieur du Belley," cited in Emma Maffitt, *Life of Maffitt,* 318–19. Another annoyance concerned an imposter. Wrote Maffitt to his children: "Some rascal has assumed my name in Paris . . . a fraud has been committed" (Maffitt to "My Dear Darlings," 1 September 1863, in Maffitt Papers).

23. "Narrative of Monsieur du Belley," cited in Emma Maffitt, *Life of Maffitt,* 319–20.

24. Maffitt to "My Dear Darlings," 1 September 1863 (in Maffitt Papers); Maffitt, "Blockade Running," *United Service* 7 (July 1882): 29.

Chapter 13: Return to Blockade Running

1. David Stick, *Graveyard of the Atlantic: Shipwrecks of the North Carolina Coast* (Chapel Hill: University of North Carolina Press, 1952), 61.

2. Samuel Lee to Welles, 18 December 1863, in *Official Records of the Union and Confederate Navies in the War of the Rebellion,* 33 vols. (Washington: U.S. Government Printing Office, 1894–1922), 1st ser., 9:338–39.

3. *Florie* File, Vessel Papers, Record Group 109, Confederate Records, Military Reference Branch, National Archives, Washington, D.C.

4. Stephen R. Wise, *Lifeline of the Confederacy: Blockade Running During the*

Civil War (Columbia: University of South Carolina Press, 1988), 300; James Sprunt, *Derelicts: An Account of Ships Lost at Sea in General Commercial Traffic and A Brief History of Blockade Runners Stranded Along the North Carolina Coast, 1861–1865* (Baltimore: Lord Baltimore Press, 1920), 109.

5. "Commissioned and Warrant Officers of the Navy of the Confederate States," 1 January 1864, in *Southern Historical Society Papers*, 52 vols. (Richmond: Southern Historical Society, 1896), 3:106–7; Preble, commanding the U.S.S. *St. Louis*, to Welles, 27 February 1864 (in *Official Records of the Navies*, 1st ser., 2:613); Flag Officer Samuel Barron, in Paris, to Welles, 15 December 1864 and 22 January 1865 (in *Official Records of the Navies*, 2d ser., 2:566–67, 574–75).

6. Bourne to Fraser, Trenholm and Company, 5 March 1864, cited in Frank E. Vandiver, ed., *Confederate Blockade Running Through Bermuda, 1861–1865: Letters and Cargo Manifests* (Austin: University of Texas Press, 1947), 57–58.

7. Slidell to a member of the Maffitt family, 12 June 1864, in John Newland Maffitt Papers, Southern Historical Collection, University of North Carolina, Chapel Hill; unidentified Northern newspaper, cited in Lieutenant Robert D. Minor to Commander Catesby A. R. Jones, 23 March 1864 (in *Official Records of the Navies*, 1st ser., 9:806–7).

8. After Maffitt left the *Florie*, the ship made several forays into Wilmington before reportedly sinking of unknown causes in the Cape Fear River in the fall of 1864. "Blockade Runners Captured and Destroyed off Wilmington, N.C." (in *Official Records of the Navies*, 1st ser., 10:504).

9. Wise, *Lifeline of the Confederacy*, 301.

10. *Lilian* File, Vessel Papers, Record Group 109, National Archives; "Statistical Data of U.S. Ships" (in *Official Records of the Navies*, 2d ser., 1:127).

11. James M. Morgan, *Recollections of a Rebel Reefer* (Boston: Houghton Mifflin, 1917), 191.

12. *Bermuda Royal Gazette*, 7 June 1864; Vandiver, ed., *Confederate Blockade Running Through Bermuda*, 132–33.

13. Cited in Nelson D. Lankford, ed., *An Irishman in Dixie: Thomas Conolly's Diary of the Fall of the Confederacy* (Columbia: University of South Carolina Press, 1988), 34.

14. *An Irishman in Dixie*, 34n; W. Stanley Hoole, *Vizetelly Covers the Confederacy* (Tuscaloosa: Confederate Publishing, 1957), 114.

15. *London Telegraph*, 8 January 1897, cited in Emma Martin Maffitt, *The Life and Services of John Newland Maffitt* (New York: Neale Publishing, 1906), 329–35. An account of the voyage by Lawley also appeared in the *Illustrated London News*, 16 July 1864.

16. Sprunt, *Derelicts*, 266. See also Ella Lonn, *Foreigners in the Confederacy* (Glouchester, Mass.: Peter Smith, 1965), 304.

17. *London Telegraph*, 8 January 1897, cited in Emma Maffitt, *Life of Maffitt*, 329–35.

18. Crosby to Samuel P. Lee, 27 July 1864 (in *Official Records of the Navies*, 1st ser., 10:311–13).

19. James Sprunt, "The Chase," cited in *Tales of the Cape Fear Blockade,* ed. Cornelius M. D. Thomas (Wilmington: Charles Town Preservation Trust, 1960), iii. Maffitt relinquished command of the *Lilian* in Wilmington. The vessel made three subsequent voyages before its capture on 24 August 1864, of which the ship's pilot wrote: "Those of us who knew Captain Maffitt, the former commander of the *Lilian,* regretted very much his absence on this occasion, as he would most likely have been more fortunate in getting away." See J. W. Craig, "Blockade Running," in *Chronicles of the Cape Fear River, 1660–1916,* ed. James Sprunt (Raleigh: Edwards and Broughton, 1916), 402–3.

20. W. Buck Yearns and John G. Barrett, eds., *North Carolina Civil War Documentary* (Chapel Hill: University of North Carolina Press, 1980), 72.

21. Maury to Maffitt, 11 September 1863 (in *Official Records of the Navies,* 1st ser., 2:660–61). See also Edward Boykin, *Sea Devil of the Confederacy: The Story of the "Florida" and Her Captain, John Newland Maffitt* (New York: Funk and Wagnalls, 1959), 242.

22. Captain Sidney S. Lee, commander of Office of Orders and Detail, to Maffitt, 9 June 1864 (in Maffitt Papers).

23. Sidney Lee to Cooke, 17 June 1864 (in *Official Records of the Navies,* 1st ser., 10:704); J. Thomas Scharf, *History of the Confederate States Navy* (n.p.: Fairfax Press, 1977), 409n. Maffitt wrote of Cooke's heroic efforts: "If an admiralty commission was ever bravely and justly won, Commander James W. Cooke richly merited the honorable distinction. Some *months* after this splendid record—he was promoted to a *captaincy!*" See Maffitt to George Davis, former Confederate attorney general, 17 August 1874, George Davis Papers, Manuscript Department, William R. Perkins Library, Duke University, Durham, N.C.

24. "Confederate States Vessels" (in *Official Records of the Navies,* 2d ser., 1:812); Navy Department, Naval History Division, *Civil War Naval Chronology, 1861–1865,* 6 parts (Washington: U.S. Government Printing Office, 1971), 4:32.

25. Carroll S. Alden and Allan Westcott, *The United States Navy: A History* (Chicago: J. B. Lippincott, 1943), 260; Stick, *Graveyard of the Atlantic,* 18.

26. John G. Barrett, *The Civil War in North Carolina* (Chapel Hill: University of North Carolina Press, 1963), 227.

27. Palmer to Major Robert S. Davis, 19 July 1864, in *Official Records of the Union and Confederate Armies in the War of the Rebellion,* 128 vols. (Washington: U.S. Government Printing Office, 1880–1901), 1st ser., 40.3.343–44.

28. Wortham to Captain J. C. McRae, 2 July 1864 (in *Official Records of the Armies,* 1st ser., 40.3.751–52).

29. Baker to Maffitt, 6 July 1864 (in Maffitt Papers).

30. Baker to Seddon, 8 July 1864; and Baker to Captain John M. Otey, 8 July 1864 (in *Official Records of the Armies,* 1st ser., 40.3.752). Mallory, who had great confidence in ironclads, had undoubtedly issued the orders. He wrote in an endorsement to the collection of opinions gathered by the army that

the *Albemarle* "was not designed to act as a floating battery merely" (Endorsement of Mallory, 30 July 1864, in *Official Records of the Armies,* 1st ser., 40.3.753).

31. Commander William H. Macomb, Union senior officer on the sounds of North Carolina, to Samuel Lee, 15 August 1864 (in *Official Records of the Navies,* 1st ser., 10:385–86).

32. Maffitt to Hopkins, 31 August 1864 (in Maffitt Papers); Samuel Lee to Welles, 15 September 1864 (in *Official Records of the Navies,* 1st ser., 10:457).

33. Acting Masters Mate John Woodman, the Union reconnaissance officer who observed the *Albemarle* from the bushes across the Roanoke, to Macomb, 28 August 1864 (in *Official Records of the Navies,* 1st ser., 10:405–6).

34. Sidney Lee to Maffitt, 9 September 1864 (in Maffitt Papers); Maffitt to Preble, 18 May 1883, in George H. Preble Papers, Massachusetts Historical Society, Boston.

35. Flag Officer William W. Hunter, commander afloat in Savannah, to Warley, 10 September 1864 (in *Official Records of the Navies,* 1st ser., 15:770); *Dictionary of American Biography,* s.v. "Maffitt, John Newland." Subsequent to Maffitt's command of the *Albemarle,* on 27 October 1864, Union Lieutenant William B. Cushing in a daring nighttime torpedo-boat raid blew up the ram, assuring the North of renewed control of the Roanoke Valley (*Civil War Naval Chronology* 6:7).

36. Naval officials in Washington believed an attack by Maffitt in the *Albemarle* might drive Union ships from the sounds of North Carolina: "The Department considered that they had no vessels at their disposal fit to cope with the ram." See David D. Porter, *The Naval History of the Civil War* (New York: Sherman Publishing, 1886), 687.

Chapter 14: *Owl*, The Last Blockade Runner

1. Alexander R. Lawton, Confederate quartermaster general, to Major Richard P. Waller in St. George's, 21 September 1864, in *Official Records of the Union and Confederate Armies in the War of the Rebellion,* 128 vols. (Washington: U.S. Government Printing Office, 1880–1901), 4th ser., 3:674–75.

2. Colin J. McRae, Confederate agent in London, to Seddon, 4 July 1864 (in *Official Records of the Armies,* 4th ser., 3:525–29); Dudley to Benjamin Moran, assistant secretary of the U.S. legation in London, 10 July 1864, in *Official Records of the Union and Confederate Navies in the War of the Rebellion,* 33 vols. (Washington: U.S. Government Printing Office, 1894–1922), 1st ser., 3:99; Moran to Captain John A. Winslow, commander of the U.S.S. *Kearsarge,* 27 July 1864 (in *Official Records of the Navies,* 1st ser., 3:127–28); *Liverpool Mercury,* 21 August 1864, cited in *Wilmington Daily News,* 29 August 1864; Navy Department, Naval History Division, *Civil War Naval Chronology, 1861–1865,* 6 parts (Washington: U.S. Government Printing Office, 1971), 6:203, 278. The army had some voice in the operation of the new blockade runners.

3. Mallory to Maffitt, 14 September 1864, in John Newland Maffitt Papers, Southern Historical Collection, University of North Carolina, Chapel Hill. During the delay at Wilmington, Maffitt sent a partial list of his captures in the *Florida* to Mallory, saying his papers at the moment were in Bermuda (Maffitt to Mallory, 12 December 1864, in Maffitt Papers).
4. Mallory to Maffitt, 19 September 1864 (in Maffitt Papers).
5. Mallory to Maffitt, 25 November 1864 (in Maffitt Papers).
6. Mortimer M. Jackson, U.S. consul in Halifax, to Seward, 31 August 1864 (in *Official Records of the Navies,* 1st ser., 10:410); *Bermuda Royal Gazette,* 30 August 1864.
7. Stephen R. Wise, *Lifeline of the Confederacy: Blockade Running During the Civil War* (Columbia: University of South Carolina Press, 1988), 300; James Sprunt, *Derelicts: An Account of Ships Lost at Sea in General Commercial Traffic and A Brief History of Blockade Runners Stranded Along the North Carolina Coast, 1861–1865* (Baltimore: Lord Baltimore Press, 1920), 198.
8. Maffitt to Florie, 8 November 1864, cited in Emma Martin Maffitt, *The Life and Services of John Newland Maffitt* (New York: Neale Publishing, 1906), 343–44.
9. Bulloch to Mallory, 15 November 1864 (in *Official Records of the Navies,* 2d ser., 2:765–67); Cargoes Received from Abroad, on Government Account— Port of Wilmington (in *Official Records of the Armies,* 4th ser., 3:957).
10. Maffitt, "Blockade Running," *United Service* 7 (July 1882): 30; Mallory to Maffitt, 5 December 1864 (in Maffitt Papers). The *Owl* cargo manifest listed 145 cases merchandise, 2 bales merchandise, 4 cases hardware, 7 casks hardware, 130 sacks niter, 200 pigs lead, 24 packages hardware, and 100 bundles hoop iron. See Frank E. Vandiver, ed., *Confederate Blockade Running Through Bermuda, 1861–1865: Letters and Cargo Manifests* (Austin: University of Texas Press, 1947), 144.
11. Maffitt, "Blockade Running," *United Service* 7 (July 1882): 30.
12. John Wilkinson, *The Narrative of a Blockade Runner* (New York: Sheldon, 1877), 234.
13. Maffitt, "Blockade Running," *United Service* 7 (July 1882): 30–31.
14. J. Thomas Scharf, *History of the Confederate States Navy* (n.p.: Fairfax Press, 1977), 489.
15. William S. Hoole, *Four Years in the Confederate Navy: The Career of Captain John Low* (Athens: University of Georgia Press, 1964), 116. Maffitt was probably united with his son Eugene at about this time. As a midshipman on the *Alabama,* Eugene had participated in the 19 June 1864 engagement with the U.S.S. *Kearsarge* off Cherbourg, France. When the *Alabama* sank, Eugene offered his life preserver to Kell, who refused it. Both men were rescued. See John McIntosh Kell, *Recollections of a Naval Life* (Washington: Neale, 1900), 250. Eugene then became executive officer of the blockade runner *Susan Beirne* and on 24 December 1864 cleared St. George's for Wilmington. Encountering a fierce storm, the ship nearly foundered; it returned to Bermuda damaged and leaking. Denied the government dry

dock, the *Susan Beirne* went to Nassau. See Vandiver, ed., *Confederate Blockade Running Through Bermuda*, 144; Emma Maffitt, *Life of Maffitt*, 344–45; Sprunt, *Derelicts*, 199; Wise, *Lifeline of the Confederacy*, 322.

16. Vandiver, ed., *Confederate Blockade Running Through Bermuda*, 144.

17. Maffitt, "Blockade Running," *United Service* 7 (July 1882): 33.

18. "Blockade Running," 33.

19. James Sprunt, with the *Susan Beirne* repairing in Nassau, cited in Emma Maffitt, *Life of Maffitt*, 350.

20. Wise, *Lifeline of the Confederacy*, 213.

21. Maffitt's sudden departure from Nassau before repairs were completed on the *Owl* was probably prompted by the efforts of the U.S. consul to have him arrested for recruiting seamen in Nassau in 1862 for the *Florida* (Consul Thomas Kirkpatrick to Governor Rawson W. Rawson, 23 February 1863, in FO5/1314, British Foreign Office Papers, Public Record Office, London).

22. Cited in Lankford, ed., *An Irishman in Dixie*, 21–22. Conolly noted that the entrance at Nassau "even in day is very dangerous, being both narrow and turning, and has been the scene of many calamities." The unorthodox exit gave him "a great idea of Maffitt's coolness and capacity" and "would have scared a man of different metal [*sic*] from Maffitt" (*An Irishman in Dixie*, 21–22).

23. *An Irishman in Dixie*, 20–30, 34. Joshua G. Wright, Florie's husband, was from a prominent Wilmington family. A war hero, Lieutenant Wright fought at Sharpsburg and Fredericksburg, and was wounded during an assault by "Stonewall" Jackson's corps at Chancellorsville. See Susan Block, *The Wrights of Wilmington* (Wilmington: Wilmington Printing, 1992), 93.

24. Unidentified newspaper (clipping, in Maffitt Papers); Wise, *Lifeline of the Confederacy*, 215. Maffitt's exact itinerary during the final days of the war is difficult to establish. Scharf wrote that Maffitt left Havana "about the middle of March," evaded the U.S.S. *Cherokee* with the soft-coal smoke screen deception, "and disappeared in the darkness of night and storm" (*History of the Confederate States Navy*, 490). It is not clear if this exit by Maffitt had Galveston as its destination, but he did visit the Florida coast in the *Owl*. Lieutenant Edward C. Stiles, a Confederate naval officer on special assignment from Havana, wrote that on March 24, Maffitt landed Assistant Surgeon David S. Watson and Assistant Engineer Edward Archer safely on the Florida coast some nine miles from St. Mark's (Stiles to Mallory, 31 March 1865, in *Official Records of the Navies*, 1st ser., 27:194–95).

25. *Galveston Daily News*, 6 May 1901 (clipping, in Maffitt Papers); Henrietta Lamar, Maffitt's sister who lived in Galveston, to Emma Maffitt, n.d., cited in Emma Maffitt, *Life of Maffitt*, 350.

26. General John B. Magruder, commander of the District of Texas, New Mexico and Arizona, to Colonel Ashbel Smith, commander of defenses at Galveston, 17 April 1865, *Owl* File, Vessel Papers, Record Group 109, Confederate Records, Military Reference Branch, National Archives, Washington, D.C.

27. "Received, Galveston, 5 May 1865, of Mr. C. B. Cook, two hundred and

twenty-two 15/100 (in specie) dollars for duties on clearance of goods imported into the port on Steamer *Owl*" (Receipt of Surveyor A. P. Lupkin, of the port of Galveston, 5 May 1865, in Maffitt Papers).

28. J. G. Randall and David Donald, *The Civil War and Reconstruction* (Lexington, Mass.: D. C. Heath, 1969), 453.

29. *Civil War Naval Chronology* 2:38. The Federals were still tracking Maffitt's movements: "The *Owl*, Captain Maffitt, is in Galveston, and expected back to Havana" (Major A. M. Jackson, of the U.S. Division of West Mississippi in New Orleans, to Lieutenant Colonel C. T. Christensen, assistant adjutant general of the division, 28 April 1865, in *Official Records of the Armies*, 1st ser., 48.2.230).

30. *Register of the Commissioned and Warrant Officers of the Navy of the Confederate States to January 1, 1864* (Richmond: MacFarlane and Fergusson, 1864), 6; Jones to Emma Maffitt (?), 20 November 1905, cited in Emma Maffitt, *Life of Maffitt*, 351.

31. Mallory to Maffitt, 24 February 1865 (in Maffitt Papers).

32. Jones to Emma Maffitt (?), 20 November 1905, cited in Emma Maffitt, *Life of Maffitt*, 351.

33. *Civil War Naval Chronology* 5:118. Maffitt turned the *Owl* over to Fraser, Trenholm and Company in Liverpool.

Chapter 15: The Moorings

1. Maffitt to Eliza Hybart—his cousin, who still lived at Ellerslie—12 September 1865, in John Newland Maffitt Papers, Southern Historical Collection, University of North Carolina, Chapel Hill. Union troops, in Fayetteville 12–14 March 1865, visited Ellerslie and destroyed some of Maffitt's early letters. According to Eliza, "the soldiers would amuse themselves awhile . . . reading the letters, shouting over his graphic descriptions of events, and then maliciously destroy them"; cited in Emma Martin Maffitt, *The Life and Services of John Newland Maffitt* (New York: Neale Publishing, 1906), 45.

2. Cited in *Life of Maffitt*, 45. Among those writing letters of recommendation to the Marine Board, which issued the necessary certificate, was former Confederate Secretary of War John C. Breckinridge (Breckinridge to Marine Board of Examination, 31 August 1865, in Maffitt Papers).

3. The *Widgeon*—named after a duck-like bird of northern latitudes—was probably the vessel built as a blockade runner in 1865. It was 225 feet by 24 feet by 11 feet, and 645 tons (registered or gross not specified). See Richard I. Lester, *Confederate Finance and Purchasing in Great Britain* (Charlottesville: University Press of Virginia), 231.

4. Cited in Florie to Eugene, 24 May 1866, in Emma Maffitt, *Life of Maffitt*, 356–57. Eugene, traveling with Jefferson Davis Howell, returned to the U.S. on the steamer *Hibernian* and was captured in Portland, Maine. The two spent some time in Fort Warren, near Boston (unidentified newspaper, clipping, 6 December 1865; and Florie to "My beloved Brother," 17 December 1865, in Maffitt Papers).

5. The War of the Triple Alliance, provoked by President Francisco Solano Lopez of weak Paraguay, meant massive losses for his people. Lopez himself was killed in 1870, leaving his mistress, Elisa Lynch, to flee with money and jewels to exile in Paris. See Hubert Herring, *A History of Latin America* (New York: Alfred A. Knopf, 1968), 815; and William E. Barrett, *Woman on Horseback: The Story of Francisco Lopez and Elisa Lynch* (Garden City, N.Y.: Doubleday, 1952), 311.

6. Maffitt to "My Darling Girls," 6 January 1867 (in Maffitt Papers); James Sprunt, "Running the Blockade," in *Southern Historical Society Papers,* 52 vols. (Richmond: Southern Historical Society, 1896), 24:165.

7. Receipt of British Registry, Maffitt to A. Benites and Company, Buenos Aires, 27 March 1867 (in Maffitt Papers).

8. Maffitt to Henry Storm, a New York friend, 20 March 1875, in Henry Storm Papers, Manuscript Department, William R. Perkins Library, Duke University, Durham, N.C.

9. Maffitt to Preble, 15 November 1871, in George H. Preble Papers, Massachusetts Historical Society, Boston.

10. Maffitt to Preble, 24 March 1882 (in Preble Papers). Maffitt had a small income from the estate of his second wife based on the Laurens lands in South Carolina (Lord and Inglesby—a Charleston law firm that was agent for the lands—to Maffitt, 4 March 1870, 31 January 1873, and 20 July 1881, in Maffitt Papers).

11. Henry D. Shapiro, *Confiscation of Confederate Property in the North* (Ithaca: Cornell University Press, 1962), 54–55.

12. Unidentified newspaper, 5 May 1886 (clipping, in Maffitt Papers).

13. In 1870, the Moorings was valued at $8,000, and Maffitt's personal property at $4,000 (Ninth Census of the United States, 1870: Population.)

14. David McRae, a family friend from Scotland, cited in Emma Maffitt, *Life of Maffitt,* 379.

15. Barron to Maffitt, 4 June 1870 (in Maffitt Papers); Emma Maffitt, *Life of Maffitt,* 363–76.

16. Maffitt—over the signature "Harry," which he used during this period—to Emma Martin, his future wife, 27 July 1870 (in Maffitt Papers).

17. Maffitt, by his third wife, Emma, had three children—Mary Read, Clarence Dudley, and Robert Strange. See Samuel A. Ashe, "John Newland Maffitt," *Biographical History of North Carolina,* ed. Samuel A. Ashe, 8 vols. (Greensboro, N.C.: Charles L. Van Noppen, 1906), 5:211.

18. Ashe, "John Newland Maffitt," 211.

19. Maffitt continued to love adventure and retained his physical agility. After a visit to the Moorings, his Savannah friend Edward C. Anderson recalled Maffitt's "cat-like proclivities." Wrote Anderson: "I remember that Gilpino ride well [after William Cowper's "John Gilpin's Ride," which contains many ludicrous adventures on horseback], and have more than once congratulated myself that I came off with whole bones." Anderson was confident that in the event of an accident, Maffitt "would have somehow or other lit on [his] feet" (Anderson to Maffitt, 14 December 1872, in Maffitt Papers).

20. John A. Grier, Maffitt's engineer on the *Crusader,* to Maffitt, 10 November 1882 (in Maffitt Papers). During the late 1870s and early 1880s, Maffitt was a justice of the peace of New Hanover County, an honorary member of the Third North Carolina Infantry in Wilmington—and at times addressed memorial groups in Wilmington—and a local supervisor of public roads (miscellaneous documents, in Maffitt Papers).

21. The most colorful correspondent was Frank Rivers, a seaman on the *Florida,* who after the war had been a hotel chef, hotel and restaurant owner, store owner, land and cattle owner, Texas ranger, buffalo hunter, mule whacker, prospector, and miner (Rivers to Maffitt, 20 April 1883, in Maffitt Papers).

22. Maffitt to Preble, 22 March 1879 (in Preble Papers).

23. Maffitt remained on cordial terms with President Davis after the war, but blamed him for neglecting the navy: "All the official consideration of Mr. Davis was for the army, he cared but little for the navy, until it dawned upon him, that an efficient navy—which he could have had by early industry—would have thwarted many important military combinations of the Federals" (Maffitt to Preble, 22 May 1879, in Preble Papers).

24. Frank L. Owsley, Jr., *The C.S.S. Florida: Her Building and Operations* (Philadelphia: University of Pennsylvania Press, 1965), 45; *Dictionary of American Biography,* s.v. "Mallory, Stephen Russell."

25. Maffitt, "Reminiscences of the Confederate Navy," *United Service* 3 (October 1880): 509–13; Navy Department, Naval History Division, *Civil War Naval Chronology, 1861–1865,* 6 parts (Washington: U.S. Government Printing Office, 1971), 5:118.

26. Cited in Virgil C. Jones, *The Civil War at Sea,* 3 vols. (New York: Holt, Rinehart, and Winston, 1960–1962), 2:447n.

27. Charles B. Boynton, *The History of the Navy During the Rebellion,* 2 vols. (New York: D. Appleton, 1868), 2:450.

28. Cited in Emma Maffitt, *Life of Maffitt,* 380. Stephen R. Wise, author of *Lifeline of the Confederacy,* contends that the Confederacy made one of its biggest mistakes of the war by removing Maffitt from his position of overseeing blockade running at Nassau since he had the knowledge and the skill to administer a government-run system. Wise allows that Maffitt enjoyed a better reputation as commander of the *Florida* than he would have had he remained as administrator of the blockade-running system. Personal communication, 13 January 1992.

29. Carroll S. Alden and Allan Westcott, *The United States Navy: A History* (Chicago: J. B. Lippincott, 1943), 138.

30. Charles L. Dufour, *The Night the War Was Lost* (Garden City, N.Y.: Doubleday, 1960), 9.

31. Maffitt to Preble, 5 June 1881 (in Maffitt Papers).

32. Cited in Emma Maffitt, *Life of Maffitt,* 422–23.

33. Cited in Emma Maffitt, *Life of Maffitt,* 424–25.

34. *Wilmington Morning Star,* 16 May 1886. Maffitt was buried in Oakdale Cemetery in Wilmington.

Bibliographic Note

The John Newland Maffitt Papers are located in the Southern Historical Collection, University of North Carolina, Chapel Hill. Maffitt's granddaughter, Mrs. Albert Ward of Redding, Connecticut, deposited the papers in August 1950. The Maffitt Papers cover the period 1833–1911, consist of six hundred items, and include business, official, personal, and family correspondence, as well as manuscripts of Maffitt's writings. The collection also includes some of the papers of his third wife and widow, Emma Martin Maffitt, and his daughter Florie. "Maffitt's Journal" (13 April 1861–30 April 1863) includes some material concerning the first cruise of the *Florida,* and "Notes" (4 May 1862–9 April 1863) is an unnamed partial log of the *Florida*. Both appear to be in Maffitt's handwriting, but might have been written in later years.

Many of Maffitt's papers did not survive the Civil War. First, an accidental fire in Charleston in 1861 destroyed a trunk of Maffitt's valuables, left with his brother-in-law, John Laurens, including his U.S.S. *Crusader* accounts and letters relating to his Mediterranean cruise. Most unfortunate (and needlessly, as it turned out) was the submergence of official documents from the blockade runner *Owl* in 1865 when capture by Federal blockaders seemed imminent. Hence the wartime log of the *Florida* kept by Maffitt sank in a weighted pouch in fifteen fathoms of water off Charleston. Shortly afterward, more of Maffitt's papers, including correspondence with his family, were destroyed by Sherman's troops at the family home, Ellerslie, near Fayetteville, North Carolina.

Maffitt's literary pursuits after the war were considerable, although he did not leave a complete memoir of his naval service. One of his major efforts, which focuses on his early career as a midshipman and gives considerable insight into the events of his Mediterranean cruise, was published as a novel. First titling the work "*Oreto,* or the Adventures of a Midshipman's Cloak," Maffitt finally settled on *Nautilus, or Cruising Under Canvas* (1871). Maffitt's articles consist of "The Life and Services of Raphael Semmes," *South Atlantic* (1878); "Reminiscences of the Confed-

153

erate Navy," *United Service* (1880), which contains a sketch of Lieutenant James W. Cooke and the building of the C.S.S. *Albemarle* that was later quoted by J. Thomas Scharf in his history of the Confederate navy; and "Blockade Running," published in two parts in the *United Service* (1882). Maffitt also left unfinished another novel about piracy in the West Indies, set during the War of 1812 and based on his experiences while in command of the *Crusader*.

Unlike Admiral Raphael Semmes, to whom he is often compared as a sea raider, Maffitt's postwar writings were not vindictive. That he had the capacity to be so, however, his private letter of 11 April 1880 to his friend Admiral George H. Preble firmly attests. (In this letter Maffitt replied to Mrs. Martha Williams's criticisms of him as commander of the C.S.S. *Florida*.)Both Semmes and Maffitt were subjects of Northern invective, but only Semmes (who by accounts treated prisoners less well than Maffitt did) in his postwar memoir *Service Afloat* (1887) struck back in public print. Here Semmes defended Maffitt: "This man—who was pursued by the Yankee, after his resignation [1861], with a vindictiveness and malignity peculiarly Puritan—to his honor be it said. . . . His fame will survive the filth thrown upon it by a people who seem to be incapable of understanding or appreciating noble qualities in an enemy, and devoid of any other standard by which to try men's characters, than their own sectional prejudices."

Maffitt aided others with postwar publications, devoting an entire month to gathering material when Jefferson Davis requested information on the Confederate navy for his *Rise and Fall of the Confederate Government* (1881). After Maffitt's death, his widow saw to it that many of his papers were published. In addition to compiling *The Life and Services of John Newland Maffitt* (1906), which contains much original Maffitt material, she also made many of his documents available for publication in the *Official Records of the Navies* (1894–1922).

Index

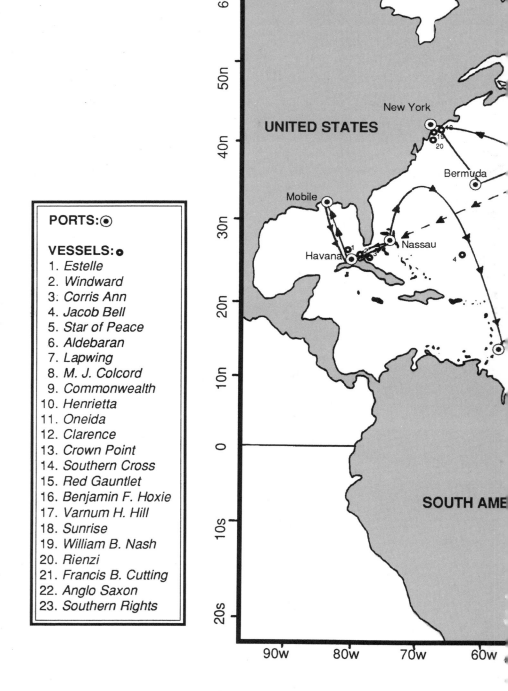

PORTS: ◉

VESSELS: ○
1. *Estelle*
2. *Windward*
3. *Corris Ann*
4. *Jacob Bell*
5. *Star of Peace*
6. *Aldebaran*
7. *Lapwing*
8. *M. J. Colcord*
9. *Commonwealth*
10. *Henrietta*
11. *Oneida*
12. *Clarence*
13. *Crown Point*
14. *Southern Cross*
15. *Red Gauntlet*
16. *Benjamin F. Hoxie*
17. *Varnum H. Hill*
18. *Sunrise*
19. *William B. Nash*
20. *Rienzi*
21. *Francis B. Cutting*
22. *Anglo Saxon*
23. *Southern Rights*